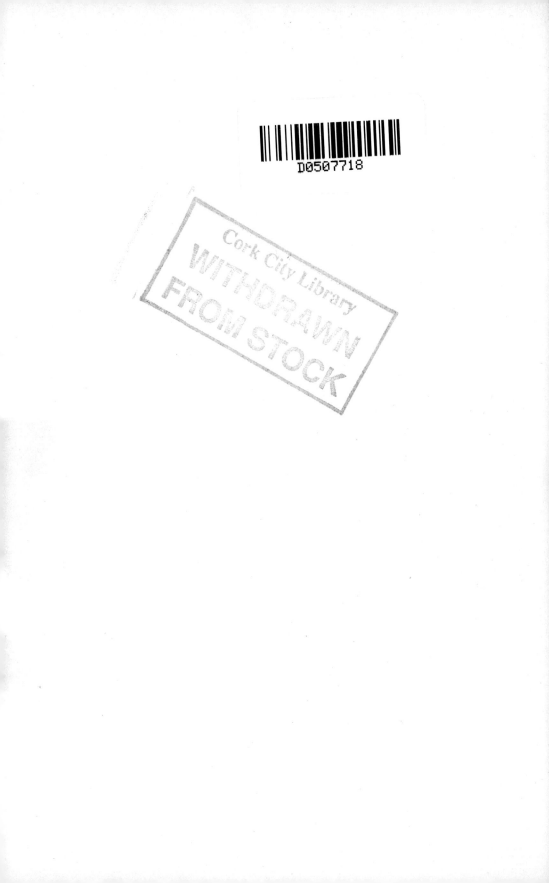

THE
LIAM MacCARTHY CUP

THE LIAM MacCARTHY CUP

SEÁN ÓG Ó CEALLACHÁIN & OWEN McCANN ～

Gill & Macmillan

Gill & Macmillan Ltd
Hume Avenue, Park West, Dublin 12
with associated companies throughout the world
www.gillmacmillan.ie

Index compiled by Cover to Cover
Typography design by Make Communication
Print origination by Carole Lynch
Printed and bound in Great Britain by
MPG Books Ltd, Bodmin, Cornwall

This book is typeset in Linotype Minion and
Neue Helvetica

The paper used in this book comes from the wood pulp
of managed forests. For every tree felled, at least one
tree is planted, thereby renewing natural resources.

A CIP catalogue record for this book is available from
the British Library.

5 4 3 2 1

And when the Great Recorder marks
Your score against your name,
'Twill matter not who won or lost,
But how you played the game.

CONTENTS

RÉAMHRÁ

*Táim thar a bheith sásta roinnt focail a scríobh
don leabhar seo agus táim ag tnúth go mór le cóip
a fháil.*

Seán Óg Ó Ceallacháin and Owen McCann are amongst the most experienced and long-serving scribes who have a link with our games and the association as a whole and, given their longevity and passion for hurling and football, their latest offering will come as a surprise to few.

The name 'Liam MacCarthy' is one of the best known in this country, synonymous with hurling, and this publication underlines the trophy's long association with the game and the GAA at large.

While Owen McCann provides a synopsis of the early finals, Seán Óg picks up from the 1938 final—a game he attended.

In the period since, his name has gone hand in hand with our games and while he is well known in Dublin circles as a result of his long involvement with that county, his unmistakable voice is known to many GAA followers through the medium of his Sunday night radio show which is amongst the longest running in global broadcasting.

The same passion shines through in this book, and its arrival is a welcome addition to the growing number of books that focus on the affairs and exploits of the association.

Our hurling championship is something we should never take for granted. Publications such as this help reinforce the impact that those heady summer games have on the Irish sporting landscape, particularly in the counties lucky enough to be involved in the eagerly awaited titanic clashes that help illuminate so many Sundays.

Congratulations to both authors on their latest foray into publishing and I wish everyone involved with the project every success.

Rath Dé ar an obair.

PÁRAIC Ó DUFAIGH
ARD STIÚRTHÓIR
CHUMANN LÚTHCHLEAS GAEL

Iúil 2009

RÉAMHRÁ

Is cuis mhór athais dom réamhra gairid a scríobh don leabhar is déanaí atá á fhoilsú ag Seán Óg Ó Ceallacháin agus ceann an-shuimiúl ar fad atá ann.

Given Seán Óg's penchant for hard work and meticulous research, can anyone really be surprised that he has yet another book to add to the GAA library—one that continues to grow year on year.

His latest offering, *The Liam MacCarthy Cup*, which sees him join up with Owen McCann, will strike a chord with hurling and GAA followers everywhere given the renown attached to the subject and the special place that the trophy has come to occupy in Irish sporting life for many years.

It is not so long ago that the GAA's library could have been viewed as a short-stocked entity, with a welcome offering every now and then thrown up to shine a light on one aspect or another of the association.

The same can no longer be said, and scribes like Seán Óg and Owen McCann have played their part in this change, contributing more than their share to a collection that has grown handsomely in recent years.

Few could be considered to be more important than this book. Its publication does a service to the GAA in providing yet another reliable reference point for those who follow our games—and hurling in particular—in minute detail.

In addition to the provision of a background to the man that was Liam MacCarthy, and the story of how his name came to rest on one of the iconic trophies of Irish sport, the book also provides details of finals through the ages, and final attendances and match officials are not overlooked either.

I wish the authors every success with this publication and look forward to delving into it when the chance presents itself.

In the meantime I look forward to seeing both Owen and Seán Óg on the GAA beat for many years to come.

Le gach dea ghuí.

CRIOSTÓIR Ó CUANA
UACHTARÁN-TOFA
CHUMANN LÚTHCHLEAS GAEL

ACKNOWLEDGMENTS

This book would never have seen the light of day without the assistance and permission of my good friend and colleague Owen McCann. Away back in 1993 Owen produced a book, published by Oisin Publications, *The Shell Book of the McCarthy Cup*. I know now that the donor of the cup for the All-Ireland senior hurling championship was Liam MacCarthy, who was born in England in 1853. His parents emigrated from Ireland following eviction two years before. Even though the name McCarthy has long been identified with the trophy and used by the media, for the sake of historical correctness I must mention that the family name was MacCarthy and I have applied that name to all written matters arising in this publication.

When Gill & Macmillan expressed an interest in publishing it, I set about building and extending the match descriptions contained in the original book compiled by Owen. I would like to point out that the first Liam MacCarthy Cup All-Ireland final game was played in Croke Park on 4 March 1923 and it was for the All-Ireland hurling final of 1921. More about that anon. In the course of research for this book we found that it was not possible to accurately record the exact line-outs of teams in the early years in the twenties and early thirties. Owen has included a brief compilation of the early finals. We start with the 1938 All-Ireland final. Since I was present at that game, it gave me a good launching pad for this historical publication.

Seán Óg Ó Ceallacháin

PREFACE

This book is dedicated to those GAA officials who had the wisdom and courage to launch the Gaelic Athletic Association in 1884 and thereafter controlled the two most exciting national games, football and hurling, which to this day attract the greatest attendances of any sport in this country of ours. The game of hurling stands alone as being one of the fastest in the history of sport, unique in style, breathtaking in its intensity and passion, and played by those gifted with the skills that are demanded in the execution of the play that forever remain part of its great ethos. One of the stories in this book relates to an American viewing a hurling final game for the first time, and very much taken by its speed and competitiveness. 'My,' he said, 'it's a game for the gods!'

This book tells the story of the All-Ireland hurling finals for the winners of the Liam MacCarthy Cup first presented in 1921. It tells of the victories and the defeats of those who took part in these games. It contains the names of the players who carved their names with pride, whether in victory or defeat, to achieve an objective, touched by the greatness of the much sought after occasion—an All-Ireland hurling final. Hurling casts a spell as illustrated by the frequent clashes of Kilkenny and Cork, Wexford, Tipperary, Offaly, Limerick, Dublin, Waterford, Clare, Galway, Laois and Antrim. Naturally, lovers of hurling will perhaps be reminded of some of the great finals which brought so much joy to followers and are still talked about to this very day.

Chapter 1 ~

THE LIAM MacCARTHY CUP

The trophy for the All-Ireland senior hurling championship com-memorates the memory of Liam MacCarthy who was prominently associated with the GAA in London. He was born in London in 1851 to a Bruff (Co. Limerick) mother and Ballygarvan (Co. Cork) father. Liam was distraught when his mother died in 1877. A very special bond had existed between them. From his mother he inherited a deep love of Ireland and all things Irish—its politics, history, language and mythology—and as a result he never forgot his roots. From his father he inherited discipline, organisational ability and a strong sense of duty. In 1890 his father died, at which time Liam had established his own cardboard box manufacturing business, a trade he had learned from his in-laws.

As the business progressed and developed, he formed a company called William MacCarthy and Sons Cardboard Box Factory in Peckham, London. His levels of mental and physical energy were such that he was able to be actively involved in a wide range of activities. He was vice-president of the Gaelic League and gave generous support to Pádraig Pearse's school, St Enda's. When the first county board was formed in London in 1895, he was appointed treasurer and became its president three years later. He loved the game of hurling and it wasn't surprising that he should have donated a trophy for the All-Ireland senior hurling championship. The new trophy was made in Dublin to Liam's design at a cost of £50—a lot of money at that time.

The first winners of the Liam MacCarthy Cup were Limerick in the All-Ireland championship in 1921. They were captained by Bob McConkey and the final was played in March 1923.

In 1992, after 70 years of service, the Liam MacCarthy Cup was replaced. The new trophy was an almost exact replica of the original but was heavier. A thicker gauge of silver was used to create the new trophy, and the handles were strengthened to allow for the inevitable wear and tear. Modifications raised the weight from two and a half kilos to nearly

four kilos. The height remains at 33 cm and diameter 22 cm. Master craftsman James Mary Kelly, gold and silversmith, Kilkenny, made the new
trophy. The last man to receive the old cup was Tipperary captain Declan
Carr in 1991. It is now displayed in the Croke Park Museum.

Liam Fennelly of Kilkenny has a personal record all his own where the
Liam MacCarthy Cup is concerned. In 1983 when Kilkenny won their 23rd
All-Ireland crown, he returned to the Noreside with the original cup. Nine
years later, in 1992, Kilkenny won their 24th All-Ireland title. Liam was captain again, and so he collected the new MacCarthy Cup. In so doing he
became the only captain in the history of the GAA to have been presented
with both cups.

Liam MacCarthy, a teetotaller all his life, was in failing health from 1906
onwards and died on 28 September 1928. At Easter 1996, on the occasion
of the centenary of the London County Board, a headstone was unveiled
over his grave before a distinguished gathering.

BACKGROUND TO THE FIRST FINAL

The first Liam MacCarthy Cup game was played at Croke Park on 4 March
1923 and was for the All-Ireland championship of 1921. Dublin were the
defending champions and holders of the Great Southern Cup, which until
then was the trophy for the All-Ireland senior hurling title winners. They
were challenged by Limerick. When the MacCarthy Cup was offered for
the championship, and accepted, Dublin became the sole owners of the
Great Southern Cup.

The day of the first final was bright but cold. Outside Croke Park the
bookies were laying the odds, and Dublin were favourites. By then the GAA
had barred betting on games inside the ground, but apparently it was
possible to engage in betting on the streets around the stadium.

Admission to the ground was 1/- (one shilling) and 2/- (two shillings)
or 5 cent and ten cent in today's currency for adults, and 6p (six pence) or
2 cent for schoolboys. The match was timed to start at 3.15 p.m.

The ground was in excellent condition and the 'proceedings were
enlivened by the Transport Workers Band and the Artane Boys Band',
to quote a newspaper report the following day. The match attracted an
attendance of 18,000–19,000 and the gate receipts were £1,680.

The final was the first between Limerick and Dublin, and a James
O'Mara, of the O'Mara Opera Company and a native of Limerick, threw
in the ball. The referee was Willie Walsh of Waterford. The umpires were

T. McGrath (Clare), E. O'Keeffe (Laois), P. O'Brien (Wexford), then chairman of the Leinster Council, and J. O'Brien (Clare). The linesmen were O'Farrell of Roscommon and P. McFadden of Antrim.

Unfortunately the standard of play was not equal to the excitement of the occasion. There was no spectacular overhead play and little clever passing. Limerick were convincing winners, captained by Bob McConkey, 'the little fellow with the grey cap—the skipper who knows more about finding the net than most', as a feature in the *Irish Independent* put it.

Dublin's captain was Bob Mockler, a native of Tipperary. McConkey scored four goals in the final. He was presented at the end of the match with the MacCarthy Cup by Dan McCarthy TD, president of the GAA, who did the honours in the absence of the donor.

The *Irish Independent* described the trophy in the sports pages as 'of racy and costly design'. Elsewhere in the same issue in a feature article on the final, the cup is referred to as a 'splendid trophy—marred by an English inscription'.

The first ten minutes of the inaugural final raised expectations of a good struggle as the pace was fast and furious, with play swinging from end to end. But then Limerick took a firm grip on the exchanges and went on to lead by eleven points at the interval, 4-1 to 0-2. Team captain McConkey scored three of the goals.

Dublin had the best possible start to the second half when they scored a goal. However, the Shannonsiders soon regained the initiative and McConkey's fourth goal of the day powered them on to a convincing 8-5 to 3-2 win.

THE GOLDEN YEARS

The fifties proved a golden decade for attendances at All-Ireland senior hurling finals. Followers flocked to the games at that period as never before.

There were a number of reasons for the extra special appeal of the MacCarthy Cup ties. Chief among them were the hurlers of Wexford and the magic of Cork's Christy Ring. Wexford proved one of the most popular teams in hurling and football during the fifties. They built up a following far outside their own county boundaries as they came from nowhere to quality for their first final appearance in 33 years in 1951. They then had to endure many disappointments and frustrations before finally taking the MacCarthy Cup for the first time in 1955.

Rejoicing was nationwide after that breakthrough as a Cinderella-like story came true in hurling. The great-hearted Wexford men, with a colourful and cavalier-like approach to the game, won the hearts of many followers. Many who rallied to Wexford's side at the time had little real interest in hurling up to that point.

Wexford dominated the decade, if not in terms of title wins, certainly with their exciting play that kept the turnstiles clicking merrily. The Slaneysiders had the happy knack from the spectators' viewpoint of bringing out the best in the opposition, with the result that a game in which they were engaged generally provided full value for money.

Then there was Christy Ring. It could be said that his career began a second stage in the fifties. He won his fifth All-Ireland medal in 1946, and a sixth in 1952. That marked the start of a great chapter in the career of the Cork man. He led Cork to their title wins of 1953 and 54 to become the first to win eight All-Ireland senior medals in either code.

Cork with Christy Ring and Wexford with the Rackard brothers, Nicky, a towering inspiration and a real personality-plus campaigner of his day, Bobbie and Willie, Nick O'Donnell and Ned Wheeler, had some great games during that period.

The meeting of the counties for the 1954 MacCarthy Cup drew, at 84,856, a new attendance record for a hurling final. That game incidentally attracted a greater attendance than the football final of 1954. Two years later it was Wexford and Cork in opposition again for the game's top prize. Although the attendance was down somewhat on that of 1954, it was still a tremendous 83,096. This is the second best for an All-Ireland senior hurling final, and the 1954 and 1956 games ranked as the only ones to bring more than 80,000 followers to Croke Park for a match in the ancient code prior to the redevelopments that have resulted in the now magnificent headquarters.

The 1937 final played at Killarney was watched by a crowd of 43,638. The game was played at the famed Kerry beauty spot as the first Cusack Stand was in the course of construction at Croke Park at the time.

The magical figure of 70,000 was almost reached for the first time in the year World War II ended—1945. Despite all the difficulties travel-wise, the Tipperary-Kilkenny encounter drew a crowd of 69,459. Then came the golden years of the fifties, and an attendance of 71,195 at the Cork-Galway match of 1953—the first 70,000 plus crowd at a hurling decider.

The only final not played at Croke Park since the 1937 game was that between Cork and Offaly in Centenary Year. Their meeting in 1984 took place at Semple Stadium, Thurles, attracting a crowd of 59,814.

The first decider for which there was seating along the old Cusack Stand side was the 1966 clash of Cork and Kilkenny, watched by a splendid gathering of 68,249.

The lowest attendance since 1958 (47,276) was at the 1986 meeting of Cork and Galway—43,451.

The extra accommodation provided by the redevelopment of Croke Park has helped bring in bigger crowds. Four finals in this new century attracted 80,000-plus attendances—2005, 06, 07 and 08. The Kilkenny-Cork show-down of 2006 leads the way with 82,275.

Top 10 MacCarthy Cup Attendances

84,856	Cork v Wexford	1954
83,096	Wexford v Cork	1956
82,275	Kilkenny v Cork	2006
82,127	Kilkenny v Limerick	2007
82,186	Kilkenny v Waterford	2008
81,136	Cork v Galway	2005
79,383	Kilkenny v Cork	2003
78,212	Cork v Kilkenny	2004
77,154	Wexford v Tipperary	1960
77,285	Waterford v Kilkenny (Replay)	1959

REFEREES

Willie Walsh of Waterford had charge of the first Liam MacCarthy Cup tie. He was a very experienced referee at the time and in fact officiated at five All-Ireland senior finals in succession from 1915 to 1919. After the initial MacCarthy Cup tie, he refereed one further clash for the trophy—the second replay in the memorable three-game saga that was the Cork-Kilkenny story for the 1931 title.

Dr J. J. Stuart, who refereed the 1943 final, became president of the GAA in 1958. A native of Clare who gave tremendous service to the game in Dublin, he became the first one-time MacCarthy Cup final referee to assume the highest office in the Association. He was a former Leinster president when he became national president.

Con Murphy, who won All-Ireland senior hurling medals with Cork in 1942, 43, 44 and 46, refereed the 1948 and 50 MacCarthy Cup ties, and was elected president of the Association in 1976.

John Dowling joined the ranks of referees who became president when he took over the principal executive role in 1988. The Offaly man handled three MacCarthy Cup ties—1960, 62 and 68.

Pádraig O'Keeffe, who had control of the whistle in the 1924 final, became general secretary of the GAA in 1929, a man who contributed tremendously in his lifetime to setting the organisation firmly on the road to the proud position it occupies today.

J. J. Callanan captained Tipperary to their success in 1930. Ten years on he was the official in the middle as Limerick beat Kilkenny for the cup.

Pat Dunphy of Laois was the first Leinster man to referee a cup tie. He earned that distinction in the second year of the competition.

Stephen Jordan (Galway) blazed the trail for Connacht in 1930.

We still have to see an Ulster man in charge of the top game of the hurling year.

Diarmuid Kirwan (Cork) followed in his father's footsteps when he took charge of the 2007 final. His father Gerry, from Offaly, refereed the 1988 All-Ireland final. Diarmuid is a native of Offaly and played with his home club, Ballyskenagh. He has been living in Farran, Ovens, Cork, for some time and also played with the local Éire Óg club there.

Twelve counties are represented in the list of MacCarthy Cup referees over the years, with Limerick setting the standard with ten representatives.

Statistics

5 Robbins S. (Offaly): 1928, 29, 31 (draw), 31 (first replay), 34 (replay).

4 Jordan S. (Galway): 1930, 33, 34 (draw), 34 (replay). Murphy D. (Wexford): 1992, 95, 97, 98.

3 Dowling J. (Offaly): 1960, 62, 68. Fitzgerald G. (Limerick): 1959 (draw), 59 (replay), 61. Flaherty J. (Offaly): 1937, 39, 46. Hatton J. (Wicklow): 1963, 66, 70. O'Connor P. (Limerick): 1999, 2001, 03.

2 Barrett W. (Tipperary): 1994, 2000. Hayes M. (Clare): 1965, 67. Hennessy M. (Clare): 1942, 44. Murphy C. (Cork): 1948, 50. Murphy F. (Cork): 1971, 81. Murray T. (Limerick): 1987, 93. McCullagh P. (Wexford): 1925, 26. MacSuibhne A. (Dublin): 2002, 04. O'Connor S. (Limerick): 1969, 75. O'Donoghue N. (Dublin): 1980, 82. O'Donoghue W. (Limerick): 1951, 52. Ryan G. (Tipperary): 1979, 85. Walsh W. (Waterford): 1921, 31 (second replay).

1 Bailey J. F. (Dublin): 1986. Baston V. (Waterford): 1945. Callanan J. J. (Tipperary): 1940. Connell P. (Offaly): 1953. Daly T. (Clare): 1935. Delaney P. (Laois): 1989. Dunphy P. (Laois): 1922. Duggan N. (Limerick): 1983. Flaherty M. J. (Galway): 1949. Gleeson S. (Limerick): 1957. Harney I. (Galway): 1938. Higgins A. (Galway): 1964. Horgan W. (Cork): 1991. Horan P. (Offaly): 1966. Johnson P. (Kilkenny): 1976. Kelly B. (Westmeath) 2006. Kennifick P. (Dublin): 1923. Kirwan G. (Offaly): 1988. Kirwan D. (Cork): 2007. Lanigan D. (Limerick): 1927. Long P. (Kilkenny): 1984. Moloney J. (Tipperary): 1974. Moore J. (Waterford): 1990. Mulcahy J. (Kilkenny): 1954. O'Donnell W. (Tipperary): 1941. O'Grady S. (Limerick): 1977. O'Keeffe P., better known later as Pádraig Ó Caoimh, general secretary of the GAA (Cork): 1924. O'Regan J. (Cork): 1936. O'Sullivan T. (Limerick): 1956. Purcell P. (Tipperary): 1947. Roberts J. (Kilkenny): 1928. Rankins J. (Laois): 1978. Roche S. (Tipperary): 2005. Slattery M. (Clare): 1973. Spain Matt (Offaly): 1958. Spain Mick (Offaly): 1972. Stakelum B. (Tipperary): 1955. Stuart J. J. (Dublin): 1943.

INDIVIDUAL SCORES

The era of the new Liam MacCarthy Cup, introduced for the 1992 All-Ireland senior hurling final, has already been marked by some noteworthy individual scoring performances. However, all still pale when compared to some of the leading returns during the reign of the old trophy.

D. J. Carey set a new standard for the new trophy when he helped himself to 2-4 for Kilkenny in their 2000 win over Offaly.

Two years later another Kilkenny man, Henry Shefflin, equalled that feat with a return of 1-7 in Kilkenny's win over Clare.

Cork sharpshooter Ben O'Connor joined the ranks also on 1-7 in the 2005 success over Galway.

However, in 2008 Eoin Kelly powered his way to the top with 1-9 for Waterford in their unsuccessful bid against Kilkenny.

Impressive as those scores undoubtedly are, they are still short of older leading returns. In the early days of the old trophy Michael 'Gah' Ahearne set an impressive standard with a superb 5-4 in Cork's 1928 win over Galway. That return has still to be bettered.

It was in 1971 that Eddie Keher came closest to the Ahearne return when he recorded a splendid 2-11. It was still not enough to earn Kilkenny the honours against Tipperary. Keher's senior career with Kilkenny spanned three decades from the late fifties to the mid-seventies, and he proved by far the scoregetter-in-chief over the entire history of the cup from the inaugural campaign right up to the end of his inter-county career. The sharpshooter from the Rower-Inistioge wrote his name into the top scoring chart in spectacular fashion with that 1971 return of 2-11 (1-7 from frees).

Long before Keher's proud return in 1971, he had assured himself of a special place in the record book. He coloured his All-Ireland senior final-winning appearance debut by scoring 0-14 as Waterford went under to Kilkenny in the 1963 decider. That points tally still holds the No. 1 spot on the individual scale as far as points scored are concerned. It says much for Keher's excellent finishing in MacCarthy Cup games that he holds four of the top eight scoring records, and shares sixth position with Limerick's Eamonn Cregan. The Kilkenny man hit 7-72 (93 points) in ten final outings. His lowest return in any full game was 0-2 when Kilkenny lost the title to Tipperary in 1964. He hit 0-2 making his senior final debut when going in as a substitute in the 1959 replay with Waterford. Keher commanded the second spot in the chart until Nicholas English moved up to that position in 1989.

English did not make his MacCarthy Cup debut until 1988, and he had a quiet enough time on the scoring front, hitting just six points. Nevertheless, that return was still good enough to earn him the ranking as Tipperary's top marksman in their unsuccessful bid against defending champions Galway. However, English struck it rich in a big way the following year when he chalked up the best score of the modern era with a superb 2-12 in Tipperary's win over Antrim (0-8 from frees and a point from a penalty).

A forward who shared much of the limelight with Keher was Tipperary lethal finisher Jimmy Doyle, who also spanned three decades from the end of the fifties to the second year of the seventies in big-time hurling. Doyle scored 1-43 (46 points) in nine final appearances with the Premier County, including his last in 1971 as a substitute in the team that beat the Noresiders. He did not get on the scoresheet in that limited outing, the only time in a MacCarthy Cup game that he failed to raise a flag. He had his best return in 1964 when he rifled over ten points as Tipperary regained the trophy in a meeting with Kilkenny.

The legendary Christy Ring appeared in the finals over two decades—the forties and fifties. He had ten outings in all between 1941 and 1956, scoring in every game with a return of 3-34 (43 points). Unlike the other two marksmen, Ring did not achieve anything dramatic in the scoring line in a final. His best haul came on his last outing in 1956 when he rattled home 1-5 as Cork lost a classic to defending champions Wexford. He scored a single point as Cork made it four titles in a row and a new record by beating Dublin in 1944, and he notched just a point again as the Leesiders lost the MacCarthy Cup to Kilkenny in a superb game in 1947.

In the new era only three hurlers scored two goals in a final: Damien Quigley scored 2-3 for Limerick in their unsuccessful 1994 bid against Offaly; D. J. Carey ushered in the new century with 2-4 in Kilkenny's victory over Offaly; and a year later Mark O'Leary hit 2-1 in Tipperary's victory over Galway.

Points	Score		Year
19	5-4	M. Ahearne (Cork) v Galway	1928
18	2-12	N. English (Tipperary) v Antrim	1989
17	2-11	E. Keher (Kilkenny) v Tipperary	1971
15	2-9	E. Keher (Kilkenny) v Cork	1972
14	0-14	E. Keher (Kilkenny) v Waterford	1963
	1-11	E. Keher (Kilkenny) v Limerick	1974
13	2-7	E. Keher (Kilkenny) v Galway	1975
	2-7	E. Cregan (Limerick) v Galway	1980
12	1-9	C. McCarthy (Cork) v Wexford	1970
	4-0	B. McConkey (Limerick) v Dublin	1921
	4-0	D. Clohossy (Limerick) v Dublin replay	1934
	1-9	Eoin Kelly (Waterford) v Kilkenny	2008
11	3-2	J. Keane (Waterford) v Dublin	1948
	3-2	N. Rackard (Wexford) v Tipperary	1951
10	2-4	J. Kennedy (Tipperary) v Laois	1949
	0-10	J. Doyle (Tipperary) v Kilkenny	1964
	3-1	E. O'Brien (Cork) v Wexford	1970
	0-10	R. Bennis (Limerick) v Kilkenny	1973
	0-10	P. Moylan (Cork) v Wexford	1976
	1-7	L. O'Brien (Kilkenny) v Galway	1979
	0-10	W. Fitzpatrick (Kilkenny) v Cork	1983
	1-7	Padge Kehoe (Wexford) v Tipperary	1960
	1-7	Joe Cooney (Galway) v Cork	1990
	2-4	D. J. Carey (Kilkenny) v Offaly	2000

1-7	H. Shefflin (Kilkenny) v Clare	2002
1-7	B. O'Connor (Cork) v Galway	2005
2-4	E. Brennan (Kilkenny) v Waterford	2008

THE PIONEERING YEARS

The early years of the Liam MacCarthy Cup brought some of the shortest reigns as cup holders due to the fact that for a time competitions ran late. This resulted in two finals in the same year. For instance, Limerick were the first winners on 4 March 1923, but by September of that year Kilkenny had also put their name on the trophy for the first time.

Limerick's win was for the 1921 championship, and Kilkenny were champions of 1922 as a result of their success in September 1923. The Noresiders' show-down with Tipperary ranks as the first MacCarthy Cup tie played in September, which for some years afterwards became the traditional month for the match.

Two more finals were played in the calendar year of 1924. Galway beat Limerick in September in the 1923 final but lost the cup just three months later when they were beaten by Dublin in the 1924 decider.

The 1923 and 1924 finals, and Galway's short spell as cup holders, are linked historically: Mick Gill, of Ballinderreen, played on each title-winning side—a rare achievement that stands out on its own. Gill, a Garda stationed in Dublin, was assisting the Garda club in metropolitan competitions at the time the 1923 MacCarthy Cup tie came around. However, he had been in action earlier with Galway in the 1923 championship and so was eligible to turn out with the Connacht county in the All-Ireland final against Limerick. The westerners won that match—their MacCarthy Cup debut. There was no declaration rule in operation at that time, and when Galway met Dublin just three months later in the final defence of the trophy for the 1924 championship, Mick Gill was on duty with the metropolitans.

Dublin won that game to give Gill a unique ranking in the annals of hurling as the only man to win All-Ireland senior medals in the same year with two separate county teams. He won a third medal in the pioneering years as Dublin's captain in 1927.

One of the most interesting statistics of these early years is that the first three finals resulted in the trophy travelling in turn to each of three provinces—Munster, as a result of Limerick's 1921 final win, Leinster (Kilkenny in 1922) and Connacht (Galway in 1923). The cup has still to be won by an Ulster county.

Limerick, Kilkenny and Galway each had a winning debut. So too had Cork, who were to go on to become the MacCarthy Cup specialists. The Leesiders made history on the double in fact in the early seasons. They had their winning debut in 1926 at Kilkenny's expense, and in 1929 became the first county to make a successful defence of the cup.

Dublin, after their defeat in their first final, came back to make it second time lucky in the 1924 clash with Galway. It was also a case of second time lucky for Tipperary, who followed their initial appearance in 1922 when they lost to Kilkenny, by beating Galway for the 1925 title.

Galway appeared in more finals than any other county during the first years—five times from 1923 up to 1929. In addition, they had the lowest score of any team when they only managed a goal against Cork in 1928.

The period was also marked by a noteworthy individual achievement other than Mick Gill's unique double. Seán Óg Murphy led Cork to the 1926 and 28 titles to become the first man to captain two MacCarthy Cup-winning teams.

The 1925 final was played on 6 September, the 1926 decider on 24 October, and the remaining three finals were all played in September. The first final on 1 September was the Cork-Galway tie of 1929.

On the refereeing front, the man in charge of the 1924 decider was Paddy O'Keeffe (better known later as Pádraig Ó Caoimh), who went on to become one of the main bulwarks in the advancement of the Association.

Willie Walsh of Waterford had charge of the initial final. Patrick McCullagh of Wexford became the first to referee two MacCarthy Cup ties, in 1925 and 26.

Six counties dominated the MacCarthy Cup records in the pioneering years. Each not only won the trophy at least once but also sustained at least one defeat. Cork had the best record—three wins and one defeat.

Finally, the first six finals (1921 to 1926 inclusive) provided a new name each time on the plinth of the cup.

Statistics

Greatest attendance	26,829 in 1926
Busiest referee	P. McCullagh (Wexford) 1925, 26
	S. Robbins (Offaly) 1928, 29
Highest team score	6-12 (30 points) by Cork 1928
Highest winning margin	27 points by Cork 1928

Lowest winning margin	2 points by Kilkenny 1922
Highest individual score	5-4 by M. Ahearne (Cork) 1928
Highest individual goals total	5 by M. Ahearne (Cork) 1928
Goalless finals	None
Finals in which winning team failed to score a goal	None
Finals in which losing team failed to score a goal	None
Best points tally by winning team	12 by Cork 1928
Best points tally by losing team	6 by Tipperary 1922 and by Galway 1924
Top scoring final on aggregate	1921: 11-7 (40 points)
Lowest scoring final on aggregate	1926: 6-6 (24 points)
Replays	None
Most successful captain	S. Óg Murphy 1926, 28

Chapter 2 ~

THE EARLY FINALS

The 1921 to 1929 All-Ireland hurling finals

1921 FINAL: FOUR GOAL CURTAIN RAISER
4 March 1923   Limerick 8-5, Dublin 3-2
Attendance: 18,000–19,000   Referee: W. Walsh (Waterford)
Top scorer: B. McConkey (Limerick) 4-0

The day was bright but cold and the final was not as exciting as generally expected but featured a superb scoring performance by Limerick captain Bob McConkey who finished with four goals.

The opening ten minutes provided fast and competitive hurling as play swung from end to end. After that, however, the Shannonsiders had much the better of the first half exchanges. McConkey was in particularly fine form as he collected three goals to help his side to a clear-cut interval lead of 4-1 to 0-2.

Dublin had the best possible start to the second half when Mick Neville collected a fine goal from a difficult angle. Later on the metropolitans further boosted their morale with a goal from a mêlée.

But Limerick were in no mood to allow the trophy to slip from their gasp and quickly re-established their superiority. Tommy Daly brought off a splendid save in the Dublin goal, but before he could clear McConkey was in to finish to the net and Limerick went on for a most convincing win.

McConkey, Tom McGrath and Willie Gleeson did much up front to orchestrate the success, while further back Denny Lanigan had an outstanding game.

Daly, captain Bob Mockler and Martin Hayes were prominent for Dublin.

1922 FINAL: ONE OF THE GREAT FINALS

9 September 1923   Kilkenny 4-2, Tipperary 2-6
Attendance: 26,119   Referee: P. Dunphy (Laois)
Top scorer: R. Grace (Kilkenny) 2-0

This was one of the great finals. The pace was terrific all the way; the scoring alternated; the teams were level at the interval; and the issue was in doubt right until the final whistle.

With about ten minutes remaining Tipperary looked poised for the cup as they led by a goal, but great play by Kilkenny brought the equaliser. Dick Grace sent a 70 to the Premier County goal area. Matty Power, John Roberts, Paddy Donoghue and Dick Tobin were all involved in the action, but the ball went all the way to the Munster team's net from the free.

Tipperary regained the lead with a goal, but with just three minutes remaining, Kilkenny, captained by Willie Dunphy, stormed back to collect a brace of goals and finish cup winners for the first time.

Tipperary played with the sun towards the Canal goal in the first half and the scores were tied at the break, Kilkenny 1-1, Tipperary 0-4.

Dick Grace had an outstanding game for the Leinster side. Mark McDonald was reliable in goal, and John Holohan, Martin Lalor and Dick Tobin were other stars for Kilkenny. Incidentally, Grace played in the All-Ireland final-winning teams of 1912 and 13, and was the only All-Ireland senior medallist in the Kilkenny side.

Goalkeeper Jack O'Meara, Paddy Power, J. J. Hayes and J. Cleary were the pick of the Tipperary squad.

1923 FINAL: WINNING DEBUT AND A DOUBLE FIRST

14 September 1924   Galway 7-3, Limerick 4-5
Attendance: 15,000   Referee: P. Kennifick (Dublin)
Top scorer: L. McGrath (Galway) 3-0

This was Galway's initial appearance in a MacCarthy Cup final and their first meeting with Limerick. Moreover, the Connacht men trained specially for the game—the first time the county had adopted such preparation for a decider.

On a day of brilliant sunshine Limerick won the toss and played into the Railway end, backed by an appreciable wind. The game was a thrilling affair with goal-scoring a feature. In all, eleven were scored as against just eight points.

Team captain Mick Kenny, Leonard McGrath and Bernie Gibbs were on target for the westerners, who did not score a single point in the opening half.

Willie Gleeson and Denny Lanigan scored the Limerick goals, and the teams finished level at the break—3-0 for Galway and 2-3 for Limerick.

The gripping exchanges continued after the restart. A goal by Gibbs put Galway three points clear. Limerick battled back bravely but failed to score, and the next breakthrough was achieved by Galway with a fine goal from Leonard McGrath.

Soon after came Galway's first point when Gibbs finished off a fast and clever attack with a fine score. Limerick did not throw in the towel, however, and were rewarded for their efforts with goals from Mick Neville and Tom McGrath. Leonard McGrath regained the initiative for Galway with a goal to set the seal on a magnificent contribution to the victory effort.

Mick Gill had a superb game at midfield for Galway. Mick Derivan was another star in the defence.

1924 FINAL: UNIQUE DOUBLE FOR GILL

14 December 1924   Dublin 5-3, Galway 2-6
Attendance: No figures   Referee: P. O'Keeffe (Cork)
Top scorer: B. Gibbs (Galway) 2-1

Mick Gill completed a unique double in double-quick time in this second MacCarthy Cup tie of the year. Three months earlier Galway had captured the trophy and with it their first-ever All-Ireland senior title in the belated final of 1923. Gill, then a member of the western outfit, now played a big role in fashioning this metropolitan success.

Galway, backed by the wind and sun, started into the Railway goal in the first half and played some delightful hurling but still could not manage to take a decisive grip on the exchanges. A tenacious rearguard ensured that Dublin trailed by just three points at the break—3-0 to 2-6.

Although the elements did not favour the challengers at the change of ends, Dublin still had the better of the exchanges. Indeed, they did not concede a single score in the half.

Garret Howard, who scored the first goal of the game in the first minute, landed Dublin's first goal of the second half. The challengers went on to build up a 5-2 to 2-6 lead and later their cause was further strengthened by the brilliance of goalkeeper Tommy Daly who brought off three superb saves.

Howard's two goals and the excellence of Gill and Daly's superb goal-keeping were the brightest features of the success.

Bernie Gibbs, who scored 2-1, team captain Mick Kenny, Michael Derivan and Leonard McGrath were in the spotlight for Galway.

1925 FINAL: GOALKEEPERS STAR AS TIPP TRIUMPH

6 September 1925   Tipperary 5-6, Galway 1-5
Attendance: 20,000   Referee: P. McCullagh (Wexford)
Top scorer: T. Duffy (Tipperary) 2-1

This final produced hurling that was fast and at times brilliant, as well as some top-class individual displays. Tipperary finished decisive winners but had to work harder for the victory than the scoreline would suggest.

Two players stood out. John Mahony was in tremendous form in the Galway goal, while Mick D'Arcy had an outstanding game at midfield for Tipperary. His well-judged and lengthy pucks regularly put the Premier County forwards into good scoring positions. However, Tipperary's goalkeeper, Arthur O'Donnell, also stamped his personality on the game in style with some excellent saves.

Tipperary had the better of the first half exchanges and with D'Arcy to the fore were nicely placed at the interval with a lead of 3-2 to 0-3 after playing towards the Railway end.

The Munster men had much the better of the exchanges after the interval. Hurling with skill and polish and helped along the way by the goal-scoring exploits of Duffy and D'Arcy, they fashioned a comfortable 5-6 to 0-3 advantage.

Galway, to their credit, rallied well and hit 1-2 without reply, but Tipperary soon regained the initiative. Their scoring rate did not improve, but a point by Paddy Leahy, the last of the game, eased their pressures and they finished easy winners.

Full back John Leahy and Hayes and Duffy in attack did much to complement the play of D'Arcy and O'Donnell in fashioning the Tipperary success.

In addition to Mahony, Galway had impressive performers in Dick Morrissey, King and Shaughnessy.

1926 FINAL: AHEARNE PILOTS CORK WIN

24 October 1926   Cork 4-6, Kilkenny 2-0
Attendance: 26,829   Referee: P. McCullagh (Wexford)
Top scorer: P. Ahearne (Cork) 2-2

Cork went into their MacCarthy Cup final debut sharpened by three testing games with Tipperary in the Munster final. They benefited from those
outings if one is to judge by their convincing win over Kilkenny, who failed
to score in the second half.

Kilkenny played their best hurling in the opening stages when backed
by the sun and wind. Michael 'Gah' Ahearne scored the first goal of the
game for Cork after ten minutes. The Noresiders responded in tremendous style and put strong pressure on the Cork defence. Eventually John
Roberts got through for a goal to level the score. There was little between
the sides for the rest of the half, which ended with Kilkenny just ahead by
2-1 to 2-0.

Defences were on top in the early stages of the second half, but Paddy
'Balty' Ahearne put Cork in sight of the winning post by notching up 1-2.

Kilkenny continued to battle on bravely and with plenty of skill, but the
Cork defence, with Seán Óg Murphy and Maurice Murphy to the fore,
gave little away.

Back into the picture stepped Paddy Ahearne. He picked up a long delivery from Jim Hurly and collected another goal to ensure a win for the
Rebel County.

Paddy Ahearne, with his two goals, midfielder Eudie Coughlan and
defender Seán Óg Murphy were the Cork heroes.

Goalkeeper Dick Cantwell, who had a splendid game, Dick Grace and
Lory Meagher did best for Kilkenny.

1927 FINAL: GILL TO THE FORE AGAIN

4 September 1927   Dublin 4-8, Cork 1-3
Attendance: 23,824   Referee: D. Lanigan (Limerick)
Top scorer: T. Barry (Dublin) 2-1

Cork, bidding to become the first county to make a successful defence of
the MacCarthy Cup, started favourites. However, Dublin had a real match-
winner in Mick Gill. He played a captain's role with his good general play
and his efficient use of frees. Joe Bannon and Ned Fahy also sparkled in a

defence that did really well against the Cork attack. When the Cork forwards did get through, they found Tommy Daly in inspired form in goal. Some of his saves were electrifying.

The metropolians fielded nine of the famed Garda club and, not surprisingly, they displayed fine combination play throughout. They also lasted the pace better.

On a day of bright summer-like weather, Dublin played towards the Canal goal and landed their first score after six minutes with a point from Jim 'Builder' Walsh. Four minutes later Tommy Barry collected the first goal of the game to help Dublin on their way to an interval lead of 2-3 to 0-1.

Cork looked like getting right back into the title hunt when they opened the second half with a goal by Eudie Coughlan. However, Dublin responded with a brace of points before really strengthening their grip on the exchanges. Barry slipped the Cork defence beautifully and placed Ned Fahy for a great goal from twenty yards to give Dublin a commanding lead, 3-5 to 1-2.

Cork were always battling a lost cause after that. They scored just one point more while the metropolitans notched up 1-3, their goal coming near the end from a very industrious Barry.

Coughlan, Hurley and Seán Óg Murphy were best for a somewhat disappointing Cork, who struggled for most of the game.

1928 FINAL: TOP SCORE FOR 'GAH'

9 September 1928   Cork 6-12, Galway 1-0
Attendance: 15,000   Referee: S. Robbins (Offaly)
Top scorer: M. Ahearne (Cork) 5-4

This was Michael 'Gah' Ahearne's final. He was in sparkling form throughout with his clever hurling and, above all, his finishing that was of the highest class. His return of 5-4 still stands as the top individual score for a MacCarthy Cup tie.

Cork had taken revenge over Dublin in their semi-final for their defeat by the metropolitans in the 1927 decider. In the final they lost no time in getting into match-winning gear. They played against a fairly strong wind and sun but quickly had two points from Paddy Delea.

Although Galway, who had a bye to the final, bounced back well after those scores, they got little change from the Cork rearguard, superbly led by team captain Seán Óg Murphy.

Then 'Gah' Ahearne took a grip on the exchanges in a decisive way. He pointed a free, scored a goal and followed up with another point. Galway responded with their solitary score of the game before 'Gah' Ahearne was back in the scoring spotlight with 1-1 to leave Cork ahead by 3-5 to 1-0 at the break.

There was no way back for Galway after that—especially facing the wind in the second half. A Eudie Coughlan point a mere minute after the throw-in further emphasised Cork's superiority, and some fetching performances from the Ahearne brothers, with another grand goal from Michael, kept the Leesiders motoring along well.

Cork continued to have the whip hand for the remainder of the game in what was a disappointing encounter overall. Long before the final whistle, the spectators were winding their way homewards.

1929 FINAL: CORK DEFEND THE CUP

1 September 1929   Cork 4-9, Galway 1-3
Attendance: 18,000   Referee: S. Robbins (Offaly)
Top scorer: J. Kenneally (Cork) 2-1

Cork succeeded where they failed in 1927 by becoming the first county to make a successful defence of the MacCarthy Cup.

There was a tram strike in Dublin at the time, but followers still made their way to headquarters in large numbers for this second successive final between the counties.

The defending champions, who played against a strong sun in the first half, could not have had a better start. Paddy Delea scored an early goal, but Galway hit back with a brace of points. Galway maintained the pressure for a time, but it was Cork who proved better in the finishing stakes, with Michael Ahearne and Johnny Kenneally on the goal standard. Play was fast and exciting for the rest of the half, with Galway hurling with power and determination—so much so that they had the edge in some stirring passages, and Dick Morrissey reaped the reward the Connacht men deserved with a good goal.

However, Kenneally eased matters for Cork with his second goal, and just before the break Eudie Coughlan showed his characteristic style as he gained possession and sent a searing shot over the bar to give Cork an interval lead of 3-3 to 1-2.

Cork had the better of matters in the second half. Jim Hurley opened with a point and soon afterwards gained possession on the 70. He sent a powerful drive goalwards which was helped over the bar by Ahearne.

Although Galway battled on bravely, they found it difficult to get scores against a tenacious Cork rearguard, where Jim O'Regan was a brilliant performer, and Cork went on to retain the trophy in comfortable style.

Paddy Delea and Kenneally, who each scored two goals, O'Regan and Coughlan were prominent in the Cork triumph.

Chapter 3 ~

THE THIRTIES

The 1930 to 1939 All-Ireland hurling finals

The thirties were marked by big crowds at MacCarthy Cup finals, some gripping encounters, memorable teams and exciting personalities who were to go on to earn hurling immortality.

Cork and Kilkenny provided three superb matches before deciding the destination of the 1931 All-Ireland senior championship. The teams played a thrilling draw in September, and the replay a month later drew the greatest attendance to a hurling final up to then at 33,124.

The attendance fell somewhat below that for the second replay, but the general interest created by the three matches gave the ancient game a tremendous impetus and set the pattern for a highly successful decade.

Kilkenny and Clare drew 34,372 to their meeting in 1932 to set another new high, and a year later came the first 40,000-plus crowd at a hurling match. That MacCarthy Cup decider featured Kilkenny and Limerick.

Kilkenny were the most consistent team of the thirties. Including the 1931 final and up to and including 1937 they contested every All-Ireland decider except 1934 and won three titles. Many maintain that with a little better luck Kilkenny would have won six titles in that period!

Those were the days of Lory Meagher, Matty Power, Paddy Phelan, Johnny Dunne, Paddy Larkin and Peter O'Reilly, bright stars in a glittering galaxy, who contributed richly to the development and advancement of the game.

There were giants in other counties as well. One of the greatest and also the most colourful was Mick Mackey. He made his All-Ireland senior final debut in 1933 in that first 40,000-plus crowd puller, and over the remainder of the decade the Limerick man proved one of the most talked about personalities in the sport.

Mackey won his first All-Ireland senior medal in 1934, captained the Shannonsiders to their 1936 title and then, though not strictly in the confines of this chapter, led Limerick again to the 1940 title. They contested four successive finals in the thirties, plus one drawn game, and they won two of the deciders.

The decade also saw Clare appear in a MacCarthy Cup engagement for the first time in their history. The Banner County, like the other teams of the time, had personality-plus hurlers, among them 'Tull' Considine, John Joe Doyle, the team captain known as 'Goggle' because he wore a special pair of goggles, Tom Daly, a goalkeeper of outstanding ability who had earlier won All-Ireland medals with Dublin, and Larry Blake. Clare lost the 1932 final to Kilkenny before a then record attendance.

The decade also provided the last All-Ireland senior hurling final played outside Croke Park until 1984. In 1937 the stadium was not available because of construction work then in progress on the Cusack Stand, and as a result the final was allocated that year to Killarney. The game resulted in a Tipperary win over Kilkenny before a crowd of 43,620 and earned the Premier County their second and last MacCarthy Cup win of the thirties.

Tommy Doyle, who was to go on to prove one of Tipperary's leading performers in subsequent years, won the first of his five All-Ireland senior medals in that unique 1937 game and less than a year after his senior debut with the county side.

Waterford stepped into MacCarthy Cup action for the first time in 1938, but this outstanding team skilfully led by Mick Hickey and with other powerful hurlers in John Keane, Charlie Ware and Declan Good lost to Dublin. It would take Waterford ten more years to return to the MacCarthy Cup scene, and that outing proved a historically successful one for the county.

Cork, after that great start to the thirties with their win over Kilkenny in three spine-tingling games, surprisingly achieved only one other final appearance in the decade. That was at the end of the period, the day war was declared in 1939 and when Jack Lynch, who was to go on to carve out a unique niche for himself in the annals of the games by winning six All-Ireland senior medals (five in hurling and one in football) in succession, led the Leesiders in a final that has become part of the folklore of hurling

The 1939 show-down with Kilkenny is known as the 'Thunder and Lightning final', as much of the second half was played in an electric storm.

Cork had been rebuilding after the 1931 games. They hadn't yet got all the answers right by 1939 when Kilkenny came out on top, but from that squad emerged the great team of the forties.

Kilkenny were the leading power in the thirties with four MacCarthy Cup wins between 1932 and 1939. Dublin won in 1938.

Munster collected five championships, two each by Tipperary and Limerick, and one by Cork.

And if the decade did not end as it began with bumper crowds, an attendance of 39,302 for the last game of the thirties was still a wonderful one as Ireland and the world held its breath wondering about the future, with World War II threatening death and destruction that would extend over six long years.

Statistics

Greatest attendance	51,235 in 1936
Busiest referee	S. Jordan (Galway) 1930, 33, 34 (draw and replay)
Highest team score	5-8 (23 points) by Cork 1931 (second replay)
Highest score by losing team	3-4 (13 points) by Kilkenny 1931 (second replay) and 3-4 by Dublin 1934
Lowest winning margin	One point by Kilkenny 1935, and by Kilkenny again 1939
Highest individual score	4-0 by D. Clohossy (Limerick) 1934 (replay)
Goalless finals	None
Finals in which winning team failed to score a goal	None
Best points tally by winning team	11 by Tipperary 1937
Best points tally by losing team	6 by Limerick 1933, by Dublin 1934 and by Waterford 1938
Lowest scoring final on aggregate	1933: 1-13 (16 points)
Replays	1931: Two. 1934: One
Most successful captain	J. Walsh (Kilkenny) 1932, 39

1930 FINAL: O'MEARA SHINES FOR TIPP

7 September 1930   Tipperary 2-7, Dublin 1-3
Attendance: No accurate figures available   Referee: S. Jordan (Galway)
Top scorers: M. Kennedy (Tipperary) 1-1, P. Cahill (Tipperary) 0-4, J. J.
Callanan (Tipperary) 1-1

Although the hurling was fast and earnest, this final did not rise to great
heights. Tipperary had the first two points of the game, but overall Dublin
set the pace in the opening twenty minutes. They were the faster team and,
after playing with the sun, turned over just a point in arrears. They would
probably have been ahead but for the brilliance of Tom O'Meara in the
Tipperary goal.

Matty Power scored Dublin's only goal after twenty minutes, but near
the end of the half Martin Kennedy hit Tipperary's opening goal to put
them ahead by 1-3 to 1-2 at the break.

Tipperary reshuffled their team during the break and the changes
improved the side as they made most of the running after the restart. A
brace of points from frees by Phil Cahill and a further point from team
captain John Joe Callanan put the Munster champions in command.

Dublin continued to battle strongly, but soon after their cause
was ended by a sweeping Tipperary attack of old style flair and finishing
that resulted in Callanan banging home his team's second and decisive
goal.

Kennedy, Cahill and Callanan with their vital scores and goalkeeper
O'Meara were the principal architects of the Tipperary success.
Outstanding for Dublin were their captain, Jas Walsh, midfielder Gill and
goalscorer Power.

1931 FINAL: THRILLER BOOSTS GAME'S IMAGE

6 September 1931   Cork 1-6, Kilkenny 1-6
Attendance: 26,460   Referee: S. Robbins (Offaly)
Top scorer: D. Dunne (Kilkenny) 1-1

This was the first chapter in a thrilling sequence of games that really started
to bring the crowds to hurling matches in big numbers. The teams gave a
brilliant exhibition on a balmy autumn day, with Kilkenny taking most of
the honours in a wonderful rally that brought them from six points in
arrears with twenty minutes to play to earn a well-deserved draw.

Kilkenny played towards the Canal goal and against the sun in the first half. Exchanges were fairly even throughout, but a goal from 'Gah' Ahearne sent Cork on the way to a 1-3 to 0-2 interval advantage.

The Leesiders had the better of the exchanges in the early minutes of the second half and pushed their lead to six points, but Kilkenny's mighty captain, Lory Meagher, did much to fuel a Noreside revival after that. A Meagher free sailed into the Cork goal area and Dan Dunne sent the sliothar to the net. Meagher collected the puck-out and gave to Mick Larkin, who cut his team's deficit to just two points. Nor was Meagher finished. He pointed a free, then took full advantage of another free to level the scores. The Noreside rally continued as Dunne popped over another point to give his team what appeared to be a match-winning lead, but as the excitement built to a tremendous pitch, Eudie Coughlan sent over the equaliser.

Both sides battled strongly after that, but they failed to add to their returns before the final whistle.

1931 FINAL: FIRST REPLAY

11 October 1931   Cork 2-5, Kilkenny 2-5
Attendance: 33,124   Referee: S. Robbins (Offaly)
Top scorer: E. Coughlan (Cork) 1-2

The attendance set a new record for a hurling final, and the spectators were treated to a cracker of a match as two gifted teams provided a superb exhibition, marked by skilled play and exciting exchanges.

Kilkenny opened promisingly and a Dunne goal helped them to a five point lead after only seven minutes. Cork then began to find their style and fluency, and goals by Eudie Coughlan and Willie Clancy sent the Munster champions in at the break leading 2-4 to 1-3.

Kilkenny skipper Lory Meagher broke three ribs early on in the game, but he continued to play on and boosted his team's hopes on the restart with two early points. The hurling was top class after that with plenty of exciting passages, and Meagher proved a bright feature with his classic touches and inspiring play.

Thirteen minutes into the second half, Paddy 'Skipper' Walsh goaled to give Kilkenny a point lead. Ten minutes from the end Cork had their only score of the half—a point by Paddy Delea.

The exchanges continued to be spirited as the game ended all square.

1931 FINAL: SECOND REPLAY

1 November 1931   Cork 5-8, Kilkenny 3-4
Attendance: 31,935   Referee: W. Walsh (Waterford)
Top scorers: P. Delea (Cork) 2-0, W. Clancy (Cork) 1-3

Kilkenny lined out without Lory Meagher, whose broken ribs sustained in the second drawn game kept him on the injured list. He was joined by Paddy Larkin and Bill Dalton. Nevertheless, the Leinster men put up a much better display than Cork's victory margin would suggest. Tommy Leahy, who went in as a substitute for Larkin in the second draw, replaced Meagher, and his brother Jerry was also called into action.

The match had hardly started when Willie Clancy had Cork ahead with a point. Kilkenny stormed back and Paddy Walsh goaled. The exchanges continued to be keen, and with just two minutes remaining in the half the sides were on level terms—Cork 0-5, Kilkenny 1-2. However, Cork then struck a purple patch and goals by 'Gah' Ahearne and Paddy Delea gave them an interval lead of 2-5 to 1-2.

Kilkenny had the advantage of the breeze in the second half and they quickly set about reducing arrears. A point by Matty Power, a Dan Dunne goal and an Eddie Byrne point from a 70 yard free left them just a point behind.

Cork responded in positive fashion. Clancy boosted their morale with a fine goal and Jim Hurley followed with a point. The closing stages produced a feast of goals. 'Balty' Ahearne looked to have secured victory for Cork when he goaled, but gallant Kilkenny hit back in the best possible manner with a Jer Leahy goal.

End of goals for the day? Not a bit of it, as Delea was back to find the Kilkenny net and ensured that this third chapter of a memorable serial ended in Cork's favour. The three games attracted an aggregate attendance of 91,519 and the receipts amounted to £7,779.

The Central Council marked the special three-match series by presenting both teams with watches inscribed in Irish.

1932 FINAL: CLARE'S DEBUT

14 September 1932   Kilkenny 3-3, Clare 2-3
Attendance: 34,372   Referee: S. Robbins (Offaly)
Top scorers: T. Considine (Clare) 2-1, M. White (Kilkenny) 2-1

This was Clare's debut in a MacCarthy Cup final and one that had been earned after a thrilling Munster campaign followed by an amazing semi-final win over Galway. The westerners led by thirteen points at half-time and were fifteen points clear soon after the restart, but eventually lost by five points to Limerick on a clear day.

So, in the year of the Eucharistic Congress, Clare were a major talking point in Irish sport as they faced up to Kilkenny. It was hardly surprising that the final set a new attendance record.

Things looked good for the newcomers as Jack Glesson sent them into a one point lead with a long shot from midfield. He was to go on and give a great performance.

Kilkenny faced the Canal goal and put strong pressure on the Banner County defence, but with Jim Holohan, Patrick 'Fowler' McInerney and Larry Blake to the fore, the backs gave little away. It took the Noresiders thirteen minutes to equalise Clare's opening point—from a Martin White puck. Clare hit back with points from 'Tull' Considine and Holohan, and Kilkenny replied with a point from Eddie Doyle from a 70 to leave the half-time score Clare 0-3, Kilkenny 0-2.

Right from the start of the second half, however, Kilkenny hit top form, with Lory Meagher the commander in chief. Goals by Matty Power (two) and White helped them on the road to a 3-2 to 0-3 lead. However, Clare rallied well and two goals by Considine left them just two points adrift. Kilkenny kept their composure and White clinched victory with a point.

Meagher was Kilkenny's brightest star. Paddy Larkin and Peter O'Reilly in defence were also prominent in the success story.

Midfielder Gleeson, top scoring Considine and defender McInerney were hard workers for the Banner County.

1933 FINAL: POWER BREAKS DEADLOCK

3 September 1933   Kilkenny 1-7, Limerick 0-6
Attendance: 45,176   Referee: S. Jordan (Galway)
Top scorer: J. Dunne (Kilkenny) 1-1

The attendance set a new record not only for a hurling game but also for a football decider until then. The spectators were not disappointed.

Though it was not the greatest final for polished hurling, that was more than compensated for as two well-matched teams provided an intensely exciting game on a very hot afternoon, with the issue in doubt until the final whistle.

Limerick, beaten earlier in the year by Kilkenny in the National League final, played with their backs to the sun and against a strong wind. Scores were at a premium early on, but after twenty minutes Lory Meagher pointed a free to put Kilkenny ahead for the first time, 0-2 to 0-1. The scores were tied at the interval at 0-4 each.

The exchanges continued to prove very keen after the restart. Kilkenny's striking was fast, sure and hard in open play and overall their style was less laborious than Limerick's. Despite their best efforts, the defending MacCarthy Cup holders still only managed a point from Johnny Dunne in the first ten minutes. Christy O'Brien soon had Limerick back once more on level terms.

Then came eight minutes of power-packed hurling, laced with many thrills and some fine individual efforts before Matty Power gave Kilkenny back the lead again, 0-6 to 0-5, and they were never headed after that. An excellent goal by full forward Johnny Dunne in the 26th minute ensured that the trophy remained by the Noreside.

Kilkenny's defence, with Paddy Larkin, Peter O'Reilly and team captain Eddie Doyle setting the standard, was outstanding all through. Meagher at midfield and Dunne and Power up front also sparkled.

Limerick, who fielded a young team, had an outstanding captain and defender in Mickey Fitzgibbon. Ned Cregan and Garrett Howard in defence and midfielder Mick Ryan were other top performers.

1934 FINAL: GOLDEN JUBILEE DRAW

2 September 1934   Limerick 2-7, Dublin 3-4
Attendance: 34,894   Referee: S. Jordan (Galway)
Top scorer: D. Clohossy (Limerick) 2-2

This was the Golden Jubilee Year final and despite rain and a slippery pitch Limerick and Dublin served up an excellent game when sharing the honours. There were many thrilling passages of play in the exciting end-to-end exchanges, and the game was played at a fast pace throughout.

The Shannonsiders appeared on course for the cup as they held on to a narrow lead coming up to the final whistle, but a goal by full forward Dinny O'Neill just two minutes from the end gave Dublin a draw that on the run of play they well merited.

Limerick lined out with ten of the side that beat Dublin earlier in the year in the 1933–34 National League final and started favourites. However, Dublin took the game to the League champions from the throw-in and points by Mick Daniels and a goal by Muldowney boosted their morale. Limerick replied with a point from Timmy Ryan. Dave Clohossy (Limerick) and Dinny O'Neill each scored a goal before the interval, which ended with the Munster men ahead by 1-5 to 2-1.

The second half was a ding-dong affair with plenty of exciting play and stirring exchanges to keep the spectators on their feet. Dave Clohossy, who did not play in the earlier League final, began to stamp his personality on the decider in a big way. He scored two points followed by his second goal to put the Shannonsiders five points clear.

But Dublin did not throw in the towel. They did not allow Limerick to add to their total as they steadily whittled away at their opponents' lead. Coming up to the end came that O'Neill goal, a first-rate effort that earned Dublin a well-merited replay.

1934 FINAL REPLAY: CLOHOSSY, FOUR GOAL HERO

30 September 1934   Limerick 5-2, Dublin 2-6
Attendance: 30,250   Referee: S. Jordan (Galway)
Top scorer: D. Clohossy (Limerick) 4-0

Limerick invited famed Cork trainer Jim Barry to prepare the side for this replay. They lost their goalkeeper Paddy Scanlan on the eve of the match because of illness, but one-time Limerick and Munster net-minder

Tommy Shinney stepped into the breach, and he proved an outstanding deputy.

This was Dave Clohossy's final. He set the seal on a fine display by helping himself to one of the top individual scoring feats in a final with four goals. In a keenly contested first half, Clohossy recorded Limerick's solitary score to leave his side on level terms at the interval, 1-0 to 0-3.

Four goals in as many minutes early in the second half set the replay alight and ensured a tremendous battle for the rest of the game, one that provided followers of both sides with much to enthuse over.

Mick Mackey (Limerick) and Dinny O'Neill scored the opening goals of the half. Clohossy followed on with his second goal of the day and O'Neill was back again with a peach of a goal to leave the sides level again, Dublin 2-3, Limerick 3-0.

Dublin followed on with some good points. But once again Clohossy had a trump card to play. After 55 minutes he collected his third goal to tie the match once more at 4-0 to 2-6.

Mackey had Limerick's first point of the game after 58 minutes, and two minutes later Clohossy completed his goal harvest to clinch victory for the Shannonsiders.

While Clohossy was the man of the match, John Mackey in attack ran him close with a stellar showing, and Jackie O'Connell and Mick Mackey were also prominent.

O'Neill was a bright star for Dublin with two goals, with Steve Hegarty and Tommy Treacy in attack and Arthur Murphy in defence impressive.

1935 FINAL: LIMERICK LOSE TITLE DEFENCE

1 September 1935   Kilkenny 2-5, Limerick 2-4
Attendance: 46,591   Referee: T. Daly (Clare)
Top scorer: P. McMahon (Limerick) 2-0

A veritable downpour which resulted in the worst possible conditions did not prevent Kilkenny and Limerick from providing an attendance that established a then new record for a hurling final with a memorable encounter.

There was no score for eight thrilling minutes. Kilkenny eventually scored a point, but a Mick Mackey point, a Paddy McMahon goal and another point by Mackey swung the game Limerick's way for a time. However, Kilkenny came more into the game after that and a Jack Duggan goal spurred them on to an interval lead of 1-3 to 1-2.

The driving rain showed no sign of abating as the teams lined up for the second half. The exchanges continued to be very keen, but Kilkenny began to have the better of matters, and a cracking goal by Martin White had them five points clear with about ten minutes remaining.

Limerick, with their title slipping away, bounced back strongly to ensure a great finish. A point by Mackey, a goal by McMahon and a point by Mick Cross boosted their hopes, but Kilkenny held out for a deserved one point win.

Lory Meagher was a key figure in the Noreside success, with White in attack and defenders Paddy Larkin and Peter O'Reilly also outstanding workers.

Mick Mackey was Limerick's leading hurler. McMahon with his two goals, John Mackey in attack, Tim Ryan at midfield and Garrett Howard in defence were also in the thick of the action.

1936 FINAL: MACKEY'S CHEEKY SOLO RUN

6 September 1936   Limerick 5-6, Kilkenny 1-5
Attendance: 51,235   Referee: J. O'Regan (Cork)
Top scorers: P. McMahon (Limerick) 2-0, D. Clohossy (Limerick) 2-0

Limerick regained the MacCarthy Cup after two years with a riot of wonderful hurling. Their back division gave the Kilkenny forwards little or no room to operate and the Shannonside forwards showed a refreshing flair in front of goal, especially when it came to putting the ball into the net.

After Kilkenny opened the scoring with a Lory Meagher point, a great movement in which John Mackey was involved, ended with Jackie Power slamming the sliothar to the Kilkenny net. Goals by Johnny Dunne (Kilkenny) and Paddy McMahon (Limerick) were scored later in the half, which ended with Limerick ahead 2-3 to 1-4.

Limerick started the second half with a real flourish. Dave Clohossy had a goal in three minutes and Mick Mackey tagged on two points. After Eddie Byrne pointed for Kilkenny, Clohossy was back to collect his second goal after only four minutes. The cup was there and then out of Kilkenny's reach.

Later in the game came a real highlight. Mick Mackey, who had a star match as he led Limerick to an All-Ireland final win for the first time, went off on a cheeky solo run to set McMahon up for his second goal.

Paddy Clohossy and Tom McCarthy sparkled at the back for Limerick, while the Mackey brothers, McMahon and Dave Clohossy were the leading lights further upfield.

Lory Meagher and Tom Leahy did reasonably well around midfield for Kilkenny. Eddie Byrne was a solid worker in defence, while Jimmy Walsh and Matty Power were best up front.

1937 FINAL: ONE SECOND-HALF SCORE FOR CATS

5 September 1937   Tipperary 3-11, Kilkenny 0-3
Attendance: 43,620   Referee: J. Flaherty (Offaly)
Top scorer: D. Murphy (Tipperary) 2-1

Tipperary, with a number of bright youngsters in their side, swept past Kilkenny in a historic game at Killarney that failed completely to live up to expectations.

Tommy Doyle, one of the newcomers to the Premier County, had his side a point clear virtually from the throw-in, and the Leinster champions were always fighting a losing battle after that. Tipperary were fast and used their speed to range fast and wide over the spacious Killarney sward. They also lost no time in hitting the ball and got great length into their pucks

The Leinster champions, with a somewhat veteran team, tried hard but they could not match their speedier opponents and only managed to score a brace of points in the first half. Tipperary finished the half with 2-8, with goals by Dinny Murphy and Jimmy Coffey.

Jimmy Cooney was a tremendous worker for Tipperary in midfield. Kilkenny brought in Lory Meagher from the substitutes in a bid to improve matters, but the southerners continued to have the better of the exchanges. Meagher recorded Kilkenny's solitary score of the second half, a point and the opening score of the period. Tipperary's response was decisive—another goal by Dinny Murphy.

In addition to Cooney, Johnny Ryan in the half back line and Murphy and Coffey in attack were the hurlers who did most to orchestrate the Tipperary success. As for Kilkenny, they were so badly beaten that they had no real stars.

1938 FINAL: KEANE'S INSPIRATION NOT ENOUGH

4 September 1938   Dublin 2-5, Waterford 1-6
Attendance: 37,129   Referee: I. Harney (Galway)
Top scorer: J. Keane (Waterford) 0-4

It may or may not be significant in the review of the MacCarthy Cup of 1938 to lay emphasis on the fact that the victors, Dublin, were winning the title for the first time since 1927 when they beat Waterford 2-5 to 1-6 to gain a sixth major title. The metropolitans have not succeeded in capturing the glory of that success since. The composition of Dublin teams at that period was drawn mainly from non-natives playing regularly with Dublin clubs. As events transpired the 1938 team featured one Dublin-born player, Jim Byrne, from the Eoghan Ruadh club, the only Dublin player to have gained that precious All-Ireland medal.

Ten years later five Dublin-born players gained representation on the Dublin side which faced up to Waterford in the All-Ireland final. More about that anon. The events of the 1938 final were overshadowed by happenings in the Munster hurling championship and it became known as the Jimmy Cooney case and for the infamous 'Ban' rule which was in vogue at the time. Jimmy Cooney, a native of Carrick-on-Suir, Co. Tipperary, was living in Dublin and played with the UCD club. In early February 1938 Cooney duly signed a declaration form which indicated that he would be playing with his native county for that year's inter-county hurling championship. The declaration form was forwarded to the Tipperary County Board, which was the order of things, but it never reached the general secretary of the GAA until shortly before Easter.

On 12 February, Jimmy Cooney attended an international rugby match between Ireland and England at Lansdowne Road and was reported to the GAA authorities by the vigilance committee. He admitted his offence and incurred an automatic three months' suspension. Jimmy Cooney made a case in due course to the Leinster Council for his re-instatement and it was granted by the Council with effect from May 1938. Cooney was a very relieved man. He could now play with his native Tipperary in the Munster championship. (*Ní mar a sílter bitear.*) Now free to play for his county, Jimmy was picked on the Tipperary team which played Limerick in a Monaghan Cup match in London. It was to have a frightening aftermath for Cooney. The Central Council of the GAA held that Cooney's declaration, which was dated February 1938, was effective only from the date of receipt by them—Easter time 1938.

It was also stated by the Council that the declaration was deemed to have been made by Jimmy during the period of his suspension and was therefore invalid. He was accordingly declared illegal for the Monaghan Cup match and an automatic suspension of six months was imposed. There was consternation and outright anger in Tipperary. The county board held that the effective date of Cooney's declaration was 2 February 1938. Back came the Central Council insisting that the effective date was when the document came into their possession just before Easter. In order to clarify the matter and ensure that there would be no further misunderstanding in the matter, the Tipperary County Board was officially informed by the Central Council that Jimmy Cooney was a suspended player. That notification arrived on the eve of Tipperary's Munster semifinal against Clare.

Naturally there was fury in Tipperary. As feelings were running so high, there was a strong case for a cautionary approach. Some were suggesting that Cooney be withdrawn from the Clare match. It was not to be. Cooney lined out against Clare in the Munster semi-final at Limerick on 26 June filling his midfield role. It must be said that Clare did intimate that they would object should Cooney be included on the Tipperary team for that match if they were to subsequently lose the match. Tipperary won the game decisively 3-10 to 2-3 and while Cooney contributed to the winners' tally, his absence would not have been felt. Inevitably, Clare objected and their objection was upheld by the Munster Council, who also turned down Tipperary's counter objection in which they claimed that Clare included Michael Griffin, who was seen by Cooney at the same rugby match. The Council ruled that the evidence supplied by Tipperary involving Griffin came from a suspended player (Cooney) and was not therefore admissible.

Tipperary were still unhappy and appealed to the Central Council, but they lost their case. It was widely felt in Tipperary at the time that an All-Ireland title was there for the taking and that factor alone added immeasurably to the major discontent in the county. For Jimmy Cooney it still meant six months on the sideline. The Cooney case was a talking point in hurling circles for a long time after the dust had settled. Tipperary rightly felt annoyed over the slip-up in Cooney's declaration not reaching the Central Council by the proper date. On the other hand, the fact that

Cooney had admitted to being at the rugby match made it an open and shut case in the eyes of the Central Council. Had Cooney denied the charge, the onus would have been on the GAA to prove its case. That might have posed problems for the Council.

There were suggestions at the time that the Tipperary man was totally against the rule banning players from attending other named sports and he couldn't understand the logic behind it. He loved sport of all kinds and that was to place him on the 'against the ban' movement at official level. Certainly it would not have been approved by those who were insisting on the ban being upheld at all levels. It goes without saying that Cooney's position would not have helped his case when the declaration issue arose at Central Council. The ban had been a very emotive issue long before it 'walked the plank' at the 1971 GAA Congress in Belfast. It was to crop up again but in a very different context in 1938 which had nothing to do with the playing aspects of the national games of hurling and football.

On that occasion it concerned the newly installed President of Ireland, Dr Douglas Hyde. He was born in Castlerea, Co. Roscommon, the son of the rector of Tibohine. He was educated at Trinity College, Dublin, was awarded a Doctorate of Laws in 1888 and had spent a year at the University of New Brunswick. A great scholar, linguist and cultural leader, he founded the Gaelic League in 1893 with Eoin McNeill. He was appointed professor of modern Irish at UCD (1929 to 1932). He was a senator (1925–26). He became President of Ireland in 1938. Though he was a patron of the GAA, he was expelled from the organisation for attending a soccer international at Dalymount Park.

In 1938 Dublin won their sixth All-Ireland senior hurling title beating Waterford 2-5 to 1-6. They thus regained the premier title last held in 1927. It was a keenly contested game with level scoring and with the verdict in the balance holding interest all the way.

On their first time trying it was a bold attempt by Waterford, and their followers, while naturally disappointed, were honest enough to admit that their team had battled gamely for the title and had no reason to feel despondent. Waterford, after twice losing the lead in the first half-hour and again drawing level, were a goal behind at the interval, 2-3 to 1-3. Dublin all round were the faster team in the race for the ball, and many of the Waterford men had not adapted themselves to the craft of preventing an opponent from striking the ball without committing a foul.

For a period after the interval Dublin had much the better of the exchanges when, allowing for sturdy resistance from the Waterford defenders, their forwards might have turned their chances to fuller account. There was a good deal of faulty striking and misdirected efforts by both teams. Earnestness and determination were at no time wanting, but Dublin were the cooler in emergency while Waterford, for the greater part, played as if they staked their all on dash and daring. Tackling was keen and there were many stoppages due to injuries, but the only player obliged to retire was the Dublin captain Mick Daniels, who was assisted off towards the end and was replaced by his Army club mate J. Gilmartin, who had been with Tipperary a while back.

A feature of the game was the good goalkeeping by Mick Curley for Waterford. He was kept far busier than Christy Forde at the other end, and it was no fault of his that the Deise men had to taste defeat. The Waterford midfield pair, Seán Feeney and Christy Moylan, were outplayed by Dublin's Harry Gray and Mick Daniels. As in some of the earlier rounds Gray played a major role in Dublin's success. Against Kilkenny in the replayed Leinster final, 'Mossie' McDonnell on the '40' for Dublin was an untiring worker, and if his judgment was at fault on a few occasions, he had three great points and was a constant thorn in the side of Waterford centre back John Keane, who, as usual, bore the brunt of the play. When it looked towards the end that Waterford might yet avert defeat or even snatch victory, the Dublin half back line of Mick Gill, Phil Farrell and Jim Byrne gave a reassuring and splendid display.

It is interesting to note that Dublin had a formidable team with players drawn from Laois, Kilkenny, Tipperary, Galway, Mayo, Limerick, Cork, and one Dublin-born player, Jim Byrne. Writing in his column in *The Irish Times* the following day 'Pat O' observed: 'Jim Byrne of Eoghan Ruadh, a native of Dublin and a product of city schools hurling, was the best of the lot. Gill and Farrell [with Byrne] completed a half line on which Dublin's victory hinged. They held Waterford's attack in a vice like grip.' Waterford, Munster champions for the first time that year at senior level, got away to a good start but they were unable to sustain it. Mick Hickey, who captained the team, got great support from John Fanning, Charlie Ware and Mick Curley. Dublin's title success was to be the county's last MacCarthy Cup triumph. There was an interesting sidelight to the clash of the two counties. Waterford was captained by Mick Hickey whom I was later to play against ten years later in the 1948 All-Ireland final. Mick

Daniels captained Dublin and both players were born within hailing distance of each other—Mick Hickey in Carrickbeg in the Deise county and Mick Daniels in Carrickmore, across the River Suir in Co. Tipperary—a unique bit of hurling history. It was to be Mick Daniels' glory hour to capture his only MacCarthy Cup medal. When Daniels first lined out with his adopted Dublin in 1930, he was joining a county that had established a proud hurling tradition. They had won All-Ireland titles in 1917, 20, 24 and 27. The latter team was a superb combination. It beat one of Cork's greatest teams in that year's final.

Mick Daniels told me many years later that the 1938 team he led was as good as any team that Dublin fielded, taking into account the brilliant 1924 fifteen and of course the 1934 side who beat Kilkenny at the height of what many considered their greatest era by defeating them 3-5 to 2-2 in the Leinster final. It is well worth noting that Mick Daniels claimed that winning his only Railway Cup medal with Leinster in 1936, when they beat a star-studded Munster team 2-8 to 3-4, was one of his proudest moments. They were the days when to play for your province was a wonderful honour. It made you the envy of your colleagues. Sadly, that has changed now and the series is no longer rated. The public has lost interest in it.

1939 FINAL: THE THUNDER AND LIGHTNING FINAL

3 September 1939   Kilkenny 2-7, Cork 3-3
Attendance: 39,302   Referee: J. Flaherty (Offaly)
Top scorer: J. Phelan (Kilkenny) 2-1

War was declared on Sunday morning, 3 September 1939, and the news was on everybody's lips coming from Mass. Incessant overnight rain had flooded parts of Dublin city, augmented by a frightening intensity of thunder and lightning. The Oireachtas, recalled from the summer recess the day before, sat through the night before adjourning at 4.50 a.m. on that Sunday morning, having passed the emergency legislation presented to it by the Taoiseach, Éamon de Valera. Dev told that august gathering that 'a time of war' as defined in the Constitution covered the emergency which then threatened the country. No one was prepared to argue against that interpretation of the circumstances and legislation was quickly passed. When the news of the declaration of war gathered momentum, panic buying broke out all over the city and country. Stocks disappeared quickly, much of it under the counters in shops, to be sold subsequently at far higher prices. Elsewhere in the country the infamous border was to be sharply defined, resulting in villages and houses being bisected between Northern Ireland and 'Éire', as we were then known. The village of Pettigo in Co. Donegal was to be divided in half, one side in a 'war' situation and the other in an 'emergency', the latter description undoubtedly one of the great euphemisms of the century. My Limerick relations arrived at our house in Fairview for a quick snack before walking to Croke Park for the All-Ireland hurling final between Kilkenny and Cork. Frequent radio bulletins announcing that a state of war existed between Germany and Britain failed to dampen the enthusiasm of those with only hurling on their minds. The rain of the early morning had eased, but the sky was laden with heavy clouds, and the rumbling of thunder and distant flashes of lightning were only a foretaste of what was to follow after the game had commenced.

The heavens opened and the rain began to cascade down in sheets, accompanied by thunder and lightning. I watched it all from the steps of the Hogan Stand, where I sat beside my dad in the press box. In spite of the conditions the game between the great rivals was a thriller as flood waters poured river-like along those seated on the sideline in front of the Hogan Stand.

Spectators left Croke Park after that 1939 final saturated to the skin. My country cousins fared much better, because we were able to borrow old clothes, trousers, jackets, socks and shirts from neighbours when our own had been exhausted, and they at least had dry clothes going home to Limerick on the train. On that Sunday as the followers of Cork and Kilkenny made their way to Dublin for the All-Ireland, they missed the grim news and voice of Neville Chamberlain, the British Prime Minister, announcing on radio that his country was at war with Germany. Within hours of the broadcast six nations were at war with the Third Reich.

The 1939 All-Ireland final was a classic which Kilkenny won 2-7 to 3-3. The black and amber men had a goal and a point to their credit before Cork had their first score, a point, and the Noresiders, with Jimmy Langton in brilliant form, forged out an interval lead of 2-4 to 1-1. Cork had the advantage of a stiff breeze in the opening half. The pattern of play continued to favour Kilkenny after the resumption and appeared a foregone conclusion with the Leinster men leading 2-5 to 2-2. Cork, led by their captain Jack Lynch, came to life and his goal started a fight back. A Ted O'Sullivan (Cork) point left only two points between the teams. The thunder rumbled overhead and down came the threatening rain in torrents, but Kilkenny appeared to relish the sudden change in the playing conditions. The tempo of the match changed too as both teams went at it hammer and tongs. The thunder and lightning struck terror into the hearts of many spectators and indeed some of the players as well. So poor was the visibility, so sodden the turf, that many felt the game should have been abandoned. But despite the appeals of both captains, referee J. Flaherty (Offaly) waved on play which meant that the last quarter was played in the most appalling conditions ever experienced in an All-Ireland senior hurling final. Kilkenny forged four points clear, 2-6 to 2-2, but the Leesiders mounted another major challenge. Jack Lynch pointed a long-range delivery to leave three points between the teams. From the puck-out, with two minutes remaining, Cork were awarded a free in the midfield area. Big Bill Campbell, their right half back, stepped up to take the free and his shot was good and true. The ball slipped through a cluster of backs and forwards and the Kilkenny goalie Jim O'Connell to end up in the net. At that stage it looked as if this remarkable game would end in a draw.

Less than a minute remained when Kilkenny corner back Paddy Phelan forced the Cork defenders to concede a 70, and taking the shot himself, landed the ball short of the Cork posts. Batt Thornhill got his stick to it, but for once his clearance was weak and Jimmy Kelly, racing through, snapped up the chance and drove the ball over the bar to give Kilkenny their fourth MacCarthy Cup win of the decade. It also added another memorable chapter to the story of Kilkenny's one point triumphs over Cork in the showpiece game of the year. The backs were the architects of the Noreside success. Paddy Larkin and Paddy Grace were outstanding in the full line, and Bobby Hinks, Billy Burke and Paddy Phelan formed a powerful unit that had an outstanding influence on the success. Jimmy Langton was the prime scorer in attack as he won his first All-Ireland senior medal as a teenager. Teddie O'Sullivan, Jack Lynch, Batt Thornhill and Bill Campbell were best for Cork.

Cork captain Jack Lynch felt he could have won the game for Cork in the last minute, admitting, 'I missed an open goal when it was easier to score than to miss.' Still, there were good years ahead. The team was young in September 1939. Within the next seven years, five All-Ireland championships and two League titles would come to Cork. And Jack Lynch himself would atone for that 'miss' in the 1939 final.

Chapter 4 ⌒

THE FORTIES

The 1940 to 1949 hurling finals

T he early years of the forties proved difficult times for hurling and Irish life in general, understandable with World War II then raging in Europe and further afield. In those years travel was very difficult. Trains were infrequent, petrol for private motorists soon became a thing of the past and bus services on Sundays were suspended for a time. Despite these difficulties the senior hurling championships—and likewise football—continued, and the MacCarthy Cup games drew remarkable attendances.

Close on 50,000 watched the 1940 final, and three years later another attendance of almost the same size—48,843—saw Cork retain the cup in what must rank as one of the most unique clashes of them all. That featured Antrim. The northerners, powered by Kevin Armstrong, Sammy Mulholland, Jackie Bateson, Danny McAllister and the skilful Noel Campbell, brought a welcome change and many new talking points to a drab world as they shocked Galway in a high-scoring qualifying game, and then beat Kilkenny sensationally at Corrigan Park, Belfast, to earn a crack at Cork in the final.

Antrim were heavily beaten on their All-Ireland debut, but their achievement in giving Ulster a direct interest in a MacCarthy Cup tie for the first time must still rank as one of the major aspects of the competition's history. Cork's big win over Antrim gave them their third successive All-Ireland senior crown. The Leesiders retained the cup in 1944 and became the first and only county in hurling to win four All-Ireland senior championships in succession, which is still a record. Christy Ring was then an up and coming star with Cork. He played in all four winning finals, and thus early in his career he took a gigantic leap along the road that was to see him become the first winner of eight All-Ireland senior medals.

Another of the Leeside greats was Jack Lynch. He led Cork to their 1942 title win, played in all four MacCarthy Cup wins, and then was on duty in

1945 when the county's footballers brought the Sam Maguire Cup to the banks of the Lee for the very first time by beating Cavan in the All-Ireland senior final. Lynch's team mates in the football team included Derry Beckett who had won an All-Ireland senior hurling medal in 1942. The pair became the first dual medallists since the twenties. Cork had lost their Munster and All-Ireland titles in hurling in 1945, but the record-making days were not ended for Jack Lynch after the 1945 football medal. The Leesiders regained the MacCarthy Cup the following September, and their line-up included the man who later in life was to carve out such a distinguished career as a politician and rise to the position of An Taoiseach.

So, Lynch won six All-Ireland senior medals in succession (five in hurling and one in football), and to this day he remains the only man to achieve such a feat. There is an unusual and one can say record-breaking angle, in modern times at any rate, to Cork's MacCarthy Cup win in 1941. Believe it or not, they were not Munster champions that year! There was an outbreak of foot and mouth in 1941 and Tipperary and Kilkenny were counties particularly badly hit by the disease. The football final was played first that year, on 6 September, and the hurling final on 28 September. Cork and Dublin were nominated to contest the decider. Cork had beaten Limerick in Munster. They were to have played Tipperary in the semi-final, but that game had to be postponed because of the foot and mouth outbreak. Limerick were nominated to play Cork for the right to represent the province in the All-Ireland. Later on in the year the winners of the Cork-Limerick game would play Tipperary for the Munster title. The match between Limerick and Cork was played in the Athletic Grounds and Cork went on to score an easy victory over the Shannonsiders. Dublin had qualified for a Leinster final against Kilkenny, but that too was held up. So, it was Cork and Dublin for the MacCarthy Cup in 1941, and the Munster side won more or less as they pleased by twenty points.

The Munster final was played at Limerick on 26 October 1941 and the proud All-Ireland champions were humbled by the eager Tipperary men who won 5-4 to 2-3. The defeat did not cost Cork their All-Ireland crown, so we had the unusual situation of the MacCarthy Cup resting in Cork as champions, and the Munster title in Tipperary, also as champions, that Christmas time of 1941. As for Dublin, they fared somewhat better in that they eased the hurt of their All-Ireland final defeat by outscoring Kilkenny by a goal, 2-8 to 1-8, in the delayed Leinster final. Munster dominated the MacCarthy Cup campaign of the forties. There was the end of a great

Limerick era in 1940, when the Shannonsiders won what was to be their last title in 33 years. Then came Cork's great run, followed by a title for Tipperary in 1945, and Cork back again on top in 1946.

Kilkenny gave Leinster the cup for the only time in the decade following a classic with the Leesiders in 1947, but Waterford, with their first cup win in 1948,. and Tipperary in 1949 completed the Munster dominance. Waterford beat Dublin for that initial cup win in 1948, and thus a new name was inscribed on the trophy in the forties for the first time since the early campaigns in the championship.

Statistics

Greatest attendance	69,459 in 1945
Busiest referee	Mick Hennessy (Clare) 1942, 44
Highest team score	5-16 (31 points) by Cork 1943
Highest score by a losing team	3-8 (17 points) by Kilkenny 1946
Highest winning margin	27 points by Cork 1943
Lowest winning margin	One point by Kilkenny 1947
Highest individual score	3-2 by John Keane (Waterford) 1948
Goalless finals	None
Finals in which winning team failed to score a goal	Kilkenny 1947
Finals in which losing teams failed to score a goal	1941 Dublin; 1943 Antrim; 1949 Laois
Best points tally by winning team	16 by Cork 1943
Best points tally by losing team	8 by Kilkenny 1946
Top scoring final on aggregate	1946: 10-13 (43 points)
Lowest scoring final on aggregate	1949: 3-14 (23 points)
Replays	None
Most successful captain	No hurler captained more than one title-winning team

1940 FINAL: NAVAL SERVICE TO THE FORE

1 September 1940   Limerick 3-7, Kilkenny 1-7
Attendance: 49,260   Referee: J.J. Callanan (Tipperary)
Top scorers: J. Power (Limerick) 1-2, T. Leahy (Kilkenny) 1-2

Limerick achieved a remarkable double on 2 September 1940 at Croke Park by wresting the All-Ireland senior hurling title from holders Kilkenny before an attendance of 49,260 and also capturing their first minor crown when they easily accounted for Antrim. Limerick supporters, who were present in force, were overjoyed at the dual success, it being the first occasion for the All-Ireland double to go to the Shannonsiders. Limerick at the start of the campaign were not among the more fancied sides, but before reaching Croke Park they had proved their grit and persistence by disposing of Waterford and Cork in each case by two points in a replay. But all that was to change. The All-Ireland final that year between Limerick and Kilkenny lived up to most expectations. As the war clouds darkened over Europe a guard of honour of a detachment from the Naval Service reflected the mood of the times by appearing at a MacCarthy Cup final for the first time.

The first half abounded in thrills, the pace was fast and the hurling was of a high order. Kilkenny opened in whirlwind fashion, but the Limerick defenders lived up to the form they had shown in the qualifying rounds. Kilkenny maintained the pressure and jumped into an early lead with a brilliant goal from Terry Leahy following a dashing solo run from midfield. Kilkenny set a blistering pace in the opening half. There were plenty of thrilling duels, but close marking was the order of the day. The continuity of play suffered due to injuries to both teams and tempers flared at times. Kilkenny took up the running and a long clearance from full back Paddy Grace was finished off by Terry Leahy for a good point. The hotly tested Limerick backs were relieved when a goal by Kilkenny's P. Phelan was disallowed as the referee J. J. Callanan (Tipperary) had blown for a free seconds earlier. Kilkenny strove might and main to increase their advantage, but the tenacious marking of the Limerick defence and the agility and bravery of goalie Paddy Scanlan kept them out.

Limerick were awarded a 70 which Clohossy pointed. They were having a greater share of the play at that stage and they silenced the Kilkenny followers with two well-taken scores in as many minutes. First, a cut in by J. Roche led to a point by Jackie Power, who then broke through for a goal to put the Munster champions ahead 1-2 to 1-1. But back swept Kilkenny and after centre back W. Burke had resumed his place after suffering an injury, Leahy levelled the scoring from a free and then P. Phelan put the Leinster champions in front with another point. Paddy Scanlan in the Limerick goal earned thunderous applause for a brilliant save, but Kilkenny continued to attack and had a point from Jimmy Langton to enjoy a two point lead.

Limerick needed a boost and they got it when Jackie Power beat Kilkenny goalie Jimmy O'Connell with a neat flick to the net in the 23rd minute. Kilkenny finished the first half the stronger team to lead 1-4 to 1-2. Paddy Clohossy was the mainstay at centre back for the Munster men curbing many of Kilkenny's attacks.

The second half brought a number of switches by the Limerick selectors. Mick Mackey moved to midfield, J. Roche was moved to the left wing with John Mackey taking over at centre forward. The switches were to pay off in time. Kilkenny wasted no effort in pursuit of their objective and Paddy Scanlan had to bring off a couple of master saves from Jimmy Langton and Terry Leahy. Not to be denied, the Leinster champions quickly had a point from Jimmy Walsh, who always looked dangerous in the scoring area. Limerick's response was rapid. Points followed from E. Ryan and Mick Mackey and the goal that always looked on, arrived at a crucial stage. Limerick power and fast striking opened up the Kilkenny defence. Jackie Power got to a loose ball, turned his marker and shot low and hard, but the eagle eye of Kilkenny goalie J. O'Connell watched the incoming ball and he blocked it out of danger. But Limerick's Dick Stokes moved swiftly and cracked the ball to the Kilkenny net putting Limerick ahead for the second time 2-4 to 1-6. Encroachment in the Kilkenny goal area robbed Paddy McMahon of a goal, but Limerick were now playing with full authority and John Mackey availed of slack marking to hammer home their third goal to put the Munster champions six points clear. Stalwart Paddy Clohossy, who had been limping badly after a knock, was replaced by Tony Herbert, who filled the gap very effectively for the remainder of the game. The Limerick captain Mick Mackey sealed a famous victory when he smashed over the final score of the game to leave them winners by 3-7 to 1-7.

An attendance of 49,260 watched the game, a great muster under wartime conditions. The gate receipts were £4,120. 'Pato' writing in his match report for *The Irish Times*, had high praise for the Limerick performance. 'Power in the unit and Power en masse—these were factors that decided the fate of the 1940 All-Ireland hurling championship. John Power, of Ahane, playing all over the field, was man of the hour—he led up to every vital Limerick score; massed power of shoulder, lung and limb, wore down Kilkenny hurling artistry. For ten minutes from the throw-in, Kilkenny treated spectators to a glorious hurling exhibition. They were playing rings around the Munster champions for brief sessions. Then Paddy Clohossy opened his shoulders, and Power flashed in and out like a blue kingfisher over a stream. His first startling goal gave Limerick the lead. Kilkenny recovered and led 1-4 to 1-2 at half-time. They were four points clear after 40 minutes of play, but then the dynamic power of Ardnacrusha appeared in evidence. Limerick's weight and reach told again and again. From Stokes' wonderful goal to the end, Limerick were masters right through the field.'

Three years after their All-Ireland victory, Ahane, the Limerick champions, who included six of that 1940 victory, were invited by my club, Eoghan Ruadhs, to play a challenge game in Croke Park in aid of the Merrion church building fund. Founder of the Ruadhs club was Fr Pat Flanagan, the parish priest of the Merrion church. It was the first time any club outside the capital city was invited to play in the capital, and the first time for any club team outside the city to appear at GAA headquarters. The Ahane game signalled my first match with the Ruadhs at senior level.

The match was a real thriller and Ahane edged the verdict in the closing stages when Mick Mackey gained possession, broke through the Ruadhs defence on a solo run and brushed aside all kinds of challenges to slam the ball to the net to give the Munster side a 2-7 to 3-2 winning result. Ahane proved a mighty force and the Ruadhs were delighted they were able to match them in most facets of play. They had a commanding figure in Jackie Power who could fill any role on the Ahane team along with Mick Mackey. The story is told that after the game against the Dublin club, Power turned to Mick Mackey and said, 'You know, Mick, we have played so many challenge matches to raise funds for building churches, that there must be a place for us already in heaven.' One of the morning newspaper write-ups on the Croke Park meeting of the two clubs described Jackie Power as 'being like one of the big Ardnacrusha turbines radiating high-powered voltage everywhere and inspiring the Shannonmen to deeds of daring do that meant everything to them'. From an Eoghan Ruadh perspective I would add that we learned a lot from the visit of Ahane and respected their brilliance as a team rightly billed as the 'wonder team from the South'. I may add that the appearance of Ahane as invitees to Croke Park set a trend for other Dublin clubs to follow, and from then on other prominent club teams made their debuts in challenge matches against Dublin club opposition.

1941 FINAL: CHRISTY RING DEBUT

28 September 1941   Cork 5-11, Dublin 0-6
Attendance: 26,150   Referee: W. O'Donnell (Tipperary)
Top scorer: T. O'Sullivan (Cork) 2-2

The dreaded foot and mouth disease which affected cattle and sheep caused havoc to major GAA fixtures particularly in Kilkenny and Tipperary, and the provincial finals were not played that year. This led to an unusual situation. The provincial councils of Munster and Leinster nominated Cork and Dublin respectively to contest the All-Ireland final that year, even though neither of the two counties had won its provincial title. An effort was made to postpone the hurling final further because of the close-down of inter-county fare due to the foot and mouth scourge, but it failed. The Central Council of the GAA moved swiftly to prevent any more objections and laid down the law: teams nominated to contest All-Ireland finals would fulfil that engagement and the winning team would be awarded the All-Ireland title. In the case of the Cork v Dublin tie it proved a one-sided affair. Cork cantered away with the game 5-11 to 0-6.

Despite the wartime restrictions, all sorts of devices were used to convey followers to Dublin for the final, tractors using vapourising oil, tandems, bicycles and horse-drawn carts. The crowd numbered over 26,000 and the weather was fine all through the hour. The match opened on a bright note for Cork with a goal after just three minutes, a score that only involved two players. Long hitting Billy Murphy, the Munster team's right full back, pucked a ball from his own goalmouth to within 21 yards of the Dublin goal. John Quirke gained possession and in a twinkling had the ball nestling in the Dublin net. That score did not dishearten Dublin, who played with great fervour over the following fifteen minutes, but the forwards failed to utilise the openings created by Ned Wade and Mossy McDonnell. Cork mounted a long bout of pressure and a consequent tally of telling scores. Among the scorers was a young Christy Ring, making his debut at All-Ireland senior level, who was to become a household name and a hurling icon in subsequent years.

After twenty minutes, a fine movement involving Jack Lynch and Jim Young brought a clever goal from Ted Sullivan, and that was a signal for a flurry of Cork scores, three beautiful points from Ring, and one from Jack Barrett, Jack Lynch and Teddy Sullivan. At half-time Cork had the game virtually sewn up, leading by 2-8 to 0-3. The second half was a one-sided affair following early goals from John Quirke, Ted Sullivan and Mick 'Micka' Brennan to leave Cork winners 5-11 to 0-6. They kept a tight grip at midfield where Jack Barrett and D. J. Buckley dominated against Harry Gray and Frank White. They also had a superb defence in which Billy Murphy, Bart Thornhill and Alan Lotty were outstanding. Their forwards also taught the Dublin attack a salutary lesson by taking most of their chances. Ned Wade, Jim Byrne, Mossy McDonnell and Gerry Glenn were Dublin's best in a game well won by the Leesiders.

Cork captain Connie Buckley said after the game that he had expected a closer call from the Dublin team. 'But I must give them credit for the way they battled away to the very end. They did miss a number of good scoring chances in the first half when they put the pressure on us, but our defence was too strong for them.' The Cork captain claimed that it was one of the fittest Cork teams ever to play in a Croke Park final, thanks to the hard work of trainer Jim Barry. Towards the end of the game both John Quirke and Jack Lynch feigned injury to allow Paddy O'Donovan and Bobby Ryng the honour of playing in an All-Ireland final, a very sporting gesture.

But Cork had to first complete an outstanding arrangement before the real All-Ireland celebrations could begin. Tipperary were waiting in the long grass and a long-awaited clash with the newly crowned All-Ireland champions in the delayed Munster final. The game took place in the Limerick Gaelic Grounds on 26 October. This was to be the first major test for the champions. Tipperary were very well prepared and the match result was proof positive that they were really up for the occasion. Tipperary won the game decisively 5-4 to 2-5. Efforts by Tipperary to claim the premier title were immediately shot down by president Pádraig McNamee and the Central Council. Naturally there were murmurings in the Premier County about Cork 'stealing our rightful title', but that was the end of it. Ace Cork marksman in the All-Ireland final John Quirke told me many years later that the loss of the Munster title rankled a bit with the Cork players. The preparation and effort put into winning the title had left them very much drained when it came to playing Tipperary in the delayed Munster final. That may be so, but Cork were still overjoyed to have captured the MacCarthy Cup while Dublin had the consolation of beating Kilkenny to take the Leinster title at Croke Park on 2 November on a 2-8 to 1-8 scoreline.

1942 FINAL: CONTROLLED HURLING FROM CORK

6 September 1942   Cork 2-14, Dublin 3-4
Attendance: 27,313   Referee: M. Hennessy (Clare)
Top scorer: J. Quirke (Cork) 1-2

Cork showed no fewer than seven changes for their 1942 All-Ireland final from the side which had defeated Dublin in the previous year's decider. The selectors took a gamble on youth and that was reflected in the make-up of the team for this important outing, again against Dublin. The Cork team gelled excellently and captured a second successive title against the metropolitans on 6 September 1942. Another significant pointer was the fact that Jack Lynch was appointed captain of the team, and the result proved a great shot in the arm for the Leeside skipper, who was disappointed with the defeat against Kilkenny in the 1939 final. The newcomers mentioned at the outset were Ned Porter (in goal), Con Murphy at left full back and among the forwards were Seán Condon on the 40, Mick Kenefick left half, Charlie Tobin right full, Derry Beckett top of the left, and Paddy O'Donovan at midfield who got a late run in the previous year's final.

While the final scoreline would suggest a runaway win for the Leesiders, it must be said that only a point separated the teams at the three-quarter stage and Dublin were very much in the picture in comparison with previous clashes between the counties at All-Ireland level. Tim Horgan in his book *Cork's Hurling Story* relates an unusual feature in the meeting of the teams in that 1942 final. 'The Cork goalkeeper Ned Porter and a Dublin forward, Mossie McDonnell, had been near-neighbours at Dillons Cross in Cork. "Mossie went to live in Dublin after he joined the army," recalled Ned Porter. "His brother, Dinny 'King' McDonnell won a county medal with the Glen in 1941." Incidentally, Ned Porter lived just across the road from the son of boxing champion and bowl player, Billy Stout. It always struck me as a nice piece of juxtaposition to find Stout and Porter living in such close proximity', wrote Tim.

The district was also the home of the popular Liam 'Bowler' Walsh, the county chairman who presided over six All-Ireland victories in a row, five in hurling and one in football. Tim records that 'on one occasion at a thrilled packed Munster final "Bowler" was asked to take charge of the large bottle of water for the players at half-time. The day was hot and the game was fast and exciting, but when the interval came the thirsty players had to remain parched. In his excitement "Bowler" had finished off the entire bottle himself.'

Dublin won the toss and elected to play with the wind before an attendance of 27,313. The exchanges were keen in the opening spell, but it hardly helped Dublin's cause that it took them twelve minutes to open the scoring with a fine point from Mossie McDonnell. Cork then began to get their game together and exercised their dominance on the proceedings with some excellent points. Shortly before half-time Seán Condon put John Quirke in possession, and the Cork full forward grabbed a goal to put Cork into a 1-7 to 2-1 lead at the interval. Ned O'Brien and McDonnell hit the Dublin scores. Cork's resistance was strong in the opening stages of the second half, with Derry Beckett proving very effective. The champions lost their goalkeeper Ned Porter, who was replaced by Jim Buttimer, but continued to send over match-winning points. Still they could not shake off the persistent Dublin challenge, and midway through the half the challengers were back firmly in the hunt when Donal Davitt landed a goal which left Dublin just a point behind.

However, Cork again took command and the Leinster champions' revival was beaten back by a goal from Derry Beckett. The MacCarthy Cup holders, with fast, controlled hurling went on to finish with seven points in hand. Dublin missed a glorious chance of a goal at a crucial stage of the match when only a point separated the sides. That seemed to spur Cork on to new efforts and points from John Quirke and Jack Lynch added further to the Cork winning total.

I have always admired Harry Gray's style, grace and elegance on the hurling field, especially having played against him at midfield for many years in Dublin competitions. He played the game as it should be played in a fine sporting manner. He gave great service to Dublin from 1938 to 1942 (and Laois in 1949). I asked him many years after he had retired from playing which of the five All-Irelands he contested did he enjoy the most. His reply was, 'Without any doubt I would say the 1942 final simply because we were in there with a great chance of winning at the three-quarter stage. Not alone that, we had got to within one point of a great Cork team, and they were showing signs of panic. All it would have taken was another Dublin score and we could have snatched it. Fate stepped in for Cork when Derry Beckett got in to score that vital goal and that swung the issue. Cork added a string of points to put them on the road to victory. I was marking Cork's Jack Lynch at midfield and we had a great battle for the hour. He was a wonderful hurler, one of the best I ever played against.'

1943 FINAL: FRESH WIND OF CHANGE FROM ANTRIM

3 September 1943   Cork 5-16, Antrim 0-4

Attendance: 48,843   Referee: J.J. Stuart (Dublin)

Top scorer: J. Quirke (Cork) 2-2

As World War II dragged on, Antrim brought a fresh and welcome wind of change to the sporting scene with a series of headline-making performances. They caused a major surprise by beating Galway in Corrigan Park in Belfast in a very unusual high-scoring qualifying game, 7-0 to 6-2. It goes without saying that Antrim's failure to notch even a point in that game was quite extraordinary. I played in Corrigan Park around that time and I must say it was small and very compact in comparison to other venues around the country. I also played against Antrim's Noel Campbell and Jackie Bateson, a wonderful midfield pairing that measured up to the best in hurling at that time. It can be said that Antrim's greatest drawback was the absence of competitive hurling at a time when junior and minor competitions were suspended due to the war. The Belfast venue, Corrigan Park, reminded me of Gaelic Park, New York, where the surface was uneven and there were hollows to be overcome in the race for the ball.

Galway's defeat in the qualifier against Antrim should have been a warning for Kilkenny to tread warily for their All-Ireland meeting in Belfast with the Glensmen in 1943. The venue was packed for the visit of the Leinster champions, among whom were such great players as Paddy Grace, Paddy Larkin, Peter Blanchfield, Jimmy Walsh, Jimmy Langton, Jack Mulcahy and Seánie O'Brien. The Leinster men ended up on the wrong side of a shock defeat at the hands of the home team, 3-3 to 1-6. It also constituted the biggest upset in hurling that year which still rankles Noreside whenever it is recalled. Corrigan Park as a venue was eventually replaced in time when a special committee was formed and land was bought in Andersonstown and the building of Casement Park began. It was opened on 1 June 1953 by Cardinal d'Alton, free of debt, having cost £101,000. It must be stressed that there were no handouts then. Money was scarce but the Ulster Council and their dedicated fundraising committee set an example for all others by completing the work from the money they themselves had raised.

Antrim went into the 1943 All-Ireland final against Cork, having captured the scalps of two formidable hurling forces in Galway and Kilkenny to give Ulster men a shot at the MacCarthy Cup for the first time.

It is an indication of the intense interest created by Antrim's performances that at a time when travel was difficult, the final still attracted the greatest attendance to a decider to any of Cork's four-in-a-row games, 48,843. When the Antrim hurlers ran on to the lush sward of Croke Park on that September day, they were greeted by the greatest roar ever accorded to a visiting team. No doubt about it, Antrim had captured the imagination of the neutrals, even if that support waned as the game developed. Cork, by far the more experienced team, bristled with household names such as Christy Ring, Jim Young, Jack Lynch, Con Murphy, Din Joe Buckley, John Quirke, Mick Kenefick, to mention just some of the brilliant team.

Cork were not taking any chances against a surprise obstacle to their MacCarthy Cup hopes. They viewed Antrim as very serious contenders and treated them as such. They proved that in the opening half which they started with the wind in their favour and so great was their intensity and determination that they built up an unassailable half-time lead of 3-11 to 0-2. Only a miracle could save Antrim. Sadly, the big occasion got to them. They were never able to muster a semblance of the purposeful hurling that had ended the hopes of Galway and Kilkenny. They were completely out-classed by a far more competent Cork team who ran out easy winners on a 5-16 to 0-4 scoreline. All the hard work of such accomplished hurlers as Jackie Bateson, Jimmy Walsh, Noel Campbell, Kevin Armstrong, Sammy Mulholland and others failed to ignite a spark which might have troubled the title holders, Cork. On the day, the Leesiders ruled supremely. Perhaps one of the finest sporting gestures that marked a highly sporting occasion was the giving of token gifts by the rival captains. Antrim captain Jimmy Walsh presented tea to Cork captain Mick Kenefick, who in turn offered him some butter from Cork. It was wartime and food was rationed.

The result, however, emphasised the void that existed between the two counties. Antrim have not qualified for the All-Ireland final since their clash with Tipperary in 1989. I played against Antrim in the 1948 All-Ireland semi-final and earlier in challenge and League games. They always played like men inspired and were competent in all aspects of the game. It was a major step up for them to be pitted against Cork at All-Ireland final level in 1943. Cork were the reigning champions and they captured the county's second three in a row on that occasion. They were also perhaps one of the few teams at top level capable of switching players to berths they hadn't previously played in, which proved their versatility. Kevin Armstrong and Noel Campbell were good friends of mine. Both agreed that playing in an All-Ireland senior hurling final was the ultimate aim for a player to aspire to. It was a frightening experience and one a player can never forget. The atmosphere was incredible and to be playing against such teams as Tipperary and Cork in a game of such importance was a dream come true. They also accepted the fact that hurling standards in Ulster at the time were weak and that imposed its own strictures on Ulster teams trying to compete in the top grades.

1944 FINAL: CORK SETS RECORD

3 September 1944   Cork 2-13, Dublin 1-2
Attendance: 26, 896   Referee: M. Hennessy (Clare)
Top scorer: J. Kelly (Cork) 2-3

The 1944 All-Ireland senior hurling final was memorable for two reasons. Cork were to produce a historic four in a row which has not been equalled since. They also produced the marksman of the day in Joe Kelly, who totted up a brilliant individual tally of 2-3. Kelly, tall, slim and lightning fast, had made his name as an athlete and hurler with Glen Rovers. He was runner-up in the Irish Sprint championships before the All-Ireland final. The Dublin opposition was again rather weak and never mustered a real challenge on the day. Cork were captained by St Finbarr's Seán Condon, who had won All-Irelands in 1942, 43 and 44 and was now poised to lead his county to that historic four in a row.

The feat of three successive wins had been accomplished by Cork in 1894, Tipperary in 1900 and Kilkenny in 1913. Cork were thus poised and ready to break all records. Dublin's weak response made Cork's chances on that 1944 occasion relatively easy. The Leinster men failed to measure up to the brilliant hurling artistry and commitment displayed by the Leesiders.

A feature of the game was the brilliance of the Cork forwards. Dublin appeared to have their measure in the opening stages, when they held the much vaunted Cork attack scoreless for twelve minutes. But the wind-backed Leesiders suddenly broke loose from Dublin's grip. Jack Lynch set the scene with the best score of the match—a beautiful left-handed drive from far out for the first score of the game. That was the spur Cork needed and they turned on the style with a string of points from Seán Condon (three), Christy Ring (one), Con Cottrell (one) and Jack Lynch (two) to leave Cork leading at half-time by 0-8 to 0-2. Terry Leahy scored Dublin's two points.

Dublin opened up strongly after the restart and put Cork under severe pressure, but great goalkeeping by Cork's Tom Mulcahy kept them at bay. Then left corner forward Joe Kelly opened up the sluice gates with a clever Cork point and quickly followed with a masterly goal. The *Cork Examiner* lauded the work of Kelly in the following day's newspaper. 'Time and again', wrote the match reporter, 'Kelly thrilled the 26,896 crowd with his flying solo runs, and one of the most remarkable of those ovations was given after his shot was saved by Dublin goalie Jim Donegan out for a 70. Supporters and opponents alike applauded his effort for close on two minutes.' The comment from the *Irish Press* describing Kelly's contribution to the historic game was 'Kelly was the darling of the Cork supporters.' And no wonder, because he continued to bamboozle the Dublin defenders with his cheeky solo dashes and delightful scores.

But Dublin battled gamely all through and when Harry Gray's 70 landed in the Cork net, it brought a renewed charge of energy from the local team. But this was immediately halted after a quick response from Cork. Jim Morrison fired over a point and as the champions pulled away for their convincing win, a key factor was the skilful play and accuracy of Kelly, who set the seal on his performance by scoring his second goal. Undoubtedly Kelly was the star of that Cork victory with his dazzling solo runs. Kelly thus joined the ranks of Cork's greatest performers at All-Ireland level and part of a history-making side to win a record four consecutive All-Ireland successes—a feat still to be bettered to this day. Joe would take part in two other All-Ireland finals before ending his hurling career to pursue the priestly mission in New Zealand.

The Dublin full back in that 1944 All-Ireland final was Mick Butler of the famous Faughs club (Dublin). I remember him telling me about the Cork team in that 1944 final. He said, 'Not alone were they a great team but they always produced an unknown to wreak havoc on the big day. If it wasn't a Ring or a Jack Lynch or a Condon, it was a Joe Kelly in my day. Dublin teams were confined to a panel which represented the best talent available in the forties. Munster teams came through a hard grind in the championships, and they proved too great a force when they reached the All-Ireland stages.'

1945 FINAL: PEACETIME AND ONE OF THE BEST FINALS

2 September 1945   Tipperary 5-6, Kilkenny 3-6
Attendance: 69,459   Referee: V. Baston (Waterford)
Top scorer: E. Gleeson (Tipperary) 2-0

The first final of the post-war era, and what an exciting overture to the new period it proved. Sunday morning broke clear and warm after a downpour the previous day, and a record crowd turned up (69,459) for the hurling final. Enthusiasts were treated to one of the best games in years. Tipperary built up a commanding lead; Kilkenny rallied strongly in the second half; and then the Munster champions regained their momentum to secure the MacCarthy Cup after a break of eight years. Tipperary faced a strong sun in the first half and conceded two points in the opening five minutes without reply. A goal from Eddie Gleeson after fifteen minutes, however, helped Tipperary to a lead of 1-1 to 0-3, and by the interval they had stretched their advantage, 4-3 to 0-3. Gleeson and Ryan added the extra goals.

A goal from Tom Walton after eleven minutes of the second half sparked a Kilkenny revival. The Noresiders hit a great scoring burst with a goal each from Jack Mulcahy and Seánie O'Brien to Tipperary's solitary white flag in a great spell after that, and had cut the Munster team's lead to four points with about ten minutes remaining. Indeed, but for the brilliance of Jimmy Maher in the Tipperary goal, Kilkenny would have been even closer to their rivals. John Maher, an outstanding centre back and captain, was another major stumbling block to the Kilkenny attackers. Tipperary, however, weathered the storm and hit back doggedly in the concluding stages. A goal by Tony Brennan, their full forward, steadied the Tipperary men and turned the key finally in the door to the title. If the Mahers, Jimmy and John, stole the thunder in the Tipperary defence, Jimmy Devitt at right full and Tommy Purcell at left half also did much to ensure an unyielding barrier to the Kilkenny attack when their forwards were at their best.

Tipperary's forwards showed up well in recording that worthwhile tally of 5-6, with Eddie Gleeson a two-goal hero and Tommy Brennan and Tommy Doyle also prominent. Jimmy Langton had a fine game for Kilkenny with his excellent striking, good ground play and keen sense of position, while Tommy Walton, Dan Kennedy, Jack Mulcahy and Paddy Grace were others to stamp their personalities on the game for the Leinster champions. It must be mentioned that Tipperary's Tommy Doyle had the distinction of winning his fifth All-Ireland senior medal in that 1945 final. He invariably displayed power and hunger for the game he excelled in and loved. Perhaps the fundamental difference between the teams was the approach adopted by the Tipperary defenders to the challenge presented by the Kilkenny forwards. The robust, bustling, hard-hitting methods of the Tipperary men had an upsetting effect on the Kilkenny attack. Closely guarded by John Maher, Jimmy Langton had not the same scope as in the Leinster games. His free-taking was not up to scratch either.

No doubt about it, the Kilkenny forwards tried really hard, but chances were not taken. More than once there was an inclination to go for goals when points might have proved far more beneficial. There was for once a noticeable looseness in the Kilkenny defence in the second quarter when Tipperary's effort, as it proved, meant the winning of the game. But credit was due to Willie Walsh, who came on in the second half for the Noresiders and helped greatly to curb the attacking Tipp men. It was a manly game played in a fine sporting spirit throughout, and with Kilkenny striving relentlessly to pull down the lead, the crowd did not want for thrills in the second half. The attendance at the game of 69,459 (receipts £5,563) broke all previous records for a hurling final. Previously, the best gate was £4,477 taken in 1937 at Killarney when Tipperary and Kilkenny last met in the final.

There was an interesting sequel to the commentary arrangements for that 1937 All-Ireland final in Killarney. A difference of opinion between the GAA and Radio Éireann broadcasting director Dr T. J. Kiernan over the choice of commentator for the 1937 All-Ireland final resulted in stalemate. The GAA secretary Pádraig Ó Caoimh wanted his nominee as the commentator for the game. Radio director Kiernan claimed that as they were paying the piper they were entitled to play the tune. It was evident that the GAA wouldn't relent either. Naturally the GAA, being the largest sporting organisation in the country, had always taken a rather proprietorial attitude towards broadcasts and a very keen interest in how the games should be portrayed by its commentators. The feud between the GAA and Radio Éireann over the right to select match commentators continued right through the 1937 season. The impasse was still unresolved by the time the All-Ireland semi-finals came round; they were not broadcast. Public interest and disquiet about the conflict mounted with the All-Ireland hurling final imminent. Additional complications arose from the fact that

Croke Park wasn't available either for the All-Ireland hurling finals because the Cusack Stand hadn't been completed in time due to a builders' strike at a crucial stage of the construction. It was decided to play the games in Fitzgerald Stadium in Killarney. Radio Éireann set in train an alternative arrangement to ensure that listeners would get the best service possible.

Dr Kiernan sent for my father, Seán senior, and Eamon de Barra and told them he had made arrangements to cover the finals in Killarney. On the day before the game the national papers carried a statement from Dr Kiernan which read: 'In view of the widespread interest in the match the Broadcasting Authorities have now decided to alter the original arrangements of having eye witness accounts broadcast at 6.15 p.m. Seán Ó Ceallacháin will attend the minor match and wait for the first half of the senior game, and commencing at 4.15 p.m. he will broadcast his impressions from Killarney Post Office, where a microphone will be ready. He is expected to conclude at 4.45 p.m. and from then until 5 p.m. Eamon de Barra will give an account of the second half of the senior match. While the arrangement is immeasurably less satisfactory than a running commentary from the ground itself during play, the Broadcasting Authorities feel that it is the best they can do in the circumstances.' Eamon de Barra and my dad performed their duties and brought the news of the 1937 All-Ireland minor hurling final (Cork 8-5, Kilkenny 2-7) and senior (Tipperary 3-11, Kilkenny 0-3) to an avid listenership. It certainly was novel, but at least those fans who couldn't make the journey to Killarney didn't have to wait until 11 o'clock that night for a report on the game. The steps taken by the station brought matters to a head with the GAA. For the All-Ireland football final some weeks later the GAA agreed to accept the station's suggested commentator, Fr Michael Hamilton of St Flannan's College, Ennis, who was also chairman of the Clare County Board. It was a tactful ending to a conflict in which both sides gained little but lost much. The cold war had ended and normal relations were restored between the two parties. I must say that the Radio Éireann stance was the proper one in the light of modern day relations between sporting bodies and the broadcasting services.

1946 FINAL: RING JOINS THE CAPTAINS' TABLE
1 September 1946   Cork 7-6, Kilkenny 3-8
Attendance: 64,415   Referee: J. Flaherty (Offaly)
Top scorer: C. Ring (Cork) 1-3

One of the features of this game was the fact that the captaincy was handed to the illustrious Christy Ring for the first time in his career. Even though Cork showed a number of changes from the side that completed the coveted four in a row two years earlier, the majority of their hurlers were fully experienced and steeled for the big-time occasion. Ring was very determined to bring Cork back to Croke Park after they had missed out in 1945. The fact that Kilkenny were providing the opposition posed another challenge for the Glen Rovers skipper, because the Leinster men had beaten them by a point six years earlier. It could also be said that the Cork players were incensed because they had been written off by a prominent sportswriter with a leading morning newspaper. Never was a Cork team more determined to prove itself than the Ring-led team of 1946. Con Murphy was back at full back replacing Batt Thornhill; Jim Young, a forward in 1944, was back in the half back line, and the Riordan brothers Mossie and Gerry filled berths in the full forward line with the flying Joe Kelly. Rain which fell heavily until the end of the minor game did not affect the senior match unduly.

Kilkenny showed their mettle from the start, notching two quick points before Christy Ring got Cork's first point after twelve minutes. The Kilkenny midfield partnership of Dan Kennedy and Terry Leahy were dominating the area in the first half but the Kilkenny attack were finding scoring chances few and far between. Such was not the case with Cork. Their first goal came in the 29th minute from Gerry O'Riordan, who was placed by his brother Mossie. After the puck-out, referee Jim Flaherty (Offaly) decided to play 'lost time' and it was then that Ring acted. Running out towards midfield to collect a sideline ball from Billy Murphy, he careered away at full speed, raced through the Kilkenny defence and smashed the ball past Jimmy Donegan in the Kilkenny goal.

At the interval Cork led 2-3 to 0-5, a margin which did not reflect the power and precision of the Leesiders' first half efforts. But they were to make amends on the changeover. Ring fired over an opening point from a free and burly Gerry O'Riordan outwitted the Kilkenny defenders to whip home a goal in the space of two minutes. It took Kilkenny ten minutes to respond, but they did it in style. The hard-working Terry Leahy gathered from Jack Mulcahy, went off on a typical solo run before finishing for a classic goal. That score raised the tempo of the game and while Connie Murphy pulled a goal back for Cork in just three minutes, Terry Leahy quickly responded. He collected from a neat Liam Reidy lay-off pass and virtually walked the ball to the Cork net. The excitement was now intense. With ten minutes remaining Kilkenny were only two points adrift, and the outcome was now in the melting pot.

Ring marshalled his forces and called for a greater effort. This was to be a last ditch stand in the face of intense pressure from a gallant Kilkenny side. But Cork finished the stronger team. Mossie O'Riordan once again broke through for a Cork goal, followed by an opportunistic point from captain Ring, and then came the clincher, a goal from Joe Kelly, and once again the red brigade had taken custody of the MacCarthy trophy in what was considered a majestic encounter between two great teams.

There were no recriminations from the Kilkenny men following the game. It was admitted that Cork created more scoring chances which were duly finished off for telling scores. Some of the key players on the Kilkenny side were closely marked and that applied especially to the losers' attack. The Leinster men knew there would be another day, but it was to come sooner than they expected.

1947 FINAL: LEAHY POINTS THE WAY

7 September 1947   Kilkenny 0-14, Cork 2-7
Attendance: 61,510   Referee: P. Purcell (Tipperary)
Top scorer: T. Leahy (Kilkenny) 0-6

No matter when old hurlers meet, they generally agree that the 1947 All-Ireland senior hurling final was the most exciting one of all for thrills, excitement and a most heart-palpitating climax. Indeed, the following day a match report opened with this paragraph: 'One might call upon a whole store of superlatives and still fail to do justice to the thrill packed All-Ireland Hurling final at Croke Park yesterday, when, with practically the last stroke of the game, centre forward Terry Leahy gave the Leinster champions Kilkenny victory over the holders, Cork, by 0-14 to 2-7.' I still recall that epic encounter vividly because of its pure hurling content and the brilliance of the approach adopted by both counties. Kilkenny of course were out to avenge their 1946 defeat at the hands of Cork, and that factor gave a cutting edge to the proceedings.

Every minute of this great game produced its quota of thrills, but the match reached a wonderful climax with a nerve-tingling and tension-filled last quarter. Those last few minutes were breathtaking as both sides sought a winning score. With the crowd on their feet, Leahy gathered a pressured clearance by Cork goalkeeper Tom Mulcahy to score the all-important winner from 30 yards. The level scoring, sweeping end to end play, first time striking in the air and on the ground, were among the chief qualities that made the final such a majestic event. This was, to a large extent, a personal triumph for Terry Leahy, who was here there and everywhere in the last ten minutes when the real pressure came on. At that stage Kilkenny were holding on grimly to a two point lead when a sideline cut by Jim Young went via Connie Murphy to Mossie O'Riordan through a crowded Kilkenny goalmouth and in for a Cork goal to give the Leesiders the lead for the first time in the match.

A Kilkenny point from Tom Walton put the sides level and a further point from the irrepressible Leahy edged the Leinster champions in front again. When the centre half forward followed with another point—greeted with thunderous applause from the black and amber supporters—he scored what most people thought was the winning score. But the drama was to continue. Excitement was at fever pitch at that stage and gallant Cork showed their true champion qualities as they battled their way into Kilkenny territory. In a hectic mêlée in the Kilkenny goalmouth Joe Kelly scrambled the ball over the line to put Cork back in front again. Now the Leeside flags were being waved in ecstasy. But Kilkenny—and Leahy—were not finished yet. A long clearance from the Kilkenny defence reached Jimmy Langton, who was fouled about 30 yards out from the Cork posts. Time was practically up as the ice cool Leahy stepped up to take the free. A hush descended. Then the Kilkenny supporters rose in a frenzy as the centre forward calmly stroked over the equalising point. From the puck-out Kilkenny gained possession and the ball was returned to the Cork goalmouth where Con Murphy and D. J. Buckley were hard pressed to clear from there by Bill Cahill and Shem Downey. Eventually the ball came into the hands of Cork goalkeeper Tom Mulcahy, whose attempted clearance was fatally short. It was gathered by the iconic Leahy some 30 yards out and he sent it straight and true over the bar for the winning score of a sensational game.

Despite the fact that the Kilkenny full forward line could make little headway against a staunch Cork full back line of Billy Murphy, Con Murphy and D. J. Buckley, the Leinster men were able to pick off points from outfield. Scores from 30, 40 and even 50 yards were nothing to Walton, Leahy, Reidy and Mulcahy. Cork on the other hand may have erred in the first half when, with wind advantage, they were inclined to go for goals. A great Kilkenny defensive bulwark saw to it that there was little to gain from that game plan. Writing on the outcome of that famous match, Cork reporter Walter McGrath said: 'It would be difficult to overemphasize the part which Langton and Leahy played in their team's success. Seldom did a puck goalwards from either of them go wide of the posts. Cork forwards were away behind in their ability to turn opportunities to advantage, and chance after chance, especially in the first half, was lost.' It was the fifth time that Kilkenny had pipped Cork by a single point in an All-Ireland.

The defeat by Kilkenny brought to an end Cork's great run of successes at All-Ireland level at the time. But Jack Lynch's magnificent record still stands to this day. An Taoiseach from 1965 to 1969 and 1975 to 1981, he is the only winner of six All-Ireland senior medals in a row, hurling 1941, 42, 43, 44 and 46, football 45. Some critics at the time hinted that the opposition mounted against the Leesiders in their pursuit of MacCarthy medals in that period of hurling dominance was mediocre, but this is really a case of sour grapes. It must be stressed that Cork achieved more success in that nine year period than any other team in the history of the game. One thing is sure. The game of hurling has no equal to that served up by Cork and the rest of the hurling greats in this land of ours. The story is told about an American visitor viewing hurling for the first time at Croke Park at the 1947 All-Ireland decider. The New Yorker was fascinated by the speed of the game as the ball travelled the length of the famous venue in non-stop deliveries. The performance of Kilkenny's Terry Leahy captured his imagination especially during that exciting last quarter. He exclaimed, 'What a game . . . what a finish . . . What a player!'

1948 FINAL: FIRST FOR WATERFORD

5 September 1948   Waterford 6-7, Dublin 4-2
Attendance: 61,430   Referee: C. Murphy (Cork)
Top scorer: J. Keane (Waterford) 3-2

The ease with which Dublin battled their way to success against Laois in the Leinster final, 5-9 to 3-3, and later when they demolished Antrim 8-13 to 2-6 in the All-Ireland semi-final may well have been a factor which led to their undoing when they faced Waterford in the All-Ireland final. Laois had created a great shock when they beat the reigning All-Ireland champions Kilkenny in the Leinster semi-final that year. Laois and Dublin lined out in Tullamore in the provincial decider, which drew a huge crowd to the Offaly venue. The sideline was overcrowded and the game had to be stopped to allow players from both sides room to take sideline cuts. At the end of a well-contested hour Dublin were winners by a twelve point margin. When news of Waterford's win over Cork in the Munster final was announced at the Offaly venue, there were cheers from the Dublin supporters. They were relieved to hear that the Leesiders were out of the championship because of previous results between the two counties at All-Ireland finals.

Dublin, with just one Dublin-born player, Jim Byrne (Eoghan Ruadhs), when they beat Waterford in the 1938 All-Ireland final, had a far greater local representation ten years later. St Vincent's club supplied the Donnelly brothers Liam and Paddy and Donal Cantwell. Eoghan Ruadhs had Seán Óg Ó Ceallacháin, Kevin Matthews, Ned Dunphy and Seán Cronin, county champions UCD provided four players, Mick Hassett (Dublin), Frank Cummins (Tipperary), Davy Walsh (Kilkenny) and Jimmy Kennedy (Tipperary), while Faughs players included Jim Prior, Joe Butler, Tony Herbert and Mick Williams.

Playing in an All-Ireland final is every hurler's dream and I was no exception when I lined out at left half forward against Waterford hoping to win the MacCarthy Cup for the county. My immediate opponent was the tall Waterford right half back Mick Hickey, who didn't allow me many opportunities to display my hurling talents. Mick had captained the Waterford team beaten by Dublin ten years earlier and was part of a very strong team which stole our thunder on the occasion of the 1948 decider. To strengthen the Deise defence Mick Hickey was called out of retirement to fill the wing back berth. Earlier that year the selectors had recalled Christy Moylan to the team at right half forward. It was a very experienced team that faced Dublin. John Keane, Christy Moylan and Mick Hickey had been there in 1938 and were now supported by such great veterans as Jim Ware (captain), Andy Fleming, Vin Baston and Mick Hayes.

There was a 'photographer's' start to the game as Dr Kinnane, Archbishop of Cashel and Emly, threw in the ball. When the game began in earnest, Dublin attacked and Mick Hassett was narrowly wide from long range. Dublin goalie Kevin Matthews showed his brilliance when he saved from Waterford star John Keane, but a weak clearance from defence allowed Willie Galvin to open the Waterford scoring with a snappy point. Waterford continued to pressure the Dublin defence and Galvin broke through for an opportunist goal. Twenty-two minutes elapsed before Jimmy Kennedy opened the Dublin scoring with a point, but then at minute intervals came a succession of Waterford scores from Keane (goal), Baston (pointed free) before Kennedy had Dublin's second point. But Waterford had the final say of the half when Christy Moylan shot over the bar to leave the interval score Waterford 2-5, Dublin 0-2.

When the game restarted Jimmy Kennedy (D) and Ned Daly (W) exchanged goals in the early stages before Carew (a point) and Keane (a goal) increased the Deise men's lead. Dublin rallied for a spell and Kennedy and Cummins shot a goal apiece, but back came Waterford through Keane with a goal and a point. With time running out Ó Ceallacháin smacked home a Dublin goal which was answered by a Moylan goal for Waterford, who were in complete control by the time Con Murphy (Cork) blew the final whistle.

The proudest man that day was the Waterford captain Jim Ware, who not alone saved brilliantly throughout the game, but had the unique satisfaction of leading his team to a first ever All-Ireland senior title and the coveted MacCarthy Cup. It was a unique day for the county because the Waterford minor hurlers made history too by capturing their second All-Ireland title beating Kilkenny 3-8 to 4-2.

The senior success fully atoned for the defeat suffered at the hands of Dublin in 1938. The Munster champions left nothing to chance. Confident from the start, they outmanoeuvred and outplayed a more youthful and less experienced Dublin team by their dashing play. Such an achievement placed Waterford among the elite counties, and they certainly deserved the honour. The one bright spell for Dublin came in the sixth minute of the second half when Jimmy Kennedy scored a goal—one of the best of the ten in the match. But in virtually every position throughout the field Waterford were the masters. Even when the Leinster champions revived interest by scoring two goals in quick succession with seven minutes to go, there was never the feeling that Waterford would be deprived of their first title. It was perhaps fitting that their centre forward John Keane—always the inspiration in the half forward line—should consolidate the Munster team's position by adding a goal and a point.

Dublin continued to battle dourly and scored a goal, but to show that they still had reserves of energy, Waterford closed with a well-taken goal from Christy Moylan. That was the climax to a brilliant display by Waterford, a display which showed that the years had made little difference to such veterans as Ware, Hickey, Moylan and Keane. All four played a major part in the victory, but each and every one of the fifteen struck top form. Idle for 30 minutes, Jim Ware was ready when needed in the second half, as were all six defenders. Once again Vinny Baston deserves the highest credit. Whether his opponent was Mick Hassett, Donal Cantwell or Jim Prior, it was all the same. He was always first to the ball and cleared without delay and to good purpose, unlike the opposition who, more often than not, failed to find a colleague. At midfield, Johnny O'Connor and Eamon Carew linked defence and attack admirably.

When it comes to the winners' attack the name of John Keane at once springs to mind. Whenever Dublin seemed likely to make a recovery, he rallied his side to greater efforts and he scored the goal and point in the first half which finished Dublin's hopes of being within striking distance at half-time. Again it was Keane who pegged Dublin back midway through the second half with another goal following a free by Baston, and he stepped in later on with another point and a goal after Dublin had goals from Cummins and Ó Ceallacháin. In centre half back Joe Butler and Jimmy Kennedy, Dublin had two players who were not overcome by the strength of the opposition, but they were the only Dubs to measure up to Waterford's high standards.

1949 FINAL: SPECIAL PLACE FOR PAT STAKELUM

4 September 1949   Tipperary 3-11, Laois 0-3
Attendance: 67,168   Referee: M.J. Flaherty (Galway)
Top scorer: J. Kennedy (Tipperary) 2-4

This was a debut for Laois in a MacCarthy Cup game, the county's first All-Ireland senior hurling appearance in 34 campaigns. Laois had raised hopes of presenting a serious challenge for the title as a result of good wins over Offaly, Dublin, Kilkenny and Galway. But the unique clash was a huge disappointment resulting in one of the dullest finals on record. Tipperary lost no time in setting out on the victory trail, their captain and right half back Pat Stakelum pointing from a 70 in the opening minute. Laois did make a brave enough bid in the opening half, in which the Munster men played into the Railway end and with the aid of a slight wind. Laois kept their cause alive until the 25th minute. Paddy Kenny banged home the first goal of the game. Kenny was called into the attack from the Tipp substitutes bench after only twelve minutes as Tipperary rearranged their team when centre back Flor Coffey had to retire injured. The Kenny goal put Tipperary 1-5 to 0-3 ahead at the interval, and Laois failed to score in the second half.

It was all Tipperary in the second half. A goal and a point in quick succession from star forward Jimmy Kennedy midway through the period tightened the Munster men's grip on the final and sent many Laois followers heading for the exits. Whether it was the occasion that affected Laois or not, many of their followers were shocked at their very poor showing, and the writing was on the wall even at the half-time whistle. Tipperary wasted no time in settling the issue after the restart. They were on top in virtually all areas of the field and but for the brilliance of Tom Fitzpatrick the Leinster title holders would have suffered an even heavier defeat. Fitzpatrick saved shots from all angles and could not be faulted for the three that beat him. Pat Stakelum at 21 years led Tipp with the coolness of a veteran as he became the county's youngest All-Ireland winning captain in years. Tommy Doyle took over at centre back when Flor Coffey retired and starred in that berth, while Mick Byrne was tenacious and unbeatable in the full back line.

Incidentally, John Doyle, who was to equal Christy Ring's record of eight All-Ireland senior medals, came through his first final outing with flying colours at left full. Jimmy Kennedy stole the scoring honours, but Sonny Maher, Seamus Bannon and the Kenny brothers earned the plaudits in a very impressive attacking set-up. During periods when they caught the eye, Laois did have a number of great triers. In the early stages they had a grip at midfield where Billy Bohane and Joe Styles ruled the roost for a twenty minute period before surrendering ground to Tipperary's Seán Kenny and Phil Shanahan thereafter. Paddy Rustchitzko, of Polish origin, was having a splendid game in defence when he had to retire with a leg injury, but Paddy Lawlor and Jimmy Murray were the best of a Laois defence which kept trying to the very end. Tipperary held a distinct advantage in fitness and ground striking, qualities which played a major role in their success on the day. It was a very disappointing contest from a spectator's viewpoint. While play was never really rough there was plenty of hard pulling by both sides, which necessitated the referee's intervention, and thus the continuity of play suffered.

When Tommy Doyle was asked to recall his memory of the 1949 final many years later, he said it was too one sided as a contest. He felt that the first round Munster championship win over Cork that year had far more relevance. His task that year was to mark Cork maestro Christy Ring and the importance of curtailing Ring featured very much in the match previews. But Doyle rose to the challenge. The game ended in a draw and the Cork maestro's contribution was one point. Came the replay and the final whistle. Once again it was a draw and incredibly Ring was on this occasion held scoreless from play. Doyle was carving a name for himself among the hurling immortals. The game went into extra time. When the marathon ended Tipperary were in front and Ring had but one point to his credit. So after 150 minutes of play Doyle's name had entered history for his magnificence in containing the Cork maestro and, apart from one point, rendering him ineffective where scores were concerned. The fairy-tale didn't end there. Tommy went on to win three more Munster and All-Ireland titles as well as two National League awards.

Chapter 5 ～

THE FIFTIES

The 1950 to 1959 All-Ireland hurling finals

This was the decade of Wexford, the Rackard brothers, Christy Ring, a record making eighth All-Ireland senior medal win, big crowds and some memorable games—the decade when hurling, it can be safely said, reigned supreme in Irish sport. There was no real inkling of what was to come when Tipperary retained the MacCarthy Cup in a more or less traditional style decider with Kilkenny in 1950. But the following September, Wexford arrived and the scene was changed dramatically and to the benefit of the game itself. Wexford qualified in 1951 for their first ever appearance in a MacCarthy Cup tie, and their initial final engagement at senior level since the decider in 1918. Right away they captured the imagination and affection of the whole country.

It was not until 1955, however, that Wexford finally reaped the reward for their efforts. Prior to that they lost to Tipperary in 1951 for the Premier County's last treble of MacCarthy Cup wins, and to Cork in 1954 before putting their name at last on the trophy after a showdown with Galway. Those were the days when Christy Ring was again a dominant force in hurling. He did much to spark a Cork revival in the early years of the decade, a revival that led to the return of the trophy to the Leeside in 1952 after an absence of six years. Cork went on to make it three All-Ireland titles in succession from 1952 to 1954, and Ring set the seal on a remarkable career and one that was to continue in the top bracket for a further nine years by becoming the first man in hurling to win eight All-Ireland senior medals.

It could be said that at that period there was a 'Ring around Wexford'. Christy was Cork's captain for the second successive year when the Leesiders put the Liam MacCarthy Cup on the line in 1954 against Wexford and the Rackard brothers, Nicky, Bobby and Willie, Nick O'Donnell, Jim English, Ned Wheeler and Padge Kehoe and their colleagues in the exciting and colourful company of hurlers from the Leinster county. Interest in the game was so high that the greatest attendance until then—and one that still ranks as the record for a hurling All-Ireland tie, a mighty crowd of 84,856—turned up for the eagerly awaited clash. Cork won with a goal by Johnny Clifford, and Ring collected that record making eighth medal. He was to prove a central figure in one of the folklore moments of hurling when the Slaneysiders took revenge over Cork in the 1956 final

Wexford really came of age in that 1956 game. After the immediate delight that surrounded their win over Galway the previous September had faded, there were many who argued that it was a pity that the Model County had not met one of the 'Big Two' from Munster, Cork or Tipperary, in their glorious championship run. Limerick were southern champions in 1955 when a young and speedy outfit upset the odds by regaining the provincial crown after a break of fifteen years. The Shannonsiders were beaten by Wexford in an All-Ireland semi-final. However, Wexford left no doubt as to their right to rank as one of the great MacCarthy Cup winners of all time by outscoring Cork for the successful defence of the trophy in 1956. The build-up for that match had everything required to set the pulse of the nation racing: Wexford out to prove their right to greatness, Ring bidding to build on his eighth medal win, and hurlers from both counties who had thrilled and delighted so many in the period with their skills and very sporting play. No wonder the final attracted a huge attendance of 83,096. Art Foley in the Wexford goal was at his brilliant best, and had to be, when he brought off the save of a lifetime from Christy Ring three minutes from full time to ensure that the cup stayed in the Leinster county after a never to be forgotten contest. And at the end came one of the most wonderful sporting gestures of all time, and one that was an indication of the sporting qualities of the Wexford men. Nick O'Donnell and Bobby Rackard, in their moment of greatest triumph thought not immediately of their own success, but right away carried Ring shoulder high off the field. Never before or since has such a spontaneous gesture of sporting acclaim ever been accorded to a player on a losing side as on Christy Ring on that historic Sunday in 1956. Yes, a final with many magical moments. That was the 1956 MacCarthy Cup clash.

A year later, Kilkenny, with a stylish hurler at right half back who was to become not only a future president of the GAA but also the man to lead the Association up to and through the Centenary Year of 1984, Paddy Buggy, returned to the top. Kilkenny beat Waterford. The last great hurrah of the decade, though, fell to the Waterford men as they wiped out the disappointment of 1957 by beating Kilkenny in a replay for the 1959 crown. That was to prove, as time went on, a bitter-sweet hurrah for the Deise men, as the county has not since tasted success. Munster won seven of the ten championships of the fifties and Tipperary and Cork were most the successful. Tipperary won in 1950, 51 and 58 and Cork took three titles in a row, 1952 to 54 inclusive.

Statistics

Greatest attendance	84,856 in 1954
Busiest referee	W. O'Donoghue (Limerick) 1951, 52; G. Fitzgerald (Limerick) 1959 draw and replay
Highest team score	7-7 (28 points) by Tipperary 1951
Highest score by losing team	3-12 (21 points) by Waterford 1957
Highest winning margin	13 points by Cork 1952
Lowest winning margin	One point by Tipperary 1950; Kilkenny 1957
Highest individual score	3-2 by N. Rackard (Wexford) 1951
Highest individual goal tally	3-0 by T. O'Connell (Kilkenny) 1959 drawn game
Goalless finals	None
Finals in which winning team failed to score a goal	None
Finals in which losing team failed to score a goal	Galway 1952; Dublin 1953
Best points tally by winning team	14 by Cork 1952; 14 by Wexford 1956
Best points tally by losing team	12 by Waterford 1957
Top scoring final on aggregate	1951: 10-16 (46 points)
Lowest scoring final on aggregate	1953: 3-11 (20 points)
Replays	One 1959
Most successful captain	C. Ring (Cork)

1950 FINAL: JOHN DOYLE'S GOLDEN HOUR

3 September 1950 — Tipperary 1-9, Kilkenny 1-8
Attendance: 67,629 — Referee: C. Murphy (Cork)
Top scorer: J. Langton (Kilkenny) 0-6

A heart palpitating grandstand finish which yielded the two goals of the game brought this final at Croke Park to an exciting climax after interest had flagged somewhat in the second half. A minute from the end Paddy Kenny hit the first goal of the game to put Tipperary four points clear. The Tipp right corner forward took a pass from Ned Ryan and beat Kilkenny goalie Ramie Dowling with a rasping shot. Tipperary hats, scarves and coats were still flying through the air when Kilkenny struck back. Right from the puck-out Jimmy Kelly, Kilkenny's right half back, sent the ball to the Tipperary net from 70 yards. But as the Leinster champions gathered their forces for one last assault, referee Con Murphy (Cork) blew full time, leaving the Munster men one point clear and MacCarthy Cup winners. Kilkenny, who were the one point specialists, having won five All-Irelands by that margin, were at the wrong end for once. Looking back they had only themselves to blame.

Playing against a near gale force wind and glaring sunshine, they certainly made light of the conditions and played like men inspired. Try as Tipperary might to break Kilkenny's stranglehold, they just could not match the speed and skill of their opponents. At half-time Kilkenny held a slender two point lead, 0-7 to 0-5, as the large attendance sat back and awaited developments. Eager to maintain their first half dominance, the Leinster men were pegged back by the force of Tipperary's new found challenge. Whatever was said in the dressing room at the interval saw Tipperary in a new light after the restart, and the men who had come through against Limerick, Clare, Cork and Galway cut loose in typical fashion with first-time ground striking that paid rich dividends. Kilkenny, irrepressible in the first half, slackened off surprisingly in their approach on the change of ends and became goal conscious.

With points there for the taking, the Leinster men instead changed tactics and literally threw away easy chances of scores. Noted free-taker Jimmy Langton faced up to a 21 yard free for Kilkenny and looked certain to level the game, but the Éire Óg sharpshooter's effort for a goal flew inches wide of the post. In the succeeding minutes Langton was presented with two similar chances, but on each occasion he made the goal his objective and the Tipperary defence cleared. Tipperary captain Seán Kenny, who had switched to the centre forward berth from the wing, began to make his presence felt in a big way. He rampaged at will to the complete bewilderment of his marker Paddy Prendergast. He made two great solo runs which left opponents helpless and which ended in well-taken points by Paddy Kenny and Seamus Bannon. Apart from these brilliant individual efforts, Seán Kenny pulled more than his weight and but for him

Tipperary might not have prevailed. It must be stressed, however, that the Tipperary backs in fact won the day for the defending All-Ireland champions. John Doyle had one of his best ever displays in a MacCarthy Cup tie and Tony Brennan and Mickey Byrne were other key players in the defence.

Mark Marnell shone most for Kilkenny at left half back. He was here, there and everywhere breaking up Tipperary raids and neither Eamon Ryan nor Paddy Kenny could match him. Phil 'Diamond' Hayden was sound at full back where he curbed Tipperary danger man 'Sonny' Maher very effectively. Jimmy Kennedy, normally a matchwinner on his own, never reached the heights of other outings in the Tipp colours. He contributed only two points to his team's total and missed a few scorable frees which normally would have been dead easy for him. Kennedy, none the less, had a good hour. Kilkenny's midfield partnership of Dan Kennedy and Shem Downey, who performed so brightly in the first half, never reached the same heights after the resumption when Seamus Bannon and Phil Shanahan beat them fairly and squarely, but Downey, who was on a roving commission, had evidently played himself to a standstill earlier on.

1951 FINAL: ARRIVAL OF WEXFORD

2 September 1951   Tipperary 7-7, Wexford 3-9
Attendance: 68,515   Referee: W. O'Donoghue (Limerick)
Top scorer: N. Rackard (Wexford) 3-2

Wexford, who had regained the Leinster senior hurling championship in July after a break of 33 years, brought a new enthusiasm to the game, and there was great nationwide interest in their bid to complete a fairytale story as they challenged championship hardened Tipperary in the Model County's debut in a MacCarthy Cup game. The final was played at a scorching pace up to the final quarter and followers were treated to plenty of thrills. In the end the match proved a triumph for experience and class over a physically superior team. Wexford, playing into the Railway end after winning the toss, conceded a point from a Paddy Kenny free in the opening minute but were right in the match two minutes later when a long free by Bobby Rackard was finished to the net by brother Nicky. Coming up to the end of the first quarter, another Wexford goal from play by Nicky left the challengers from the east very well placed as they led by five points, 2-3 to 0-4.

Tipperary refused to panic and goals by Seamus Bannon and Tim Ryan revived their hopes. Then in added time, a midway free led to a Ned Ryan goal to give the champions a 3-6 to 2-6 lead, but Wexford had had enough chances up to that period to have at least turned over on level terms. Tony Reddan was brilliant between the Tipperary posts as the colourful challengers made strenuous efforts to get back into command in the opening quarter of the second half. However, it was the Tipperary men who struck first when Sonny Maher got the opening goal of the period after ten minutes. Then three rapid goals in a spell between the 21st and 25th minutes from Tim Ryan, Seamus Bannon and Mick Ryan ensured that the MacCarthy Cup would go to Tipperary for the third successive year.

Wexford refused to concede defeat, but the gritty and great-hearted Slaneysiders were fighting a losing battle in the final moments, even though Nicky Rackard hit a consolation goal. Paddy Kenny was Tipperary's brightest star, but he had strong challengers in Tony Reddan, Pat Stakelum, solid as a rock at centre half back, and left half back Tommy Doyle who became the first hurler from the county in 50 years to win five All-Ireland medals. Nick O'Donnell and Bobby Rackard were giants in every sense of the word for Wexford in defence, and Nicky Rackard and Tim Flood powered the attack with drive, grit and no little skill. While defeat was to be their lot, the Model County men paid the price for inexperience against a Tipperary team bidding for three in a row. Perhaps the same fault surfaced in the 1950 Leinster final against Kilkenny which they lost by a goal. They still talk about that scoreline, 3-11 to 2-11, and the controversial Kilkenny goal that wasn't in the final played in Nowlan Park.

Art Foley, the great Wexford goalkeeper, whipped a ball off his goal-line and cleared it, but the referee deemed it had crossed the line and awarded Kilkenny a goal after the umpires had expressed conflicting views. Had the goal not been given, Nicky Rackard wouldn't have had to attempt to blast a closing 21 yard free into the Kilkenny net for the equaliser. He would only have had to tap the ball over the bar for the winning score.

The arrival of Wexford changed the scene in Leinster. Between 1951 and 1960 inclusive, Wexford contested nine of the ten Leinster finals. They won five of them: 1951, 54, 55, 56 and 60. In the same period they carried off two of the most memorable National League titles and stamped their undoubted class on the games they contested. Perhaps the most famous league victory was the 1956 final against Tipperary. They were fifteen points down at the interval and looked dead and buried. But aided by a stiff second half wind, they chipped away at Tipperary's intimidating lead. Nicky Rackard played an inspired role in the supercharged atmosphere as Wexford picked off score after score to run out winners 5-9 to 2-14 in an unforgettable contest.

1952 FINAL: CREEDON UNBEATABLE IN GOAL

7 September 1952   Cork 2-14, Dublin 0-7
Attendance: 64,332   Referee: W. O'Donoghue (Limerick)
Top scorers: C. Ring (Cork) 0-6, L. Dowling (Cork) 2-0

The brilliant goalkeeping of Dave Creedon for Cork was one of the high points of this final. He brought off some tremendous saves, especially in the first half as Dublin exerted plenty of pressure, and it was a long clearance by Creedon that led to Cork's first goal by Liam Dowling after fifteen minutes. The Cork team was reported to have been the lightest ever to represent the county in a senior final, and after a keen first half pulled away in the second for a clear-cut win. Cork had suffered badly from injuries and illnesses on the path to the final. Matt Fouhy suffered a broken finger and missed the Munster final against Tipperary. He was fit enough to join the All-Ireland panel later, but then came another blow for the Leesiders' selectors when Josie Hartnett was hospitalised with appendicitis. So a few changes had to be made for the All-Ireland final against Dublin.

Mattie Fouhy was brought into the team at right half back and his club mate Willie John Daly was moved to the attack. Willie Griffin, who had replaced Mossie Riordan in the All-Ireland semi-final against Galway, was retained at right half forward. The Dublin team created a big impression after defeating a much fancied Wexford team in the Leinster final. One change was made at midfield where Norman Allen replaced his club mate Marcus Wilson for the final against Cork.

Dublin won the toss and captain Jim Prior opted to play with the wind into the Railway end and against a glaring sun. Christy Ring wasn't long making his presence felt. He grabbed the ball from the throw-in and went on a solo run before the rest of the forwards had reached their positions. He was fouled and cracked the resultant free over the bar for the game's opening score. The lead changed hands many times in the opening half as Dublin measured up to the Cork challenge. Norman Allen and Connie Murphy were very prominent in the midfield tussles with Cork's Gerald

Murphy and Joe Twomey. Dublin put plenty of pressure on the Cork defence and it took some excellent play from left full Tony O'Shaughnessy and goalkeeper Dave Creedon to keep their lines intact. As it was, Dublin went ahead after eleven minutes with a point. But within four minutes Cork were in front again, and from that stage on they never lost control of the match.

The Cork defence tightened their grip and inspired their outfield players. Excellent points from Ring, Paddy Barry, Willie Griffin and Joe Twomey offset Dublin points from a hard working Roger McCarthy, Norman Allen, Connie Murphy and Gerry Kelly. One of Dublin's best forwards on the team was Jack Finnan. He suffered a knee injury a few weeks before the final in a challenge match against Kilkenny but had it well strapped for the Cork match. In the opening quarter he grabbed possession 40 yards out from the Cork goal and as he cracked the ball over the bar he was subjected to a wild tackle by a Cork defender. The referee, Willie O'Donoghue (Limerick), immediately awarded Dublin a free instead of allowing Finnan's point to stand. The free was subsequently missed and Finnan had to leave the field because of his injury. Liam Dowling scored the crucial goal to give Cork a half-time lead, 1-5 to 0-5. The second half was brimful of exciting hurling. One of the features was the great work of Dessie Ferguson for Dublin, who kept a very close eye on the irrepressible Ring and confined the Cork maestro to two points from play. Dublin goalkeeper Kevin Matthews made it a good day for keepers when he brought off a sensational save from Christy Ring which brought the house down. But Cork steadily added on the points, and when Liam Dowling got through for his second goal of the day, the issue was finally sealed. If Creedon was Cork's brightest star, Tony O'Shaughnessy, Liam Dowling with his brace of goals, Ring for his accuracy from frees and his general play, and team captain Paddy Barry, left indelible marks. For Dublin, Des Ferguson was brilliant in the half back line together with team captain Jim Prior and goalie Kevin Matthews. Norman Allen at midfield and Roger McCarthy and Tony Herbert in attack were their hardest workers.

1953 FINAL: O'SULLIVAN GOAL WINS THE DAY
6 September 1953   Cork 3-3, Galway 0-8
Attendance: 71,195   Referee: P. Connell (Offaly)
Top scorer: C. Ring (Cork) 1-1

The final played on a scorching day attracted the greatest attendance at a hurling decider until then, the first 70,000 plus crowd to a MacCarthy Cup tie. Cork's success was founded on a powerful full back line, and forwards with the ability to snatch goal-scoring chances. The match was always interesting but was marred by unsporting play, resulting in comments by officials from both counties for some time after. For all that, the game had its bright moments, culminating in Christy Ring captaining the Leesiders for the second time in his career to a title, as he also collected his seventh All-Ireland medal. It must be said that the occasion was spoiled from a hurling viewpoint due to the tactics employed by some rival players. Some of the incidents fuelled the passions of spectators present and as a result Christy Ring was booed by some Galway supporters every time he challenged for the ball. Ring was being very closely marked by Galway captain Mick Burke from the start of the game, and that did not go down too well with the Cork fans. Unfortunately the 1953 final was remembered for all the wrong reasons (which this writer felt was unfair to both counties).

Cork had the advantage of sun and breeze in the first half and opened well with goals by Josie Hartnett and Christy Ring, and a point by their 1952 captain Paddy Barry. Joe Salmon had a great game at midfield for Galway in the period, but the challengers still turned over four points adrift at the interval. Galway came back strongly in the second half, however. A point from Josie Gallagher raised their spirits and they increased the pressure on Cork that brought a great save from Dave Creedon in the Cork goal. The men from the west never relaxed in their quest for scores and their patience was rewarded as they continued to stroke over points to bring the scores level. The excitement was intense, but Cork's dander was up. Visions of losing an All-Ireland quickly disappeared when Christy Ring stepped into the breach. He gained possession and strode forward, only to be fouled by a rash challenge. A free was awarded. The Cork captain took the puck and sent it over the bar and Cork were ahead. Willie John Daly also responded when he was neatly placed and fired over another point. John Killeen kept Galway hopes alive with a superb point as the final minutes kept ticking away. Once again Cork were not to be outdone. They geared themselves for one last assault and it ended when right full forward Tom O'Sullivan smashed the ball to the Galway net to ensure another title for Cork in a low scoring final.

That powerful Cork full back line of Gerry O'Riordan, John Lyons and Tony O'Shaughnessy proved the big stumbling block to Galway's cherished hopes of All-Ireland glory. Willie John Daly was the pick of the Cork forwards that found the going tough against a powerful Galway defence, brilliantly led by Colm Corless. Mickey Burke, like Christy Ring, was injured during the game but continued to the end. Josie Gallagher, Billy O'Neill and John Killeen were best in the Galway attack. John D. Hickey, writing in the *Irish Independent* the following day, stated: 'I have no hesitation in parading the last line of the Cork defence, Riordan, Lyons and O'Shaughnessy as the men entitled to most of the plaudits, but the winners' forwards, including Ring, met their match in the Galway backs. However the ability to take crucial scores when most needed was again the big weapons in Cork's armour on the day.'

In all my years watching Christy Ring in action in major contests, I have never seen him pulling a foul stroke on an opponent or being responsible for his match opponent leaving the field injured. I have played on him during league matches and admired him as the complete hurler that he always was. Interestingly, I spoke to Dessie Ferguson, who was a near neighbour of mine, about Ring, and he left me in no doubt that the Cork star was the best opponent he ever played against. The duels between Ferguson and Ring in the Dublin and Cork 1952 All-Ireland final proved the point—not a foul stroke in sight.

1954 FINAL: EIGHTH MEDAL FOR RING

5 September 1954	Cork 1-9, Wexford 1-6
Attendance: 84,856	Referee: J. Mulcahy (Kilkenny)
Top scorer: C. Ring (Cork) 0-5	

Some fifteen minutes before the senior game the Croke Park gates were closed and hundreds of fans remained outside. By then a record attendance had passed through the turnstiles. An unbelievable goal by Cork's Johnny Clifford three minutes from time deprived gallant Wexford of a first MacCarthy Cup win, but also made history in its own right as the score ensured a record eighth All-Ireland senior medal for Christy Ring. There may have been more classical finals, but surely none to match the tension and atmosphere which prevailed in Croke Park in that 1954 All-Ireland decider. Despite some weird strokes—and mistakes too—there was not a dull moment in a match in which every man was utterly unmindful of his personal safety. Here were 30 men locked in stupendous battle to produce an end result of unparalleled effort. Men hit with all they knew, but legitimately on every occasion, and it is a tribute to their hardi-hood that there were only two casualties in an hour that was worthy of a great occasion. No doubt about it, Cork deserved their triumph, but how they had to fight to fashion it!

In the early stages of the second half Cork were very definitely rattled, and had Wexford recorded the scores that their outfield approach work deserved, the title might now rest in the Model County. Wexford won the toss, played into the Railway goal end, but it was Cork who drew first blood with a second minute point from Eamon Goulding. Ring, the man very much in the spotlight, kept Cork in touch with some fine points, but a palmed goal by Tom Ryan and some grand points from Nicky Rackard had Wexford ahead at the interval 1-3 to 0-5. Wexford had an excellent spell after the restart, with Tim Flood delighting with some brilliant solo runs, and it took a marvellous save by Dave Creedon in Cork's goal from Nicky Rackard and solid defensive play by Tony O'Shaughnessy, Vince Twomey and Mattie Fouhy to keep Wexford out. Nevertheless, Wexford were still four points clear and looking good. The game was distinctive in another way, inasmuch as it stamped the incomparable Christy Ring as a hurler apart, having captured eight All-Ireland medals. This feat eclipses the record shared by Kilkenny's Sim Walton, 'Drug' Walsh, Dick Doyle and Jack Rochefort in hurling and Kerry's football goalkeeper Danno O'Keeffe.

There is no denying that Wexford were unlucky. What Cork man would positively assert that the champions would have survived, had not the Leinster county lost their eminently capable full back, Nick O'Donnell, six minutes after the restart. Christy Ring was still playing excellent hurling. He collected a long drive from midfielder Gerald Murphy and powered the sliothar goalwards. The ball struck Nick O'Donnell, broke his collar bone and it sped out for a 70. The big full back was taken off, and Bobby Rackard was moved back from centre half to the No. 3 spot. He turned in a super show in the position, so much so that with three minutes remain-ing, Wexford were hanging on grimly to a lead of two points. Yet again Ring emerged to exercise a decisive influence. He sent a shot along the ground past Jim English, the opposing right half back. The shot appeared to be going wide, but right corner forward Johnny Clifford, who had just changed places with Paddy Barry, refused to accept that fact. Goal scoring Cork hero Clifford tells it as it happened. 'Wexford were leading by two points,' he began, 'and the game was drawing to a close. Paddy Barry and I were corner forwards and we were having a fairly bad time of it with the strong Wexford backs. Josie Hartnett realised this and suggested that we swap places. Then the golden opportunity arrived. I saw three players going for the ball. Christy was there and Wexford defenders Bobby Rackard and Jim English. The ball broke between them and was heading for the end line. I ran out for it and got to it before it crossed the line. I took a left swing at it and it hit the back of Art Foley's net to a deafening roar from the crowd.' Johnny Clifford's match-winning goal was indeed the most vital score in MacCarthy Cup history as Josie Hartnett and Ring himself added a point apiece to climax one of the most famous of All-Ireland senior hurling victories.

Before the game I went into the Cork dressing room and asked Christy if he would allow me to bring him to Radio Éireann should he collect his eighth All-Ireland medal. He said quietly, 'Of course we will win, no ifs or buts. We will definitely win today.' He duly won as he predicted. My interview with Ring on radio that Sunday night was not alone historic but noteworthy for the sincere and genuine way he answered my questions on the programme. He told me afterwards that he was very conscious of the fact that he was talking to the nation, and some of his answers gave that impression too. He laid great stress on fitness and made repeated references to practice. He claimed that a player would never be great unless he devoted a lot of time to practising the skills of hurling. I asked him would he now consider retiring from the game. I can still see those steely blue eyes boring into mine when he replied, 'I have no intention of retiring. I'll keep hurling for as long as the good God above gives me the strength.' His pious wish was granted; he kept hurling away until he retired from inter-county hurling in 1965. And it can be truly said that Ring made a huge contribution to the 1954 All-Ireland victory and sealed it with a great point from play. The *Cork Examiner* the following day wrote: 'Were the match to be recorded stroke by stroke, no name would be printed more often than that of the Cork captain because he won the game for his county. All the superlatives of the dictionary have from time to time been used to describe the ability of the hurling wizard of the age, so much so that when one endeavours to find adequate praise for his performances, words fail. Perhaps it can all be summed up in one phrase—it was Ring's game.'

In my opinion Christy Ring was undoubtedly the most fabulous hurler of his time. He supplied touches which stamped him as a genius of his craft during his period at the top of his career. But mention must be made also of the performance of Wexford's Bobby Rackard in that 1954 final. He too was unmindful of the flailing hurleys; time and again he came through a forest of them, ball in hand, to get in magnificent clearances. Such a display by a man who had not a moment's training for such a test of endurance and skill proclaimed him as one of the greatest backs in the game. Nor should we forget Wexford defender Jim English, who was allotted the task of marking Cork's danger man Ring. He performed an unenviable task with great courage and fortitude, as indeed did Tim Flood with his flying solo runs.

Other top performers on the day were the Rackard brothers, Nick and Willie, and Ned Wheeler. To my mind I thought Vince Twomey was the man of the match for Cork. Time and time again he came to his side's rescue when Wexford appeared likely to mount an offensive that could not be staved off. Not far behind was the incomparable Tony O'Shaughnessy who was the dominant figure in the full back line even after suffering a head injury. On numerous occasions he averted possible disaster. And it was to full back John Lyons's great credit that he curbed Wexford's prime marksman Nicky Rackard to achieve his greatest hour ever on the field of play.

1955 FINAL: O'DONNELL AND THE RACKARDS

4 September 1955   Wexford 3-13, Galway 2-8

Attendance: 72,854   Referee: R. Stakelum (Tipperary)

Top scorer: N. Rackard (Wexford) 1-3

After Wexford's first All-Ireland senior title in 1910, they captured their second title and first MacCarthy Cup at the expense of Galway at Croke Park by an eight point winning margin. It was a fast, tough and tremendously exciting game. Galway won the toss and elected to play with a slight breeze behind them into the Railway end, but within two minutes they were a goal down when Nicky Rackard, the towering Wexford full forward, had the first score of the match. A minute later Tim Flood stretched the Wexford lead with a fine point, but soon afterwards the Galway fight back began with a point from midfielder Billy Duffy. Duffy and Joe Salmon then took over control at midfield and with good support from John Molloy and Mickey Burke in the half back line, Galway took a grip on the exchanges. Despite excellent defensive play by Wexford, the Tribesmen turned over at half-time leading by 2-5 to 2-3.

But for the brilliance of the Wexford backs, Galway might well have done enough in that opening period to have won the day. As it was,

Wexford came more into the picture in the second half. They broke Galway's dominance at centrefield with the aid of the Jim Morrissey and Seamus Hearne partnership, which started to blossom. Five points in the second half in the first sixteen minutes without reply set the Slaneysiders firmly on the road to success. Then in the 21st minute came the deciding score. Nicky Rackard got the ball out on the left flank and sent it to Paddy Keogh close to the end line. He drew the defence out of position before passing to Tom Ryan. The right full forward flicked the ball on to Tim Flood and the man in the No. 15 jersey sent a stinging shot unerringly past Tom Boland in the Galway goal. That gave Wexford a 3-8 to 2-6 lead and the MacCarthy Cup for the first time.

The powerful hurling of Nick O'Donnell, the Rackards, Bobby and Willie, and Jim English did much to keep Wexford in the hunt as Galway had done in the opening period. Then the defensive work was set off by the ability of Nicky Rackard, Tim Flood and Ned Wheeler, in particular, to take scores in a manner which the Galway forwards could not match. So, a good all round performance by Wexford and one that finally compensated for the many disappointments that preceded the historic breakthrough. Salmon, Duffy, Jimmy Burke and Paddy Egan were the pick of a determined Galway side that battled all the way but lacked the forward finesse and accuracy necessary to clinch a major title on the day.

1956 FINAL: WHAT A SAVE!

23 September 1956   Wexford 2-14, Cork 2-8
Attendance: 83,096   Referee: T. O'Sullivan (Limerick)
Top scorers: N. Rackard (Wexford) 1-5, C. Ring (Cork) 1-5

'The greatest disappointment of my hurling career,' said Nicky Rackard, 'was the All-Ireland final of 1954 when we were beaten by Cork. After that match I resigned myself to the fact that I'd never win an All-Ireland medal and I announced my retirement. Despite this, I was prevailed upon to line out again the following year and we went through to the All-Ireland and beat Galway in the final. It was like a dream come true to win that medal. But there was something hollow about it, probably because our opponents were Galway and not as great a team as Cork and reverse the 1954 result. So I was glad I stayed on in 1956 and was there for the final against Cork. When we won that game my greatest hurling ambition was fulfilled.'

Nicky's dream of beating Cork in the 1956 decider seemed about to be realised three minutes from the end when one of hurling's legendary saves by Wexford goalie Art Foley coloured a memorable game and ensured a successful title defence by the Slaneysiders after an hour of fast, exciting, sporting hurling of a high standard. Wexford led by two points at the time, as the final minutes ticked away. Cork left half back Paddy Philpotts sent a long clearance upfield where it was grabbed by Christy Ring and he headed goalwards in a darting run, tapping the ball on his hurley. Then from 25 yards Ring cracked a powerful shot that had goal written all over it. But Art Foley proved he was the man for the big occasion with a never to be forgotten save under the crossbar. In a wonderful sporting gesture Christy Ring raced in to congratulate the Wexford keeper. Foley's save proved inspirational for Wexford as Nicky Rackard hit back for a goal and Tom Dixon pointed to make assurances doubly sure.

Wexford played into the Canal goal on a bright sunny day at Croke Park, and in the space of three minutes had a point from Tim Flood and a goal from Padge Kehoe before Cork had raised a flag. Soon afterwards the challengers lost their captain and left corner back Tony O'Shaughnessy with an injury. Good points scoring, especially from Christy Ring, had Cork very much in touch at the interval as they trailed the holders 0-5 to 1-6. Wexford started the second half smartly and after thirteen minutes were seven points clear. Then into the scene strode Christy Ring to orchestrate a golden last quarter. He sent a 21 yard free all the way to the Wexford net and immediately afterwards reduced the Cork arrears further with a left-handed point. Padge Kehoe revived Wexford spirits with a point, but a goal inside a minute from Paddy Barry had Cork on equal terms. The excitement was intense as Ring palmed a glorious point to put the southerners ahead. Back came Wexford once again and inspiring full forward Nicky Rackard levelled matters. As Cork conceded frees in the face of strong pressure, Rackard popped over two more points, but with three minutes still left, this game had still not dealt a full hand of magical moments. It started with Philpott's long delivery to Ring and ended with Art Foley's masterful save from the Cork wizard—a fitting climax to a marvellous occasion.

Nicky Rackard was an inspiring leader; elusive Tim Flood and Jim English, Nick O'Donnell, Bobby and Willie Rackard were impressive for a great Wexford team. Ring, Paddy Philpotts and Jimmy Brohan were the leading lights for Cork. At the end of the final, Nick O'Donnell and Bobby Rackard carried Ring off the field—a noble gesture. While there was bitter

YEAR	WINNER	RUNNER-UP
1887	Thurles, Co. Tipperary	Meelick, Co. Galway
1888	Unfinished	
1889	C. J. Kickhams, Dublin	Tulla, Co. Clare
1890	Aghabullogue, Co. Cork	Castlebridge, Co. Wexford
1891	Ballyduff, Co. Kerry	Crossbeg, Co. Wexford
1892	Redmonds, Cork	Faugh-Davitts, Dublin
1893	Blackrock, Cork	Confederation, Kilkenny
1894	Blackrock, Cork	Rapparees, Dublin
1895	Tubberadora, Co. Tipperary	Tullaroan, Co. Kilkenny
1896	Tubberadora, Co. Tipperary ...	Dublin, Commercials
1897	Kilfinane, Co. Limerick	Tullaroan, Co. Kilkenny
1898	Tubberadora, Co. Tipperary	Three Castles, Co. Kilkenny
1899	Moycarkey, Co. Tipperary	Blackwater, Co. Wexford
1900	Two-Mile-Borris, Co. Tipperary ...	London, Desmonds
1901	London Irish	Redmonds, Cork
1902	Dungourney, Cork	Brian Boru, London
1903	Blackrock, Cork	Hibernians, London
1904	Tullaroan, Co. Kilkenny	St. Finbarr's, Cork
1905	Kilkenny, Erin's Own	St. Finbarr's, Cork
1906	Thurles, Tipperary	Faugh's, Dublin
1907	Tullaroan, Kilkenny	Dungourney, Cork
1908	Thurles, Tipperary	Kickhams, Dublin
1909	Mooncoin, Kilkenny	Thurles, Tipperary
1910	Castlebridge, Wexford	Castleconnell, Limerick
1911	Kilkenny	Castleconnell, Limerick
1912	Kilkenny	Blackrock, Cork
1913	Kilkenny	Toomevara, Tipperary
1914	Clare	Leix
1915	Leix	Cork
1916	Tipperary	Kilkenny
1917	Dublin	Tipperary
1918	Limerick	Wexford
1919	Cork	Dublin
1920	Dublin	Cork
1921	Limerick	Dublin
1922	Kilkenny	Tipperary
1923	Galway	Limerick
1924	Dublin	Galway
1925	Tipperary	Galway
1926	Cork	Kilkenny
1927	Dublin	Cork
1928	Cork	Galway
1929	Cork	Galway
1930	Tipperary	Dublin
1931	Cork	Kilkenny
1932	Kilkenny	Clare
1933	Kilkenny	Limerick
1934	Limerick	Dublin
1935	Kilkenny	Limerick
1936	Limerick	Kilkenny
1937	Tipperary	Kilkenny
1938	Dublin	Waterford
1939	Kilkenny	Cork
1940	Limerick	Kilkenny
1941	Cork	Dublin
1942	Cork	Dublin
1943	Cork	Antrim
1944	Cork	Dublin
1945	Tipperary	Kilkenny
1946	Cork	Kilkenny
1947	Kilkenny	Cork
1948	Waterford	Dublin
1949	Tipperary	Leix
1950	Tipperary	Kilkenny
1951	Tipperary	Wexford
1952	Cork	Dublin

An honour board showing the winners and runners-up of the All-Ireland hurling championship from 1887 to 1952.

Action from the second replay of the All-Ireland hurling final between Cork and Kilkenny at Croke Park in 1931. (*Cork Examiner*)

Two of the all-time greats shake hands at the beginning of the 1931 final: Lory Meagher of Kilkenny (*left*) and Eudie Coughlan of Cork. (*Cork Examiner*)

The great Jack Lynch leading Glen Rovers in the parade before the Cork County senior hurling final at the Cork Athletic Grounds in 1940. (*Cork Examiner*)

Cork's Joe Kelly in action against Dublin in the 1944 final. Cork won the championship each year from 1941 to 1944, a unique four in a row. (*Cork Examiner*)

The 1947 final between Cork and Kilkenny at Croke Park. Kilkenny repulse a Cork attack. (*Cork Examiner*)

The 1947 Cork team. (*Cork Examiner*)

One of the game's most
famous photographs
featuring two immortals:
Mick Mackey (*left*) by then
retired and umpiring, and the
injured Christy Ring.

The greatest: Christy Ring
playing in the Railway Cup
for Munster around 1950.

The Tipperary side of the late 1940s and early 1950s was one of the all-time greats. This is the 1951 team which defeated Wexford in the final. (*Cork Examiner*)

The immortal Rackard brothers: (*from left*) Bobbie, Nicky and Billy.

The legendary
Ollie Walsh of
Kilkenny, in the
view of some the
greatest of all
goalkeepers.

The scene before the start of the 1955 All-Ireland final between Wexford and Limerick. Nicky Rackard is in the centre of the Wexford group with his left hand on his hip. Number three is the great Nick O'Donnell.

The last Waterford side to win the championship: the 1959 team photographed before the final. (*Sportsfile*)

The 1960 Wexford team that defeated Kilkenny in the Leinster hurling final. (*Cork Examiner*)

The all-conquering Tipperary team of the mid-1960s, led by Jimmy Doyle, parading before the 1965 final against Wexford. (*Sportsfile*)

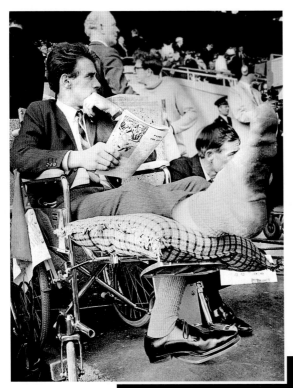

The precociously talented Justin McCarthy won an All-Ireland medal with Cork in 1966 but had his career cut cruelly short by a road accident in 1969. Here he watches the 1969 final from the sideline. He went on to become one of the most gifted and respected hurling coaches and the author of one of the best books written about the game. (*Cork Examiner*)

Pat Hartigan and Eamonn Grimes hold the Liam MacCarthy Cup aloft at the home-coming in 1973, the last time to date such scenes have been witnessed in Limerick.

Eddie Keher, an automatic choice on most people's best team ever. (*RTÉ*)

The victorious Limerick captain Eamonn Grimes walks up the steps of the Hogan Stand to accept the Liam MacCarthy Cup in 1973. (*Sportsfile*)

When this Tipperary team beat Kilkenny in the 1971 final, few believed it would be another eighteen years before the championship would return to the Premier County. (*Cork Examiner*)

disappointment in Cork that their favourite son had not collected a ninth All-Ireland medal, nobody could begrudge gallant Wexford on their splendid success on the day.

Pádraig Puirseal, writing his piece on the match in the *Irish Press* stated: 'This was a game that had everything. Fierce hip to hip clashes, dazzling solo runs, glorious goals, unbelievable saves, swaying fortunes, flashes of dazzling stickwork that might have been equalled but could hardly have been surpassed by Cuchulainn or Fionn McCool, and to crown it all, the ever exciting exchanges, hard fast and fair, were leavened by a spirit of sportsmanship that set the true seal of greatness on victors and vanquished alike.'

The great difference between the 1954 and 1956 finals was explained by Nicky Rackard. 'We had learned a great deal from the experience of playing against Cork in the first final. I had a very unhappy hour that day because of all the tension I felt as a result of the pre-match publicity. Several newspapers had speculated on whether I would score more than Ring and they built up a sort of rivalry between us which made me very tense and uncomfortable during the match. On top of that, of course, I was marked by John Lyons, a great Cork full back, but more than anything else, the pressure from being billed as Ring's counterpart was too much for me. I had overcome that by the time we met Cork in 1956. I was probably more mature as an All-Ireland hurler, as were the other Wexford players, and I must say I really enjoyed the 1956 All-Ireland final best of all.'

1957 FINAL: HURLING IN THE MOVIES
1 September 1957   Kilkenny 4-10, Waterford 3-12
Attendance: 70,584   Referee: S. Gleeson (Limerick)
Top scorer: P. Grimes (Waterford) 1-6

This was a hurling epic, and a final associated prominently with a film of the time entitled *Rooney*. The film was shot in Dublin and the hero of the picture was a young man who was a keen hurler. John Gregson, an English actor, played the title role, and he lined out with the Kilkenny hurlers wearing the famed black and amber jersey for part of the match parade in Croke Park. Some of the shots taken at the final were also used in the film. But back to the game.

From the throw-in Waterford took up the running and inside 50 seconds John Kiely sent over the opening point. Grimes added another from a free following a foul on Donal Whelan, and then a rasper from Whelan whipped past Ollie Walsh but it rebounded off the upright. Six minutes had elapsed before Kilkenny opened their account, Kenny from a line ball, pointing from 40 yards. From the puck-out, however, the Noresiders took their first positive step to victory. Kenny sent the return into the Deise square and Rockett flicked the ball past Dickie Roche for a goal and the lead. Heaslip and Kenny (2) added further points for Kilkenny and after Grimes had sent a 70 over the bar for a Waterford point, Seán Clohosey pulled on a ground ball for another Kilkenny score. In the 22nd minute Waterford started their great fight back which was to turn a deficit into a lead before half-time. Kiely had a point; two minutes later Grimes pointed from a free and then came a rather controversial decision by referee Gleeson. A centre by Johnny O'Connor was dropping in the Kilkenny square and in the mêlée that followed Larry Guinan scooped the ball to the net. Having consulted the umpires, the official awarded a 21 yard free to Waterford and Grimes nearly burst the net with a fast rising shot. From the puck-out Martin Óg Morrissey sent to Tom Cheasty who placed Whelan for another point and the lead just on half-time.

Waterford improved their situation after three minutes of the second half when Whelan blasted the ball past Ollie Walsh for a goal, and Grimes from a 50 yard free increased their advantage with a point. Kilkenny, fully alive to the danger, struck back a minute later when Rockett chased a ball to the end line, though harassed by two Waterford defenders, flicked the ball to Billy Dwyer who gave Roche no chance. Two minutes later, Mickey Kelly reduced the arrears with a further point, but back bounced Waterford and from the puck-out the ball travelled via Grimes and Kiely to Whelan and the left corner forward again left Ollie Walsh helpless. Frankie Walsh and Kenny (from a 70 yard free) exchanged points and after Willie Walsh had replaced the fading John Sutton at midfield for Kilkenny, Whelan and Cheasty added Waterford points to stretch their lead to two goals. The challenge was there and Kilkenny rose to it magnificently. Johnny McGovern lobbed the ball upfield, Clohosey flicked it on to O'Dwyer and the stocky full forward set Noreside followers hearts alight with a fast ground shot past Roche in the seventeenth minute. Grimes (2) and Kenny exchanged points from frees before Kenny in the 22nd minute put the Leinster champions on the threshold of victory. From a typical Ollie Walsh clearance, the ball reached the centre half forward Kenny, who from about 30 yards crashed the ball to the net to leave but a single point between the sides. Excitement, seldom below fever pitch throughout the hour, was now really intense, and with five minutes left for play Clohosey jinked his way past Tom Cunningham and Morrissey to loft the ball over the bar for the equaliser. Both sides strained every sinew for the deciding score and it came two minutes later. Kilkenny captain Mickey Kelly fastened on to a long clearance from John Maher and from an acute angle on the left wing the Bennettbridge farmer reaped a rich harvest with a beautifully judged shot which Dickie Roche got his stick to but could not prevent from dropping over the bar.

Where all contributed (including referee Gleeson) to a joyous hour, it may seem ungenerous to single out any man in the winning side for special mention. However, those three miraculous saves by Kilkenny goal-keeper Ollie Walsh in the first half demands that he be accorded particular mention. Three times within seconds in the 18th minute he brought off saves from point-blank range—twice when off balance. At other times too he proved in no uncertain manner that he was a great hurler as well as a goalkeeper of astonishing ability as he advanced from his goal to beat opponents and get in lengthy clearances. In the half back line the work of Johnny McGovern was invaluable. Time and again he averted the peril that seemed about to encompass his side. Paddy Buggy on the other wing, who was to become the Centenary Year GAA president, also turned in a majes-tic display of cool confident hurling all through the game. Thanks mainly to an inspired display by John Sutton, the victors 'owned' the ball at mid-field in the first half. In an effort to break the Leinster champions' domi-nance in that area, Waterford switched Mickey and Johnny O'Connor, but the move was not very effective. On the turnover the losers finally made the switch they should have made five minutes after the throw-in. They brought Seamus Power into that vital territory, and instantly the Kilkenny midfielders seemed to dissolve.

The best of the winners' attacking sector that at times played bambooz-ling hurling was Mick Kenny. His efforts were brilliantly supported by Denis Heaslip, Mickey Kelly and Billy Dwyer. Dickie Roche in the losers' goal was very well covered by the splendid work of the full back line of Tom Cunningham, Austin Flynn and John Barron. Mickey O'Connor, and Martin Óg Morrissey for his second half, deserve warm commendation. But Seamus Power, when he moved to midfield, was the star of that department, and Phil Grimes's accuracy off placed balls was quite excep-tional until the occasion when most depended on him. In the losers' forward line, Donal Whelan, John Kiely and Tom Cheasty earned the most plaudits. Whelan's second goal was as magnificent a score as was ever seen in a top match. The other three Waterford attackers, Mick Flannelly, Larry Guinan and Frankie Walsh, could not be faulted for lack of effort. Kilkenny were the masters on this occasion when capturing their 14th All-Ireland crown, but whatever little bit of luck was going was gladly snapped up by the Leinster champions on the day.

1958 FINAL: THE BOY WONDER

7 September 1958   Tipperary 4-9, Galway 2-5
Attendance: 47,270   Referee: Matt Spain (Offaly)
Top scorers: D. Nealon (Tipperary) 1-2, T. Kelly (Galway) 1-2

Galway had a bye to the final, which did not necessarily help to create the talking points necessary to excite followers about the match. All the more so as Tipperary beat Kilkenny, the defending champions, in a wonderful semi-final. Little wonder then that the attendance of 47,270 proved to be the lowest in a final in fourteen years. The match was played in fine but blustery conditions and was a real anticlimax. Tipperary played against the wind into the Canal end and it only took them two minutes to stamp their dominance on the match with a smart goal from Larry Keane. Yet, despite their convincing winning margin, the Munster men still fought a losing battle at midfield. There Joe Salmon had an outstanding match for Galway and proved one of the brightest stars of the day. But it must be said that from the minute of Keane's goal there was never any doubt in the minds of neutrals as to where the title was going, and in the strict sense of the word this match was never a contest. Supporters of the losers may argue that they did well to hold the new champions to a 4-4 to 1-3 scoreline at the interval, but that proved to be a false dawn.

Galway made a shrewd move at the interval with the transfer of Fergus Benson, an experienced man between the posts, from left half back to goal, and this did much to boost Galway's morale. Benson's performance between the posts demonstrated that he was in the first flight of goalkeepers. It was contended that had the Loughrea man been between the posts all the time, he would have made the Tipperary men play much harder than they had to. With the interval score 4-4 to 1-3 in Tipp's favour, it was inevitable that nothing short of a hurling miracle could redeem the Connacht men. Benson tried to fashion it, but a goalkeeper cannot prove a saviour in such circumstances. He can only avert disaster, and that he did. Heartened by his work, the team responded gamely, but it was evident that the Tipperary backs, inspired by their brilliant captain Tony Wall, were not to be outwitted by a Galway forward line utterly lacking in leadership or constructive ideas. There was no doubt about it, Tony Wall was the winners' star performer. He never gave Galway danger man Joe Young an inch, and his powers of recovery against the unorthodox Mattie Fox were mighty effective.

But as well as Wall played, he was strongly challenged by Donie Nealon for top rating in the winning side. The UCD man was easily the outstanding Tipperary forward, and when he went to midfield late in the game to mark P. J. Lally, he did much to offset Salmon's complete dominance of Theo English after the Tipperary man had started brilliantly but later faded. The young Jimmy Doyle must also be picked out for his performance on the day. Dubbed the 'boy wonder' of hurling, the teenager was to go on to prove one of the leading scoregetters of all time in senior hurling. Although the Tipperary defence never had to hurl with the abandon that was demanded of them in earlier ties, all proved more than adequate to the occasion. Mick Maher at full back quickly closed down the efforts of Galway full forward Billy O'Neill, while the display of Mickey Byrne was awesome when pitted against Galway's best forward, Tommy Conway. John Doyle, Kieran Carey and Jimmy Finn completed a most capable half back line that rarely in the heat of battle conceded an inch. Goalie John O'Grady was soundness personified; his one lapse will be completely overlooked because of his many spectacular saves. There was no doubt about Galway's midfield dominance for the greater part of the hour. Joe Salmon and P. J. Lally completely outplayed Tipp's Theo English and John Hough. It must be said that Salmon was the man of the match with his superlative brand of hurling, and it was only when Tipperary moved Donie Nealon to the area that Salmon's vicelike grip was subsequently broken. Indeed if Galway had had a few more players of the calibre of the Glen Rovers men, Frank Benson when in goal, Jim Fives, Tim Sweeney, T. Conway, P. J. Lally and Jimmy Duggan, it would have been an incomparably better match. Tipperary's marksman, Jimmy Doyle, came up against the tenacious Galway defender Jimmy Duggan, and while the young Doyle only managed three points, he did create the opening for Donie Nealon's excellent goal. Best of the other Tipp forwards were Liam Devaney, Larry Keane, Liam Connolly and Tom Larkin.

Because Galway got free entry to the All-Ireland final that year, this did not help their cause and they were obviously lacking in the proper preparation for such an important occasion. John D. Hickey in his match report for the *Irish Independent* was critical of the decision to give the Connacht men free entry to the final. In the course of his match report he stated: 'Indeed as I left the ground deflated that an All-Ireland final should prove so disappointing the thought uppermost in my mind was that the match could yet have a redeeming feature if, as a result of the moderate fare we saw, Galway were never again allowed a free entry to the final. They sought an easy way themselves but now I feel sure the county must feel that there is no short cut to an All-Ireland crown. You win it the hard way, or else you do without it.'

Giving a county a free entry to an All-Ireland final was indeed a major decision at the time, and it boomeranged on luckless Galway. It was never repeated. After that 1958 final Galway made their debut in the Munster championship where they remained until 1969. Accordingly, the semi-final sequence was suspended until 1969 when London returned to the championship scene.

1959 FINAL: SIX GOALS

6 September 1959   Waterford 1-17, Kilkenny 5-5
Attendance: 73,707   Referee: G. Fitzgerald (Limerick)
Top scorer: T. O'Connell (Kilkenny) 3-0

This was a memorable drawn match. Waterford set a blistering pace for most of the way as they twice forged what looked like winning leads, but in the end they had to battle back for scores that tied the decider. Waterford won the toss and played into the Railway goal. They hurled brilliantly as they built up an 0-9 to 1-3 lead at the interval. Soon after the restart they went six points clear, and during the exchanges Tom Cheasty was very prominent, However, two goals by Kilkenny 19-year-old left corner forward Tommy O'Connell in the ninth and tenth minutes brought the Leinster champions level 3-3 to 0-12. Once again Waterford pulled away to a four point advantage. But a long delivery from Kilkenny midfielder Paddy Kelly was sent to the Waterford net by full forward Billy Dwyer to open up the match once more. After Philly Grimes gave Waterford a two point lead with time running out, Dick Carroll bagged a goal and two points for the men from the Nore and the match then looked all Kilkenny's. However, a last ditch Waterford attack ended with Seamus Power grabbing a great goal to give his team a deserved draw.

1959 FINAL (REPLAY): FLANNELLY GOAL A MATCH WINNER

4 October 1959   Waterford 3-12, Kilkenny 1-10
Attendance: 77, 265   Referee: G. Fitzgerald (Limerick)
Top scorers: T. Cheasty (Waterford) 2-2, F. Walsh (Waterford) 0-8

While Waterford started well in the first game, they got off to an unsettling one in the replay. Kilkenny were completely on top in the opening ten minutes and well deserved their lead of six points at the end of that period. But at the close of a thriller Waterford supporters were the ones doing the cheering after the final whistle had sounded. The Deise men had won their second All-Ireland hurling crown beating a Kilkenny team that was glorious in defeat. Croke Park was a mass of colour as a record attendance for a replay watched two very fit teams battle gallantly for the MacCarthy Cup. After trailing Kilkenny for twenty minutes in the opening stages of the first half, Waterford shot into the lead with two fast second half goals. The first from Mick Flannelly was the decisive score that transformed the Munster men, a cracking shot that beat renowned Kilkenny goalie Ollie Walsh. Fired up with Flannelly's goal, the revitalised Munster men got into their stride and goals followed from Tom Cunningham and Tom Cheasty. While Kilkenny chased them all the way home, Waterford continued to play coolly and confidently against stiff opponents. The verdict was never in doubt in the closing ten minutes. Undoubtedly the Waterford men were not in the mood to allow victory to slip from their gasp, and their composure brought the rich reward their efforts deserved. As their captain Frankie Walsh, who played a storming role in the scoring department with eight great points, stepped up to the dais on the Hogan Stand to receive the MacCarthy Cup from GAA president Dr Joe Stuart, a storm of cheering broke out around the ground.

The Deise men deserved it; they played as a team in which every man played a noble part in a victory that was well received. The men who stood out at peak times were Tom Cheasty, Frankie Walsh and Mick Flannelly in attack and Austin Flynn, Martin Óg Morrissey and John Barron in defence. Top forwards for Kilkenny were Billy Dwyer, Eddie Keher, Denis Heaslip and Seán Clohosey, while their defensive laurels went to Paddy Buggy, Johnny McGovern and the Mahers. Vanquished. Kilkenny and victorious Waterford men embraced and congratulated each other wholeheartedly. It was a sporting finish to a sporting game.

Chapter 6

THE SIXTIES

The 1960 to 1969 All-Ireland hurling finals

The sixties saw the emergence of Eddie Keher's influence on MacCarthy Cup games, an influence which was to extend well into the next decade. He made his debut in an All-Ireland senior final as a teenager in 1959 when he went in as a substitute for Kilkenny in their unsuccessful All-Ireland final replay against Waterford and had to wait until 1963 for his next appearance in the top game of the year. And, what a return by the Kilkenny man! He stamped his personality on the match in brilliant fashion by scoring 0-14 (ten points from frees) as Kilkenny took revenge for the 1959 defeat by Waterford in a high scoring match. Keher won a second All-Ireland senior medal in 1967, and then saw out the decade in the best possible way by captaining his county to their 1969 final win over Cork—his only year to lead the Noresiders to the MacCarthy Cup.

The period saw the last of the golden years of Tipperary hurling. The Premier County was the dominant power in the game in the opening years of the sixties, despite a bad start that saw them fail to live up to their favourites rating against Wexford for the 1960 championship. But Tipperary came back to regain the title in 1961, and they retained the championship the following September. After failing to come out on top in Munster in 1963, they were All-Ireland champions in 1964, and a year later they beat Wexford in a match that marked two major milestones in the annals of the competition.

That win over Wexford gave Tipperary their 21st All-Ireland crown, and John Doyle at right full back won his eighth medal. Until then Christy Ring of Cork was the only winner of eight All-Ireland senior medals in hurling or football. That was to prove the last hurrah for Tipperary hurling. The county did win one All-Ireland senior medal in the seventies, but those successes of 1964 and 65 proved to be the end of an era. Tipperary returned to the final scene for their next outing in 1967, and John Doyle was again on duty as they faced up to Kilkenny. But his chance of a place in history was ended by the Noresiders who made it their day with a win that ended a long-standing bogey. Starting that game, Kilkenny had not beaten Tipperary in a senior championship in a period stretching back to September 1923 (the final of 1922). Tipperary lost to Wexford in 1968 in their concluding MacCarthy Cup tie of the decade.

Cork came in out of the shadow of Christy Ring in 1966. They beat Kilkenny for a first All-Ireland senior hurling final win without the great Cloyne star since as far back as 1931, when they beat Kilkenny in a second replay. Cork's next All-Ireland senior crown was 1941, when Christy Ring was one of those who helped to shape the record-winning four in a row. Dublin put up a gallant display when losing by a point to Tipperary in 1961, and the county has not appeared in an All-Ireland senior final since. Nick O'Donnell led Wexford to the 1960 final, and became the first man to captain two All-Ireland senior hurling championship winning teams from the Slaneyside.

Jimmy Doyle was the only man in the decade to captain two MacCarthy Cup winning teams. He led Tipperary to victory over Wexford in 1962 and was skipper again when the Slaneysiders were again beaten three years later. There was an even share of the titles between Munster (1961, 62, 64, 65 and 66) and Leinster (1960, 63, 67, 68, and 69) with five championships each.

Statistics

Greatest attendance	75,039 in 1962
Busiest referee	John Dowling (Offaly) 1960, 62, 68
Highest team score	4-17 (29 points) by Kilkenny 1963
Highest score by losing team	6-8 (26 points) by Waterford 1963
Highest winning margin	14 points by Tipperary 1964
Lowest winning margin	One point by Tipperary 1961
Highest individual score	0-14 by E. Keher 1963
Highest individual goal tally	3 by Seamus Power 1963, Donie Nealon 1964 and C. Sheehan 1966
Goalless finals	None
Finals in which winning team failed to score a goal	1961 Tipperary
Finals in which losing team failed to score a goal	1960 Tipperary; 1965 Wexford

Best points tally by winning team	0-17 by Kilkenny 1963
Best points tally by losing team	12 by Dublin 1961 and by Tipperary 1968
Top scoring final on aggregate	1963: 10-25 (55 points)
Lowest scoring final on aggregate	1967: 5-15 (30 points)
Replays	None
Most successful captain	Jimmy Doyle (Tipperary) 1962, 65

1960 FINAL: WEXFORD CAUSES UPSET

4 September 1960   Wexford 2-15, Tipperary 0-11
Attendance: 67,154   Referee: J. Dowling (Offaly)
Top scorer: P. Kehoe (Wexford) 1-7

The Assyrian came down like a wolf on the fold
And his cohorts were gleaming in purple and gold

'Composing these lines many years ago, Lord Byron was commemorating in verse the Destruction of Sennacherib. But just as aptly he might have been describing the All-Ireland Hurling Final of 1960, for this was the destruction of Tipperary, red hot favourites who fell easy prey to the hungry hurling wolves from Wexford gleaming in purple and gold. Here in an astounding torrent of glory for Wexford was the most sensational final in many a championship season. Not only did these champions of Leinster record herein a fourth All-Ireland triumph that marks the golden jubilee of their first hurling title win, but they did it, incredibly, with far greater facility than any of us in the harvest-hit 67,154 attendance dreamt of. Tensed-up like ravenous beasts of prey, they leaped into this game straining for the kill. With deadly fangs protruding from every sector of the side they swept down on their victims.' That is how *Irish Press* sportswriter Mick Dunne began his report on this 1960 All-Ireland senior final in which the champions of Leinster demolished their Munster counterparts.

It was one of the biggest upsets in the history of the MacCarthy Cup. Tipperary started red-hot favourites, but a gallant Wexford team, with an exciting display of fast, flamboyant hurling allied to good teamwork, powered to one of their greatest wins ever, and in the process became the first side to beat Tipperary in an All-Ireland senior final since 1922. On the scoreboards stood a 2-15 to 0-10 win for Wexford. But into the record books goes the correct result: Wexford 2-15, Tipperary 0-11. For in a moment of frenzied confusion at the end, that eleventh Tipperary point was overlooked by the spectators. But not by referee John Dowling (Offaly) who informed the waiting sportswriters afterwards that Tipperary were rightly credited with Willie Moloughney's late point. As the umpire waved the white flag for that score, he was surrounded by jubilant Wexford supporters who went swarming over the pitch after hearing what they and others believed was the final whistle. But that whistle was not blown by referee Dowling. A thoughtless spectator seated on the Hogan Stand blew a whistle as Tipperary pressed into attack three seconds before the end. Hence the confusion. The referee, aided by players and officials, cleared the pitch because a restart had to be made to allow for the puck-out after Moloughney's late score.

Wexford had got off to a dream start with a point from Oliver 'Hopper' McGrath in the first minute and they were never headed in the hour. However, the game was finally balanced at the interval as the Munster champions trailed by only two points, 1-7 to 0-8. But it was Wexford who struck first again after the restart and McGrath was again on target. He cleverly slipped left full back Kieran Carey and sent a rasping shot to the Tipp net after a minute. Wexford were the masters from then on, even though the hurling continued to be exhilarating and brimful of exciting individual touches. But it was the sheer power and majesty of the Slaneyside play that was the dominant feature and brought Wexford to a memorable fourth title and a third MacCarthy Cup success.

John Nolan, after a shaky start to this, his All-Ireland debut, in which he had to encounter the famed Jimmy Doyle, the Oylegate-Glenbrien man, outhurled and outwitted Doyle to a degree not previously achieved by any defender that year. The measure of Nolan's success is indicated by the fact that Doyle's only score came from a free, although the Thurles player in the 24th minute, when he did break through, slipped as he charged towards goal. From the abundant service that flowed from that compact and great half back line of Jim English, Willie Rackard and John Nolan, Wexford's half forward line laid the basis for this victory. In the centre Padge Kehoe was an elusive and constant worry to Tony Wall, and although the Tipp captain battled bravely to stem the tide, he couldn't prevent Kehoe picking off important scores or opening up the play for the Wexford attack.

Padge's flankers, Jimmy O'Brien and Seamus Quaid, fast and agile, were rarely halted by John Doyle and Mick Burns. And what a birthday celebration it was for full back and captain Nick O'Donnell who was 35 the day before. Never once was this stout-hearted defender caught out. He whipped the ball off the ground, belted it in the air, and once towards the end magnificently picked a threatening Donie Nealon lob out of the air amid a forest of hurleys. Every Wexford man played a noble part in this victory, especially John Mitchell and Tom Neville who tied up Tipp corner forwards Seán McLoughlin and Liam Connolly. Few of the Tipperary men rose to the big occasion. Those who did were Theo English, who turned in a superb first half despite a troublesome leg injury, Tony Wall, who never lacked courage against ever mounting odds, and John Doyle, who never lost heart although pitted against a difficult opponent who roamed continuously.

After the game the Wexford captain Nick O'Donnell, who became the first hurler from the Slaneyside to captain two Wexford MacCarthy Cup winning teams, said: 'We are charmed to have won. I thought we were a certainty after ten minutes of the second half when the Tipp lads appeared to lose heart and we got well on top. I would like to thank our lads for playing so well. But fair dues to Tipperary. They were great battlers and didn't make our job easy on the day.' The Tipperary captain Tony Wall was very gracious in his tribute to the winners. 'Congratulations to Wexford. There was no doubt about the result. The better team won on the day. Wexford's big and strong team had the beating of us and were well worth their success. Our best wasn't good enough on this occasion.'

1961 FINAL: DEVANEY SPARKLES IN TWO ROLES

3 September 1961   Tipperary 0-16, Dublin 1-12
Attendance: 67,666   Referee: G. Fitzgerald (Limerick)
Top scorer: J. Doyle (Tipperary) 0-9

This was a final of contrasting halves. The opening one was dull and insipid; the second was a wonderfully exciting and competitive affair. Dublin were yards faster than their opponents, had a majestic figure in Des Foley at midfield, and a powerful defence steeled by the inflexible spirit of Des Ferguson. But they did not get the scores to reflect their share of the play. Dublin concentrated a little too much trying for goals and found Donal O'Brien on top of his game in the Tipperary net. By contrast,

Tipperary's forwards focused on snatching up every point-scoring chance on offer. Jimmy Doyle proved a master in this regard and was a key figure in the success, scoring nine wonderful points. Liam Devaney also left his mark on the final—on the double in fact. He was a tireless centre half forward for much of the match and then shone at centre back late in the game. There is an old adage which says that scores are the food which keeps a team's spirit alive, and that certainly applied to the Munster champions. For, more than anything else, their ability to grab scores, even when the game appeared to have turned against them, was the decisive and determining factor in a tremendously tense and exciting final.

This was the major difference between the Tipperary and Dublin teams. It gives one yet another All-Ireland crown and it leaves the other and its supporters lamenting what might have been. In a pulsating and nerve-wrecking second half, those freely offered odds were nearly made to appear ridiculous for the second year in succession. For speed and fitness and considerable hurling ability count for nothing in the white heat of championship hurling if they are not translated into decisive scores. So Dublin's superiority, so marked during this game, went without reward in the only place it mattered most—on the scoreboard.

Tipperary lost the toss. They played into the Railway end on a day when there was no wind to speak of, and in humid conditions. The Munster men had a blistering start, with three points in three minutes before Billy Jackson opened Dublin's tally with a fine point. Tipperary continued to have the better of the exchanges and had pushed to a 0-10 to 0-6 lead at the interval. In that first half when Dublin appeared somewhat nervous, the game meandered along, but the flood of full blooded, pulsating hurling that we saw from the restart right to the final whistle made this a contest in every way worthy of the occasion.

It was that glorious second half—daring, desperate, supercharged and often classic hurling—contested at pace and with a legitimate fury that charmed the neutrals and the supporters. Within seven minutes of the restart the losers, who can be proud of their part in providing fare of such splendour, had wiped out Tipperary's lead. The goal came in the sixth minute. Larry Shannon whipped the ball across to Mick Bohan, who placed the inrushing Billy Jackson for a brilliantly executed goal. Dublin supporters went wild with delight and they had cause for even greater joy a minute later when Achill Boothman took a pass from Fran Whelan and dropped over the equalising point. The fat was now very much in the fire.

The game became a hurling inferno, blazing brilliantly to the very end. But never was the folly of unqualified predictions more strikingly illustrated than in that tempestuous second half, when Dublin, hurling like men inspired, often had the Munster men reeling. Dublin were now in the driving seat and rattled over a brace of points to edge a point clear after fourteen minutes. Although the exchanges were now very keen and competitive, let it be said that a great sporting spirit prevailed between two marvellous sides until a brief flare-up earned Tom Ryan (Tipperary) and Lar Foley (Dublin) their marching orders. But Tipperary finished with the stronger challenge. Matt O'Gara knocked over a long-range point to level the game. With nine minutes to go and the sides still level, Tipp calmly hit back. Donie Nealon, brilliant all through the game once again, came to his side's rescue. He evaded two firm challenges and pointed. The accuracy of sharpshooter Jimmy Doyle proved Dublin's undoing. He stroked over a free and stretched Tipp's lead to two points. Two and a half minutes remained when Achill Boothman pointed the final score of the game. Dogged Dublin still battled strongly for a possible winning goal, but it was not to be. Two factors backboned Tipperary's success: Jimmy Doyle's magnificent free-taking and accuracy from play, and the switch of Liam Devaney to centre back from centre forward at a time when Dublin looked like upsetting predictions.

Tributes were paid to Dublin for their part in making the game such an epic occasion. Tipperary captain Matt Hassett said: 'This was a harder and faster game than I expected and I was really relieved when the final whistle sounded. Dublin were the best and the fastest team we met this year and it was really hard on them that they should have lost so narrowly. Still, it is a great consolation for us after last year's disappointment.'

Jimmy Doyle said: 'It was a great game and Dublin played terrific hurling at times. It was a pity they had to lose, but I will be surprised if there is not an All-Ireland in that squad.'

John Doyle, who won his fifth All-Ireland medal, said that Dublin's speed was their strong suit and admitted that he had never played against as fit and fast a team as Dublin. 'I expected it to be close. They are a grand team.'

Liam Devaney, the hero of the Tipperary side, said: 'It was a great game and Dublin were unlucky to lose after such a grand display. I knew it was going to be close as any team that can beat Wexford, as Dublin did, had to be good.'

Naturally there was a lot of disappointment in the Dublin dressing room after such a heart warming display. Dublin captain Noel Drumgoole said: 'I'd love to have another crack against Tipp now that they are champions. It is a great consolation for us to have gone so close to winning and it proves that Dublin hurling is back at the top. Congratulations to Tipperary on their win and I hope we can meet them in the Oireachtas and maybe reverse that result.'

Dessie Ferguson, who was hoping to add an All-Ireland hurling medal to the football medal he had won in 1958, said: 'We were a bit unlucky but Tipperary played with wonderful spirit and we do not begrudge them the win. I knew we would give them a great fight but I think we surprised a lot of people including our own supporters as things turned out.'

1962 FINAL: FULL BACKS MIGHTY BULWARKS

2 September 1962   Tipperary 3-10, Wexford 2-11
Attendance: 75,039   Referee: J. Dowling (Offaly)
Top scorer: S. McLoughlin (Tipperary) 1-2

This was a magnificent and deliriously spellbinding game of hurling splendour that so fittingly marked the completion of 75 years of All-Ireland championship hurling. Conjure up a selection of rich superlatives and you would still fall short of adequate words to describe the 1962 All-Ireland hurling final that kept the MacCarthy Cup in Tipperary. Magnificent Tipperary! Magnificent Wexford! Above all, magnificent hurling, still surely the greatest ball game on earth. Tipperary won and just deserved their narrow victory for the wonderful way they fought back through the last ten minutes, just when Wexford seemed set to snatch away the laurels, after recovering from that stunning shock of having two goals chalked up against them after only six pucks in the game.

Tom Moloughney and Seán McLoughlin were the early villains of the piece with that brace of goals that was to turn this final into a hurling frenzy as Wexford battled back courageously to play their part in a memorable match which they subsequently lost by only two points. In the 1950s Wexford brought a new glamour to the game, uplifted it to a new status and won even greater renown when mocking and almost defying adversity. Submerged by Tipperary's lightning-like start, they quickly surfaced to fight back like men affronted, men whose honour had been besmirched. But when they had only one point to their credit, and five wides to their discredit after seven minutes, it seemed that the champions would coast to an easy victory. But the Slaneymen rallied and in some exciting exchanges during which both sides shared points, they were suddenly back in the hunt in the 24th minute when Ned Wheeler got through for a goal to level the scores 2-3 to 1-6. But Tipp finished the stronger, Jimmy Doyle pointing two frees and Seán McLoughlin hitting another from play to hold the edge at the interval, Tipperary 2-6, Wexford 1-6.

Tipperary restarted in promising style with a Jimmy Doyle point after just ten seconds, but once more Wexford displayed a great fighting spirit and when Jimmy O'Brien lashed home a goal and Willie Rackard and Ned Wheeler put over a brace of points, the Leinster men looked possible winners. Disaster struck when Tipperary lost their great score-taker Jimmy Doyle with a broken collar bone, but the defending champions showed their true character by sticking to their task and were rewarded in the twentieth minute when Tom Ryan (Killenaule) boosted his team's hopes with a well-taken goal. The quick silvered Donie Nealon, moved to midfield by the team mentors, covered acres of ground making his presence felt, and indeed sparked off the charge that was to lead his team to subsequent victory. The Ryan goal was also a factor which at the time was crucial in turning the game in Tipperary's favour. Padge Kehoe followed Ryan's goal with a superb point, but the Munster men were not to be denied and had the last say with Nealon and McLoughlin sending over a point apiece. Nealon was a commanding figure all through the hour but particularly in the testing closing quarter when his speed and stamina proved mighty weapons in his side's winning charge. And it must be said that in the end, Tipperary had the stamina, the fitness, the zest and the buoyancy of youth that was in their side. Those, combined with the stubborn defiance of their defence and the opportunistic alertness of their attack, swept Tipperary to yet another All-Ireland victory.

But Wexford had no need to mourn, for their young men rose wonderfully to the occasion and the deeds of Pat Nolan, Tom Neville, who gave an exhibition of defensive play, Phil Wilson, Martin Lyng, Jimmy O'Brien, 'Hopper' McGrath and Paul Lynch will as the song says, 'Never be forgot by the sweet Slaneyside'. Not to be forgotten either were their great veterans Willie Rackard, Nick O'Donnell, Jim English and Tim Flood, who recovered so ably after that nightmare start, Padge Kehoe and above all Ned Wheeler who, had Wexford won, must surely have earned a statue in the Bullring—though it will always be a mystery why he wasn't switched to centre forward in the last twenty minutes. In a great contest like this was, there had to be some degree of messing and fumbling which is brought on by the importance of the occasion, but that aspect of the exchanges was outshone by the sheer brilliance of the hurling throughout.

For Tipperary, solid Tony Wall played as great a game as any he had turned in. He kept a firm grip on Wexford danger man, Padge Kehoe, as evidenced by the move of Tim Flood to the central role in attack in an effort to break Wall's dominance. John Doyle put in a lot of hard work under pressure during the match while Michael Maher kept more than a watchful eye on Ned Wheeler. Kieran Carey had his hands full against the lively 'Hopper' McGrath, whose roving tactics demanded a lot of Tipperary defensive attention. Unexpectedly, the Munster men were not too well served in the middle of the field until the arrival of Donie Nealon, who proceeded to break the stranglehold exerted by Wexford's Phil Wilson and Martin Lyng.

But the eager Tipperary attackers saw to it that the chances created by the outfield men were put to good use. A good example was the excellent work carried out by Tom Ryan and Mackey McKenna who pounced on any slip or opening to set up a scoring chance for better placed colleagues. McKenna on one such sortie charged down the centre in the 50th minute to provide Tom Ryan with his goal chance. Aye, it was a great day for Tipperary, a great day for Wexford, a great day for the Kilkenny minors, a great day for hurling, and a great day for Ireland.

1963 FINAL: THE SKILLS OF EDDIE KEHER

1 September 1963   Kilkenny 4-17, Waterford 6-8
Attendance: 72,123   Referee: J. Hatton (Wicklow)
Top scorer: E. Keher (Kilkenny) 0-14

This was the start of the Eddie Keher influence on the All-Ireland scene in a big way. In a match of fluctuating fortunes, he was a glittering star as he contributed fourteen points to a high scoring game. Surprisingly enough, however, the final produced few scores in the opening minutes. It can be said that never before have so many scores, 35 in all, come in an All-Ireland decider up till then. But it was the man of the match Eddie Keher who set a personal record with his prolific marksmanship in a match in which several players earned stellar rating. It may seem irrational to those who were not at the match to say that a side which scored 6-8 did not deserve to win, but on the run of play Kilkenny were considerably more than three points the better side. Rarely does an All-Ireland final provide as many transformations as this one did.

Waterford won the toss and played with a slight breeze into the Railway end. But after six minutes only three points were on the scoreboard, Keher in the third minute to start his scoring spree, Phil Grimes in the fifth and Keher again. After that the scoring rate quickened, but amazingly, despite that tally of thirty-five scores in all, both teams missed many good scoring chances. Waterford, who started favourites, struggled all through at centrefield. They trailed by seven points at the interval, 3-6 to 1-5, and they appeared in dire straits when they conceded a point from a free by Keher and a goal by Tom Walsh. They also had to depend on two super saves from Percy Flynn, who had replaced Ned Power in goal. And all this happened in the first three minutes after the restart. However, the Munster men brought the game to life again with two marvellous goals.

Tom Cheasty broke the Noreside cover, and after a great solo run on the right wing, he squared the ball and the inrushing Seamus Power cracked the ball to the Kilkenny net. Within a minute Ollie Walsh pulled off a great save from Power, but Mickey Flannelly was in like a flash to smack the rebound home. The two goals by Waterford revitalised the exchanges and gave the losers the encouragement they so badly needed to lift the game. But if Waterford improved, so too did Kilkenny when the challenge was put up to them. Waterford were quickly and effectively chastised for each breach of the Kilkenny defence, usually by Keher and on two vital occasions by team captain Seamus Cleere, who had a superb game, being one of the most elegant and commanding strikers of the ball in the game.

A Waterford goal in the 25th minute of this half cut the victory margin to a precarious two points, but once again Keher strode the scene and put over a superlative point. It was followed by two more points from Murray and Keher, who it seemed could not miss when he essayed a score to allay the fear of Kilkenny supporters that their side might be victims of larceny on a grand scale. Again, however, the Kilkenny supporters must have been beside themselves with anxiety, if not fear, when Seamus Power cleverly stealing away from his marker, gained possession and beat Ollie Walsh in the Kilkenny goal to leave only two points between the teams with a minute to go. But the score came too late to alter the state of the parties materially, and Kilkenny came thundering back. The last score of the match, a point, was fittingly recorded by Keher, who had four points from play and ten from frees.

Majestic as was Keher's scoring feat, the real source of the Kilkenny victory was the splendour of their half backs, captain Seamus Cleere, the commanding Ted Carroll and Martin Coogan, who rarely gave the opposing forward line proper space. They were backed by a splendid display from the Noreside midfield pairing of Seán Clohosey and Denis Heaslip.

While Keher was the master in attack when it came to scoring, he got a great service from the other scoring forwards, the youthful Tom Walsh and Murphy. It was not to be Waterford's day, in spite of a tremendous resurgence in the second half which failed to offset many first half shortcomings, but they did at least throw a mighty scare into their opponents before the finish. The Deise full back line were never allowed to settle in after a horrendous opening period. Martin Óg Morrissey was their best defender, ably assisted by Larry Guinan, with Seamus Power, Phil Grimes and Mickey Flannelly the prime score-takers. Tom Cheasty for once never rose to the occasion and was prevented from doing so by the magnificent Ted Carroll. It can be stated that the failure of the Waterford team officials to take corrective action at crucial stages to improve areas which were under extreme pressure did not help the Deise cause. It showed the unease on the line with the switch of John Barron and right half back Guinan with time ticking away. What could have helped would have been the transfer of Philly Grimes to the 40 in place of Cheasty, which would have been a more productive move. Without labouring the point, it was not to be Waterford's day as Kilkenny, hurling well within themselves, conjured up the scores that mattered to take their fifteenth All-Ireland crown.

1964 FINAL: KEATING POINT PROMPTS WIN

6 September 1964   Tipperary 5-13, Kilkenny 2-8
Attendance: 71,262   Referee: A. Higgins (Galway)
Top scorer: J. Doyle (Tipperary) 0-10

Tipperary had only five wides as they powered to a huge win over the defending champions. The Munster men hallmarked the game with a mighty display all through, but really excelled in the second half with their machine-like play. Nobly and majestically Tipperary in hurling stood apart from all others and were All-Ireland champions again. They are now the leaders of the championship list with their twentieth title, one ahead of Cork on the honours roll. This was a complete and overwhelming triumph and it was etched into the annals of hurling by what must surely be a performance which was as near perfection as any winning side from the famed county since the foundation of the Association 80 years ago. Here was hurling power controlled with machine-like precision and unleashed so devastatingly when the need arose with skilled effectiveness. Tipperary regulated this hurling power with such efficiency that they had Kilkenny overthrown long before the final whistle. Having edged into a pace-setting lead, they clung to it with a smooth and adept mastery of the exchanges through the second quarter, and then when it seemed that their dominance was about to be threatened, let loose the full potential of their power.

In a match played in ideal conditions they looked every inch a championship side as they carved out a win that was as convincing as the fourteen point margin suggests. Jimmy Doyle enhanced his ever growing reputation as one of the game's top marksmen by totting up ten points of his team's total. One sided, though, as the second half turned out, it was always a very entertaining match and splendid as a spectacle, if not for the Kilkenny followers who had to sit and watch the overthrow of their champions. The most telling difference which surfaced at key stages appeared in attack, an area where Tipp really excelled and the scoreboard backs up that assertion. Apart from Jimmy Doyle, who left a vivid imprint with his cool efficiency in his free-taking role, his work was complemented by Donie Nealon who smacked home three goals and also great scoring returns from the redoubtable Mick 'Babs' Keating, John McKenna and Seán McLoughlin. That attacking formation posed too many problems for the Kilkenny defensive set-up who were outsmarted in many quarters.

There was some apprehension within Tipperary circles that the age factor on their side might limit their effectiveness in the cauldron of championship heat, but it was never a factor in the match itself. Indeed much of the glory was deservedly grasped by the older members of the squad who were operating in key positions, and each emerged with match honours. The full back line of John Doyle, Mick Maher and Kieran Carey was as solid as the Rock of Cashel, rendering the Kilkenny full forward line virtually ineffective. John O'Donoghue's goalkeeping was masterly and anything missed by his front men was coolly, positively and calmly dealt with when danger appeared. There was also power in abundance in the half back line, brilliantly marshalled by Tony Wall, whose presence was always going to be inspirational and who never flinched in the face of Kilkenny pressure. Tipperary lost full back Mick Maher with a leg injury, but his replacement Mick Lonergan took over to retain the grip which Maher had held before his departure.

Mick Murphy won the toss for Tipperary on a day that conditions offered no favour to either side. The challengers elected to defend the Canal end and were rocked virtually from the throw-in as midfielder Paddy Moran won possession, passed to Seamus Cleere who sent over a picture point. A great start for Kilkenny, but as things materialised that was to be the only time they led in the final.

Ollie Walsh and John O'Donoghue in turn were called on to prove their reputations as net minders with fine saves before Jimmy Doyle levelled the score with a point from a free after five minutes. Two minutes later Tipperary were on their way. Babs Keating burst through a cluster of Kilkenny defenders to lash over a smashing point, and almost immediately afterwards John McKenna took a pass from Theo English to beat Ollie Walsh from ten yards in the Kilkenny goal. The Munster men never looked back after that.

Tipp were 1-8 to 0-6 ahead at the interval, and early after the restart excitement rose as Kilkenny rallied strongly. After a couple of fierce attacks, John Teehan connected an Eddie Keher free with an overhead swipe to give the cup holders a marvellous tonic with a smashing goal. Jimmy Doyle and Tommy Walsh added to the excitement by exchanging points, but after about eight minutes Donie Nealon got his second goal, and there was no way back for Kilkenny after that. Pa Dillon, Ted Carroll, Pat Henderson and Willie Murphy were hard workers for the Leinster men, who were unable to match the brilliance of Tipperary on the day.

1965 FINAL: McLOUGHLIN'S GOAL TOUCH DECISIVE

5 September 1965 Tipperary 2-16, Wexford 0-10
Attendance: 67,498 Referee: M. Hayes (Clare)
Top scorer: S. McLoughlin (Tipperary) 2-1

A two goal barrage from gangling Seán McLoughlin paved the way for Tipperary's successful defence of their senior hurling crown at Croke Park against challengers Wexford. Adding to a momentous occasion was the feat of Tipp's right corner back John Doyle, who was chaired off the field after winning his eighth All-Ireland senior medal. He now stands shoulder to shoulder with the illustrious Christy Ring of Cork. It is fair to suggest that this latest Doyle achievement was accomplished in a more facile fashion than some of his earlier successes. It was an interesting but by no means memorable game as Tipperary emphasised their special brand of hurling at that time by pulling away in the second half for a comfortable win.

When Cardinal Conway presented Tipp captain Jimmy Doyle with the MacCarthy Cup, he became another in a long line of illustrious captains who have heaped more honours on Tipperary than any other county. But the crowd reacted with controlled enthusiasm for such a remarkable occasion. Perhaps it just appeared in retrospect that Tipperary supporters were conditioned to an inevitable result, which was really far from the truth. The truth was that Tipperary hurlers had outgrown all opposition at this time. They stamped their class on proceedings in Munster when seeing off the threat posed by Cork and Clare, and then a spirited challenge from Wexford in the All-Ireland final which was nipped in the bud. Wexford just trailed in Tipperary's wake at half-time when the holders led 2-5 to 0-6, having played against the wind. If the signs were ominous then, after fifteen minutes of the second half the champions were ahead 2-11 to 0-9 and all hope of a Wexford resurgence had been banished. Throughout, Wexford were preoccupied with handling the ball, the type of hurling practised so successfully by their teams in the mid-fifties. While Tipperary served up similar passages at times and while this provided moments of virtuosity, it robbed the hour of the more classy hurling we had come to expect.

Where it worked admirably for Wexford outfield, it broke down quite hopelessly in front of the Tipperary posts. Wexford just couldn't break down the resolute resistance mounted by the superb John Doyle, Michael Maher and Kieran Carey line, while brilliant John O'Donoghue's citadel remained intact. The Leinster champions fielded a young team, with nine newcomers to the final series. They battled bravely to try and stem the tide that threatened to swamp them, after the quick opening burst of goals from McLoughlin. The challengers reshuffled for the second half. The moves included the transfer of Jimmy O'Brien, who was their best raider, to midfield for a time and it looked as if the switch would pay dividends, as a minute after the restart Martin Codd sent over a morale-boosting point from over 50 yards. Once more, however, Seán McLoughlin stepped into the picture. After two minutes of the half he hand passed the ball over the bar after receiving from Donie Nealon. Tipperary, now cool and competent, produced top-class hurling when the situation demanded and took over control despite some spirited opposition from Wexford. Points from John 'Mackey' McKenna and Theo English, the latter a wonderful pointed sideline cut from 50 yards, put the defending champions firmly on the road to their comfortable win. McLoughlin must get much of the credit for the success as a result of his golden goals. Nevertheless, Mickey Burns stamped his name impressively on the victory with a magnificent display at right half back in the second half. Mackey McKenna was in fine form in attack. Time and time again he captured much of the limelight with a power-packed performance when opening up the Wexford defence. Poor finishing by Wexford was to prove their undoing on a day when a number of scoring chances went abegging, and that proved fatal from the Leinster champions' perspective. Pat Nolan was always alert and dependable in the losers' goal and saved his side from a heavier defeat. Ned Colfer at left full back and Jimmy O'Brien, first in attack and later at midfield, were other wholehearted stalwarts for Wexford. It was Willie Murphy at wing back and Tom Neville at centre back who were the launching pads for the series of attacks which subsequently failed to breach the Tipperary cover, brilliantly marshalled by Tony Wall.

1966 FINAL: BARRY'S FIVE STAR SHOW

4 September 1966   Cork 3-9, Kilkenny 1-10
Attendance: 68,249   Referee: J. Hatton (Wicklow)
Top scorer: C. Sheehan (Cork) 3-0

It is a strange irony that although Colm Sheehan was a three goal hero for Cork in a game that never rose to the heights expected, he still had strong opposition for the man of the match rating from his goalkeeper Paddy Barry. He brought off some great saves, and but for his vigilance Kilkenny would have made it a closer test and indeed might well have won. It was an insipid battle with the hurling rising above the mediocre only occasionally. There was far too much mishitting, poking and lapses of judgment to make it a classic final worthy of these two counties. There was no doubt that Cork were the superior team, but for a period at the start of the game it looked as if they might be overrun. Kilkenny quickly went into a three point lead and it took Cork sixteen minutes to get their first score—a point from a free by Seánie Barry. This was a final of fragmented pieces, a jigsaw of a game which was never pieced together.

Even Kilkenny, who started promisingly, became erratic. Their shooting became careless and wild and before half-time they had hit nine wides and every one of those was a wasted chance that they were to rue before the game had run its course The Leinster champions won the toss and elected to play with the contrary wind blowing into the Railway end. The first ten minutes of prodding and probing we attributed to nerves on the big occasion, but as the first half dragged on the tempo of the game rarely quickened. The opening score came in about five minutes when Eddie Keher placed John Teehan for a point. Keher pointed a couple of frees, but it was very tame stuff. But the scene was about to change dramatically, leading to a fortuitous Cork score. Cork were awarded a 21 yard free. Free-taker Seánie Barry bent down and lifted the ball with his hurley but must have taken his eye off the ball and the resultant hit was fluffed and struck weakly. The ball hit a wall of Kilkenny defenders and bounced in front of Cork's Colm Sheehan, who poked the ball over the goal-line to leave his side just two points in arrears at the break.

The Leesiders were quite happy going in at half-time with the scoreboard reading Kilkenny 0-7, Cork 1-2. Sheehan's goal was to change the whole tempo of the game. The Kilkenny team mentors, unhappy with the performance of their attacking set-up, made some switches in an effort to restore stability. Claus Dunne was shifted to right half forward, Seán Buckley to the 40, and Keher to the left wing. But the desired effects were never achieved as the Cork defenders were not for turning. Cork now with wind advantage began to dictate the trend of play from the restart and in the space of minutes Seánie Barry and Gerald McCarthy had levelled the scoring with points. The tried and trusted Keher put the Leinster champions back into the lead with a point.

Then came the spirit-rouser for Cork when the game took a definitive turn for the Munster men. John Bennett got possession on the wing and lobbed the ball to the waiting Colm Sheehan, who hand passed past the unprepared Ollie Walsh. Cork were now firmly in the driving seat. Seánie Barry pointed from the left wing, a great effort. In the closing quarter Cork were easily the dominant force and the pressure they exerted created weaknesses in the Kilkenny defensive set-up which Cork duly exploited. Indeed, for once, the Leinster men were never able to lift their game to compete on a level footing against their rampant Cork opponents. The match was over as a contest. And so all the pent up emotions that had been reluctantly locked away in yearning Cork hearts for twelve years were released when referee Jimmy Hatton (Wicklow) blew the final whistle. That was the signal for the huge Cork following to rush on to the green sod of Croke Park to greet their triumphant heroes. And it can be said that never was a victory more fitting and more deserved for the men in red who captured the 1966 MacCarthy Cup in the 77th senior hurling championship decider.

1967 FINAL: WALSH INSPIRES RARE WIN

3 September 1967   Kilkenny 3-8, Tipperary 2-7
Attendance: 64,241   Referee: M. Hayes (Clare)
Top scorer: D. Nealon (Tipperary) 2-0

This was Kilkenny's first final win over Tipperary in a senior championship since the 1922 All-Ireland final—their first MacCarthy Cup triumph played on 9 September 1923. The match was one in which the Kilkenny men displayed character of the highest standard. Ollie Walsh, for instance, lined out between the posts with a stitched wrist following an accident on the train on the way to Dublin for the final, which necessitated a pain-killing injection before the game, and yet he defied the setback with a herculean performance. Time and again in the opening half when Tipperary had the support of a stiff breeze and were moving well, Walsh kept them at bay with his utter dependability and courage in the last line of defence. Then in the second half the Leinster champions lost their sharpshooter Eddie Keher after thirteen minutes with a wrist injury, and Tommy Walsh was forced to retire in the 25th minute because of a serious eye injury. Yet after coming from six points in arrears at the interval, 2-6 to 1-3, Kilkenny took such complete control in the last quarter of the match that the territorial advantage which they enjoyed should have been reflected by a bigger scoring total at the time. Indeed, such was the power and precision of Kilkenny's authority, that Tipperary's star-laden side were confined to a single point for the entire second half—and that score came 30 seconds before the finish.

Undoubtedly, Kilkenny relished this victory over their old rivals because it shattered the hoodoo that had for so long afflicted them in All-Ireland finals against Tipperary. Kilkenny, on the evidence of their second half display, strode the scene with an elegance that betokened an unshakeable belief in themselves, while Tipperary never at any stage showed the confidence to match their rampant opponents'. It must be stressed that the performance of goalkeeper Ollie Walsh must go into this final's record as being, under the circumstances, one of sheer brilliance in the opening half. No man did more than Walsh to keep Kilkenny's championship hopes alive as Tipperary constantly surged on the prowl for scores. But the ace Thomastown goalie offered up spectacular agility, an unbridled resoluteness and an almost impregnable defence as he repelled them again and again. After three All-Ireland finals in which the total of goals against him ran into double figures, Ollie on this occasion had obviously steeled himself to perform daring deeds. He performed them with an almost incredible mobility. (Once during the first half I counted seven shots saved that had goal written all over them.)

Nor could Ollie be faulted for the first two shots that beat him in the first half as he was not very well protected by his front men, who were feeling the brunt of Tipperary pressure and the expertise of Donie Nealon, who gave a master class with his finishing efforts for those two scores. When Tipperary jumped into their five point lead with the second of Nealon's goals, it appeared briefly as if their forwards might have found the way through Kilkenny's tight defence and Ollie Walsh's resistance. However, when Tipperary had increased their lead to no more than six points by half-time, after having wind assistance, the picture looked different as Kilkenny saw it. Tipperary had played for most of the first half with an unbalanced midfield partnership. Kilkenny's Paddy Moran had too obviously and too convincingly outshone and outplayed Theo English, while big John Teehan was too formidable a match for Mick Roche. That was a major consideration when Kilkenny faced into the second half.

It was in the second half that time ultimately and mercilessly caught up with Tipperary. They were outrun and outmanoeuvred by a younger Kilkenny team that hurled with tormenting self-confidence and unrestrained fervour. This was Kilkenny's most effective display in three years. They moved the ball about with a facility and speed that shattered the spirit of the opposition, and more important still they had the players who clearly dominated the crucial key positions.

Kilkenny had their heroes apart from Ollie Walsh. Pat Henderson added considerably to his reputation that had earned him a place among the outstanding centre half backs in the game. He got great assistance from Martin Coogan who was impassable, and the stylish, elegant and exemplary ball striker Seamus Cleere. In the inside line Ted Carroll gave one of the most effective and positive displays at corner back ever given in Croke

Park. Pa Dillon and Jim Treacy contributed very much as well. There was power and efficiency in the Eddie Keher, Tommy Walsh and Claus Dunne half forward line, and but for the injuries which forced Keher and Walsh out of the game, the winners' total score would have been greater. For Tipperary, John O'Donoghue made some great saves in goal and full backs John Doyle, Kieran Carey and Noel O'Gorman fought hard and endlessly. Their best defender was Len Gaynor who lacked the support required on such an important day, while Mick Burns was very impressive in his duels with Claus Dunne.

1968 FINAL: DORAN BLUEPRINTS 'MISSION IMPOSSIBLE'

1 September 1968   Wexford 5-8, Tipperary 3-12
Attendance: 63,461   Referee: J. Dowling (Offaly)
Top scorers: J. Berry (Wexford) 2-2, J. Doyle (Tipperary) 1-5

This was the come-back of the decade and one of the greatest in the history of the MacCarthy Cup. Wexford could do little right in a moderate first half, and they trailed 1-11 to 1-3 at the interval. Conditions were ideal and Tipperary had played into a slight breeze blowing from the Railway end. With no help in prospect from the elements therefore, Wexford had it all to do, and they summoned on all their reserves of grit, power, skill, stamina and fighting heart to provide a second half of splendour, excitement and sportsmanship. Not even that gale-swept day in 1956, when another generation of purple and gold hurling heroes snatched the National League title from the canyons of defeat, could compare with the astonishingly dramatic victory that Wexford etched into the annals of the championship. With a truly astounding recovery, they thundered to another memorable win over Tipperary for their county's fifth All-Ireland senior hurling title. It was a historic day for Wexford on which they recorded the senior-minor double on their first dual appearance on All-Ireland final day. But most important of all for the game of hurling itself, this Wexford senior success, after being eight points behind at the interval, was achieved in a second half of notable hurling, which made this final one of the greatest in the history of the game.

A series of team switches in the Wexford dressing room at the interval helped transform the Leinster champions. These included the introduction from the substitutes bench of John Quigley to right half forward and the transfer of Paul Lynch from there to centre forward, while Tony Doran, who had started at centre forward but was moved to full forward late in the first half, remained camped in the Tipperary parallelogram.

And as 'mission impossible' began to take shape, Tony Doran started to exercise a decisive influence. In six minutes he goaled cleverly from a Phil Wilson pass and from then on he caused Tipperary all kinds of trouble. After Jack Berry (W) and Liam Devaney (T) exchanged points, Doran was fouled as he was moving forward. Paul Lynch took the resultant free and smashed the ball to the Tipperary net to put Wexford on level terms, 3-6 to 1-12. Wexford were now in full cry. Three minutes later Tipperary goalie John O'Donoghue brought off a tremendous save from Jack Berry, but the Model County men were not to be denied. Eight minutes from full time they were through again for another goal, and once more the man in the spotlight was Tony Doran. He caught a midfield lob from Wilson and palmed the ball to the Tipperary net. Tipperary hadn't time to regroup when Jack Berry scored another goal. The Munster champions fought back well in the closing stages, but goals from Seán McLoughlin and Babs Keating were not enough to stem the Wexford tide. Twelve years earlier, a Wexford team stepped out for the second half against Tipperary fifteen points behind but had the assistance of a gale force wind to aid them on their way to victory. The 1968 purple and gold had no strong wind, but they did possess intractable resolve, hitherto unrevealed quantities of stamina and a high degree of fitness as well as latent hurling power and skill. In that amazing second half, a combination of all of these made them the All-Ireland champions. And it could be stressed that if magic was ever conjured up in a dressing room, it must have happened in Wexford's. Perhaps the magician was team manager Padge Kehoe, a former star hurler who pounded the dressing room table during a thunderous lecture to his charges. It certainly did the trick. But it was not the only one in Wexford's magic box. The switches forced on Wexford for the second half all worked like a charm, and the team spirit was reinvigorated also to a commendable degree. In a great display by Wexford, Tony Doran shared the honours with top scorer Jack Berry in attack. Pat Nolan brought off some remarkable saves in goal for the winners, and Dan Quigley and Willie Murphy did much to mould the defence into a tightly disciplined unit, especially in the second half. Phil Wilson had a great hour in the centre of the field where he did Trojan work. It was a great day for goalkeepers. John O'Donoghue had an excellent game in the Tipperary net, despite the five goals against him. Len Gaynor and Babs Keating were other Tipperary stars.

1969 FINAL: CARROLL KEEPS KILKENNY ON WINNING COURSE

7 September 1969   Kilkenny 2-15, Cork 2-5
Attendance: 68,844   Referee: S. O'Connor (Limerick)
Top scorer: C. McCarthy (Cork) 1-6

This was Ted Carroll's (Kilkenny) day because he was truly outstanding in the first half, and when things began to go Kilkenny's way in the second, he also provided many valuable touches. Undoubtedly, Kilkenny looked doomed when they lost centre half forward Pat Delaney ten minutes into the second half with an injury. In a game played in almost ideal conditions, they were a point behind at that stage, and up to then the Leesiders were the more composed team and hurling very well. Cork played against a light breeze blowing into the Canal end, and had a dream start when Charlie McCarthy, in the Hill 16 corner, dazzled with a weaving run before opening the scoring with a goal inside two minutes. The Munster men were in control throughout the first half and were two goals clear coming up to the interval. Martin Brennan handed Kilkenny a lifeline when he grabbed a late goal, but despite that setback Cork still looked a sound bet for the title as they went to their dressing room at the break 2-6 to 1-6 ahead. With the loss of Pat Delaney, injured and carried off on a stretcher, Kilkenny, as if incensed by the summary dismissal of their centre forward ten minutes after the restart, unleashed a torrent against their rivals, who inexplicably faded. At the time, Cork were the more efficient, purposeful and hungry team and appeared set for victory against opposition who seemed afflicted by their 'underdogs' tag.

Within seconds of the restart Charlie McCarthy was back in the scoring limelight. He stretched Cork's lead with a point, but in the sixth minute the Kilkenny revival began as Joe Millea finished a Pat Delaney centre for his team's second goal. Soon afterwards a late foul on Delaney saw the centre half forward being stretchered off and Eddie Keher rifled over the equaliser from the resultant free. Kilkenny's mood changed dramatically. Rarely has a struggling side recovered more gallantly than Kilkenny did. And their elegance when they came to realise that Cork were not unbeatable was, quite apparently, something for which the losers were unprepared. How else could the manner in which they descended from the heights they were scaling be explained. Maybe the assurances with which they must have entered the fray left them psychologically not ready for an uphill struggle. But whatever the cause, they were vastly inferior to the winners in the last quarter.

Once they were on an equal footing score wise, Kilkenny were a transformed team from then on. Hurling with all the elan for which the county is famed, they took over as the pace setters. Cork had a further brief moment of glory as Charlie McCarthy put them ahead again with a pointed free, but Martin Coogan from a 70 and Pat Kavanagh, who had come on as a substitute, with a 55 yard effort, replied with points for the Leinster champions. As a result, Kilkenny were ahead for the first time with twelve minutes remaining. There was no stopping Kilkenny after that. With Pat Henderson and Martin Coogan dominating the half back line, Mick Lawlor, outstanding at midfield, and Keher, who was moved from left half forward to centre half forward at the end of the third quarter, in sparkling form, the Leinster men set a blistering standard to pull away for a convincing win. Martin Coogan, Paddy Moran and Keher, who captained the team, scored two points from frees and one from play, and indeed he had the last score of the day from a free. Kilkenny were rampant in the final quarter and Cork just had no answer to the revival. However, there were impressive performances from a number of their hurlers, particularly Ray Cummins at full forward, top scoring Charlie McCarthy, Gerald McCarthy at left half back and Donal Clifford. The Kilkenny second half resurgence might well not have been possible but for the quality hurling served up by the polished Ted Carroll at right full back. He was the man who kept the Leinster champions in the hunt when their backs were really against the wall in the first half. Carroll was truly outstanding in the first half, and when things began to go Kilkenny's way in the second half, he produced the necessary leadership and poise. The standard was by no means of classical Kilkenny-Cork vintage, but what the game lacked in that respect was more than compensated for in the metamorphosis which overtook it.

heaving bodies. They stayed in front for only five minutes. By half-time Cork were 3-12 to 3-2 in front. Not only did Wexford's ten point deficit revive memories of their fifteen point disadvantage in the 1956 National League final and their nine point defeat in the 1968 All-Ireland decider, but it gave birth to the hope that yet again we might see another astonishing come-back. Not this time. The man who saw to that was Cork's centre half forward, Willie Walsh, who created havoc among the Wexford backs by making and creating scores. Within a minute of the resumption he extended Pat Nolan with a strong shot which the Wexford goalie diverted out for a 70, and hardly twenty seconds later he collected a Gerald McCarthy puck from that 70 and from the right of the parallelogram sent it thundering to the net. Cork were then thirteen points in front and although 38 minutes remained, it was obvious that all hope for Wexford had gone.

The Leinster men continued to show persistence and it brought goals from Pat Quigley and Tony Doran, but they still could not match Cork for defensive soundness, power and cohesion in attack and overall self-confidence. It is a matter of conjecture now as to what might have been the case had Wexford been at full strength with Willie Murphy, Phil Wilson and Ned Buggy, who were out because of injuries. But it must be said that such was Cork's complete supremacy that it would not have mattered had the injured trio been available.

From goalkeeper Paddy Barry out, Cork were sufficiently competent in every department, well knit as a hurling unit and full of conviction compared to the year before. Con Roche was as sound as a bell at left half back while John Horgan at left full back made a brilliant All-Ireland senior debut. Midfield did not play any major role in the proceedings, but Seamus Looney was one player who enjoyed his freedom in that area. For Wexford, Pat Nolan, Matt Brown, Dave Bernie, John Quigley and Tony Doran strove mightily but increasingly hopelessly to turn back the engulf-ing Cork avalanche. What mattered to Cork was that they regained the MacCarthy Cup to step alongside Tipperary with 21 titles.

1971 FINAL: GOALS GALORE ON COLOUR TV

5 September 1971

Attendance: 61,393

Top scorer: E. Keher (Kilkenny) 2-11

Tipperary 5-17, Kilkenny 5-14

Referee: F. Murphy (Cork)

Chapter 7 ⌒

THE SEVENTIES

The 1970 to 1979 All-Ireland hurling finals

The emergence of Noel Skehan from the shadow of the legendary Kilkenny goalkeeper Ollie Walsh, the return of Limerick to the top after an absence of over 30 years, additions to the ranks of the dual All-Ireland senior medal winners, and a rare three in a row by Cork, were the features of the 70s. Noel Skehan won an All-Ireland minor medal in 1962, and soon after that he made his debut with the senior side. But then came a long, long spell as reserve goalkeeper to Ollie Walsh. Over a period of nine seasons and four All-Ireland senior finals, Skehan had to settle for a substitute role to Walsh. But the long wait proved well worthwhile for in 1972 Skehan not only stepped into the All-Ireland senior hurling final action for the first time but captained Kilkenny against Cork. And, as if that was not sufficient to make it a dream day for him, he had the added distinction of leading the Noresiders to victory to launch a final story that was to stretch throughout the decade and into the eighties.

Limerick won their first Munster senior title since 1955 by beating Tipperary at Thurles in the 1973 provincial final. Then came a win over London at Ennis which put the county into an All-Ireland final for the first time since the Mick Mackey era of the thirties and forties. Limerick's opponents in the decider, Kilkenny, were weakened by the loss of a number of key hurlers because of injuries, but that still could not take from the merit of the Shannonsiders' performance in marking their first final appearance since 1940 with a win. Eamonn Grimes of South Liberties led the Munster champions from midfield and became the first man apart from Mick Mackey to lead Limerick to the game's top prize since 1934.

It was a wonderful decade too for Cork. They got the period off to a splendid start in the initial year by beating Wexford in the first All-Ireland senior final in either code over eighty minutes. The Leesiders had to wait until 1976 for their next championship success, a win that started the first treble of titles by any county since Cork's own earlier three in a row from

1952 to 1954. The win over Wexford in an exhilarating game that gave Cork the 1976 title marked one of the brightest chapters in the annals of the elite ranks of winners of All-Ireland senior medals in hurling and football. As a result of that triumph, Brian Murphy, Jimmy Barry Murphy and Denis Coughlan all took their places in the exclusive club of dual medallists. Cork lost once in five final outings—1972 to Kilkenny. They won their 21st All-Ireland in 1970 and passed out Tipperary at the top of the winners chart in 1977 with title No. 23. Kilkenny bounced back from their 1973 loss to Limerick to take revenge over the Shannonsiders in the 1974 game, and retained the championship at Galway's expense a year later. After losing to Cork in 1978, Kilkenny won their 21st championship in 1979, when they were captained by Ger Fennelly of Ballyhale Shamrocks, the eldest of a great hurling family. His brother Kevin went in as a substitute during that win. Wexford lost all three finals they contested, each time to Cork—1970, 76 and 77. Galway were beaten in two deciders, that 1975 clash with Kilkenny, and 1979 when the Noresiders again thwarted their hopes. The playing period for provincial finals and All-Ireland finals was fixed at 70 minutes for all championship games in 1975.

Statistics

Greatest attendance	66,137 in 1972
Busiest referee	No referee had charge of more than one final
Highest team score	6-21 (39 points) by Cork 1970
Highest score by losing team	5-14 (29 points) by Kilkenny 1971
Highest winning margin	14 points by Cork 1970
Lowest winning margin	3 points by Cork 1977
Highest individual score	2-11 by Eddie Keher 1971
Highest individual goal tally	3 by E. O'Brien 1971
Goalless finals	None
Finals in which winning team failed to score a goal	None
Finals in which losing team failed to score a goal	None
Best points tally by winning team	24 points by Kilkenny 1972
Best points tally by losing team	14 points by Kilkenny 1971 and 73
Top scoring final on aggregate	1970: 11-31 (64 points)
Lowest scoring final on aggregate	1979: 3-20 (29 points)
Replays	None
Most successful captain	No hurler captained more than one title winning team

1970 FINAL: O'BRIEN'S BEST GAME FOR CORK

6 September 1970
Attendance: 65,062
Top scorer: C. McCarthy (Cork) 1-9

Cork 6-21, Wexford 5-10
Referee: J. Hatton (Wicklow)

This was the first All-Ireland final in either code played over 80 minutes. Although the game produced a torrent of scores, 42 in all, it was still a most disappointing match, the least rewarding in fact, many felt, since the 1958 Tipperary-Galway clash. Willie Walsh scored Cork's fourth goal two minutes into the second half to give his side a thundering thirteen points advantage. From that juncture onwards the game was particularly wearisome if not boring, contrary to what was expected. But on a day when the championship needed a heart-warming struggle, this final deteriorated into a clumsy, chaotic, dangerous and bad-tempered contest. Even though Cork's mastery was in no way exaggerated by their fourteen point win, the Leesiders did not produce the fluency and touch of class associated with former teams from this stronghold of the game. Nevertheless, the final was not without its special features. One was the exciting goal-getting technique of Eddie O'Brien, Cork's left corner forward, who found his way through to the Wexford net three times. It was he who turned the key in the door to victory for Cork with a neat goal in the eleventh minute, when he flicked the ball overhead to the net. He got his second in 34 minutes by deftly deflecting a Willie Walsh pass home, and he completed his goals haul in the 33rd minute of the second half when he soloed through the Wexford defence before fisting home another glorious goal. It was probably O'Brien's best game in the Cork jersey. Charlie McCarthy was also in sharpshooting form, while Paddy Barry was a true leader in every sense as he captained Cork with a fine showing from goal. All three were crucial figures in the destination of final honours.

Yet it was a sad day for hurling and even more distressing for Wexford. They were so completely overcome that not even their undoubted spirit could save them from an unfortunate trouncing. They whipped the lead from Cork in the fifth minute when Tony Doran dropped the ball into the net across a parallelogram where confusion reigned because of the

The first All-Ireland final televised live in colour was a rousing game and will be remembered for many features, including Eddie Keher's mighty personal return of 2-11 and a dazzling display from Babs Keating during which he played for a time in his bare feet and ended up as his team's top scorer with seven points. Tipperary were eager, tireless and took all their chances. Kilkenny did not take all the opportunities available to them, and therein lay the story of this epic All-Ireland. Another factor in shaping the Munster win was a glorious seven minute spell just after they were headed for the first time by a Frank Cummins point in the 25th minute of the second half. The game was a personal triumph for Babs Keating, who was in tremendous sharpshooting form all through that championship season. He was without doubt the biggest danger in the Tipperary attack as he, in turn, first discarded his boots and then his socks to finish with seven crucial and excellent points. On a glorious autumn day with the sod perfect for hurling, Tipperary made a match-winning move when they switched Mick Roche from centre back to midfield in the closing fifteen minutes. Kilkenny had a slight advantage in the area until then, but when Roche arrived, he and P. J. Ryan took charge and proved vital planks in the build-up to their 22nd title win and thirteenth MacCarthy Cup triumph.

Tipperary won the toss and set their backs to the Railway end as they faced into the sun. The scoring rate was low in the first eleven minutes, and Tipperary led 2-10 to 2-4 at the interval. Keher opened what was to be a new individual scoring record for a Kilkenny hurler with a goal from a 21 yard free after sixteen minutes. It was also the Inistioge scoring ace who powered Kilkenny back into the picture on the restart. His accuracy prompted a revival that had the Leinster men a point clear after 25 minutes, 4-12 to 3-14. But then came Tipperary's golden spell initiated by Roger Ryan, who tipped a well-taken Roche free to the net. The Munster men hit three more points and a Dinny Ryan goal in the 36th minute made victory assured despite a strong Noreside rally that produced 1-1 to their credit. In a game in which scores cascaded on each other, especially in the second half, those who did not see it first hand or on TV might venture the opinion that either side might have won. But only the intolerant among the Kilkenny supporters will deny that they were fortunate not to have been two further goals in arrears at the call of full time. The Leinster champions had fallen away alarmingly between the 28th minute of the second half and just before Tipperary hit that most rewarding scoring spell which was to lift the team to subsequent victory. But Kilkenny, to their credit, weren't prepared to give up the ghost. They fought back with admirable heart in the last six minutes while their supporters waited with impatience for a match-winning resurgence. Time, however, was running short. After they had cut the winners' advantage to four points with but four minutes remaining, Denis Ryan profited by an uncharacteristic hesitation by Ollie Walsh to put Tipperary seven points ahead with the game in its death throes. Kilkenny retaliated with a point and a goal, both from frees by Eddie Keher. But, as the saying goes, time waits for no man. Tipperary had one hand on the MacCarthy Cup and kept it there to the end.

It was a hard fought encounter in which both teams had their periods of ascendancy, but perhaps Tipperary had a little more fire in their bellies when it came to a quest for goals. True, there were strong challenges by both sets of players at times, and referee Frank Murphy of Cork booked four players for what could be termed venial sins. To their credit, both teams still produced marvellous hurling at times and a lot of reputations were enhanced on both sides over the game's entirety. Despite the big returns against them, both goalkeepers Peter O'Sullivan (Tipperary) and Ollie Walsh (Kilkenny) performed very well. Tadhg O'Connor kept a reasonable check on Keher in general play, while Len Gaynor at left half back was another ace in the Tipperary pack. Jim Treacy, Frank Cummins and Pat Delaney had their good moments for Kilkenny, while Keher kept the Leinster men in the hunt for long periods with that superb personal scoring barrage.

1972 FINAL: KEHER POWERS A FAMOUS WIN

3 September 1972   Kilkenny 3-24, Cork 5-11
Attendance: 66,137   Referee: Mick Spain (Offaly)
Top scorer: E. Keher (Kilkenny) 2-9

This was a game that matched the glorious weather in which it was played, especially in the second half, as Kilkenny rallied strongly to come from an apparently hopeless position to gain one of their most famous wins over their traditional rivals. The first half was interesting, without being anything above the ordinary, and Cork went to the dressing room at the interval two points in front, 2-8 to 0-12. Kilkenny lacked penetration in that opening half despite their dozen points, and fifteen minutes after the restart they were trailing by 3-8 to 0-14. But then Eddie Keher lit the fuse that exploded this game into a pulsating struggle that had supporters limp with excitement from then until the end. The great score-taker crashed home a goal after the resumption to level matters, and Kilkenny looked on their way. But the spoils seemed destined to be snatched from their grasp when Ray Cummins and Seánie O'Leary delighted the Cork followers with two goals inside the following minute. Con Roche tacked on another point before Kilkenny brought Keher out from left full forward to the wing, and immediately the Noresiders began to hum as we had not seen in the game until then. Kilkenny really struck it rich. With just 22 minutes left for play it was appropriately Keher who started the revival when he scored a goal from a free and the Leinster men never looked back after that. In that concluding spell they really scaled the heights with Pat Henderson, Martin Coogan, who had gone in as a substitute, and Jim Treacy in defence, with Keher and Pat Delaney causing all kinds of problems for the Cork backs. Kilkenny with skill and tremendous drive added 2-9 in this amazing comeback to clinch a deserved victory in a thrill-packed finish. Liam O'Brien, playing in his first All-Ireland senior final, was another who did much to set Kilkenny up for victory with his progressive work at midfield.

The Cork backs, especially Brian Murphy and Pat McDonnell, were outstanding in the first half, while Ray Cummins, who was his team's leading scorer, and Mick Malone took their scores well. In the end, Cork could not withstand that power-packed late Kilkenny onslaught. One must mention, too, that even though Cork hit five goals, Noel Skehan brought off some telling saves in the Kilkenny goal. Indeed he went on later to win the first of his seven All-Stars trophies. The win was Kilkenny's second in a final over their great rivals.

When one reflects on a scoreline where the beaten team had scored 5-11, the question could be posed, what more could Cork have done? Looking more closely at the pattern of the game, it must be said that the Cork forwards were guilty of missing a large number of scoring chances. The reason was simple. They came up against a very formidable Kilkenny defensive set-up, which, particularly in the last quarter, was not prepared to concede an inch. Even though Cork's scoring tally was very respectable on such an occasion, it is what the Cork forwards missed, or to be more precise, what they were prevented from scoring rather than what they recorded, that most followers will surely remember most. The tenacity of the Kilkenny defenders was part of the fuel that fired the men in the black and amber. I would add that in the last five minutes of the match Kilkenny shot seven points and it was demonstrative of their mastery that one of the final nails in the coffin of Cork's hopes came the easy way—from a free. In that regard the Kilkenny backs were the real masters on the day, marshalled by the brilliant Pat Henderson at centre half back.

1973 FINAL: DOWLING GOAL ENDS 33-YEAR WAIT

2 September 1973   Limerick 1-21, Kilkenny 1-14
Attendance: 58,009   Referee: M. Slattery (Clare)
Top scorer: R. Bennis (Limerick) 0-10

It rained heavily in Dublin as Limerick travelled to Croke Park for the county's first All-Ireland senior appearance in 33 years. Under the worst possible conditions they lost no time in taking the challenge to Kilkenny, the defending champions. Amidst scenes of unbridled enthusiasm that far surpassed anything I have seen in a hurling final in recent years, the All-Ireland title and the MacCarthy Cup were won back by Limerick for the first time since 1940. And seldom can the honours and the trophy have been so magnificently and so deservedly earned. Producing sustained and sometimes inspiring spells of swift, stylish and betimes brilliant hurling, under what were the worst possible conditions of constant rain, slippery sod and greasy ball, the Munster men rocked Kilkenny back on their heels from the opening whistle. Twice Limerick came from behind to peg back the Noresiders, when the holders seemed to be regaining their poise, and they had really taken command midway through the second half and confidently romped to victory in the closing stages.

Fast, fiery and resolute, this was a Limerick team playing Limerick hurling at its effective best, and no wonder their supporters, starved of victory for 33 years, had spilled over from the stands and were swarming along the touchlines minutes before the final whistle. But fair dues to Kilkenny. It takes two teams to give us hurling of the calibre we witnessed in the superlative passages of play, and considering the handicaps under which they entered the fray, these Noresiders put up a tremendous battle in defence of their title before the speed and power of the more virile Limerick lads finally wore them down. After winning the toss the Shannonsiders elected to play into the Canal end and inside a minute Frankie Nolan set their hopes soaring with a well-taken point. At the interval Limerick led 0-12 to 1-7. Five minutes into the second half, Kilkenny were on equal terms. Less than a minute later the Leinster champions were ahead when Seamus Horgan in the Limerick goal brought off a super save to turn a palmed effort from Mick Crotty from two yards over the bar. Limerick refused to give in. Ritchie Bennis had them level with a pointed free from 40 yards, and a minute later the Munster men got through for the decisive score. A puck-out from Noel Skehan was promptly lofted back to the Kilkenny goal area by Liam O'Donoghue. The Kilkenny goalkeeper saved on his own goal-line, but Mossie Dowling and Eamonn Rea were in sharply and Dowling turned the ball into the net. That was the goal that won the title for Limerick. Eamonn Grimes, a tireless worker and tremendous captain and midfielder, and Ritchie Bennis, also effective in general play and deadly accurate from frees, laid the foundation of this rare win for the Shannonsiders with their quality midfield play. But they received strong support all round, particularly from Seán Foley, who had a mighty game at left half back, matched by Eamonn Cregan, who bore the brunt of heavy Kilkenny pressure at various periods and emerged with top honours. In view of the handicaps that bore down on Kilkenny due to the absence at the start of Eddie Keher, Kieran Purcell and Jim Treacy, Limerick had to win by a respectable margin to make the success authentic. This they did, and the victory would have been even more indelibly hall-marked, had not the new champions squandered many scoring chances. Nothing was more illustrative of Limerick's authority than the fact that Kilkenny were held scoreless for nine minutes twice in the first half and also for longer spells of ten and thirteen minutes in the second period. One can pay no greater tribute to the Munster men, who have now won the game's top prize for the seventh time, than say they could still have won had the opposition been able to marshall all their forces for the day. This was a Limerick we had not previously seen in the 1973 championship. The team had a belief in themselves not previously witnessed. Never at any stage of the 80 minutes were the winners overawed by the occasion or the might of the opposition. Indeed, through most of a contest which never flagged in intensity or glamour, it was the underdogs who were hurling.

1974 FINAL: A CLASS ACT FROM HENDERSON

1 September 1974	Kilkenny 3-19, Limerick 1-13
Attendance: 62,071	Referee: J. Moloney (Tipperary)
Top scorer: E. Keher (Kilkenny) 1-11	

Eddie Keher and Jim Treacy, both of whom were unavailable for the previous year's final, and Kieran Purcell, who only went into that game as a substitute (all three nursing injuries at the time), were back in the Kilkenny team for the return with the Shannonsiders in the All-Ireland final. On this occasion the defending champions, Limerick, faced a far different proposition, as challengers Kilkenny, sharper, surer, fitter, faster in the vital stages and far more evidently imbued with a burning desire for victory, swept to their nineteenth All-Ireland senior title with unexpected ease when they finished, deservedly, a massive twelve points in front of holders, Limerick. The latter disappointed their huge following by fading steadily from the scene when the Noresiders came at them in the second half. Despite the return of the talented Keher, Treacy and Purcell, Kilkenny got off to an uncertain start. Limerick, who had won the toss, played with a sharp breeze into the Canal end and displayed a sharpness, eagerness and a brand of effective ground hurling that had them deservedly ahead after only seven minutes. But as a shower began to fall, Kilkenny turned the game completely around with a two goal blitz inside two minutes. Right full forward Mick Brennan kicked home a goal in thirteenth minute, and a minute later Kilkenny were awarded the first penalty.

Keher stepped up to take the puck and made no mistake by crashing the ball to the Limerick net. The Noresiders were ahead by 2-1 to 0-6. Further points were exchanged before Liam O'Donoghue sent Shannonside hopes soaring again with a goal in the 22nd minute. However, Kilkenny's response was both swift and decisive. Barely a minute had passed after the O'Donoghue goal when Pat Delaney sent a low 30 yard drive to the net, and Kilkenny continued to find the range and the target to lead 3-7 to 1-9 at the interval. The Leinster champions went storming through the second half with polished and clever hurling. Their defence gave little away and their forwards picked off points in fluent fashion. By the final whistle the Leinster standard bearers were twelve points clear and were worth every point of their winning margin. And those who argue that Kilkenny might not have been beaten last year had Eddie Keher been fit have facts now to back up their argument. The sprightly veteran, who had played such a prominent part in helping his county to four previous All-Ireland victories, was again in sparkling form recording the remarkable total of a goal and eleven points. And if only five of those points came from frees, at least three of them were superlative efforts that franked the claims of his admirers that he is possibly the greatest hurler ever to grace the black and amber jersey. As for the other two mentioned at the outset, Jim Treacy and Kieran Purcell, the white-haired Treacy looked to be in trouble early on, but when the rain slowed down the play to his liking, he was as dependable as ever, and no one can remember one score off his wing in the second half. Kieran Purcell, who came on as a substitute the previous year in the second half in a vain but gallant effort to save the day, showed the difference between Purcell fit and Purcell unfit, for he was again the willing workhorse, even though he shot a few wides, and was one of the mainsprings of this power-packed Kilkenny attack. Certainly those who feared that Pat Henderson was fading from his own peak of greatness at centre back had good reason to think again. The tall and gritty Johnstown man dominated the centre of the defence even more than he did when he broke the hearts of the Cork attack in the second half of the 1969 All-Ireland. There were times when he seemed to be a one man stone wall 40 yards in front of the Kilkenny goal, and not alone did he halt attack after attack, his solid clearances dropped well into hostile territory. In addition he drilled a 70 into the wind over the bar in the first half to restore the lead for his county at a vital stage of the proceedings. Noel Skehan wasn't overburdened between the posts, but he still played his part with four superlative saves during the exchanges.

Limerick, who were striving for a first successful defence of their MacCarthy Cup title, fell away badly after a bright first half. They had star hurlers throughout the field, however, with full back Pat Hartigan, midfielder Eamonn Grimes and Eamonn Cregan, and Joe McKenna up front. They were unceasing in their endeavours from first to last whistle, defiant and with a joy that suggested they were stimulated by their appearance in an All-Ireland final. The event, happily, was right worthy of the occasion and while defeat would not have done Kilkenny any harm, victory would unquestionably have done Limerick, and far more important still, hurling, a world of good. A final word. I would single out Seán Foley for special mention as being the man of the match for his brilliant hurling and upfield sallies in an effort to initiate attacks and to consolidate the work of Limerick's great half backs.

1975 FINAL: LARKIN'S DAY

7 September 1975   Kilkenny 2-22, Galway 2-10
Attendance: 63,711   Referee: S. O'Connor (Limerick)
Top scorer: E. Keher (Kilkenny) 1-6

Galway went into this first final since 1958 with sound credentials. They won the National League title in the spring after an interval of 24 years and shocked Cork in their All-Ireland semi-final at Croke Park. As a result much was expected from their MacCarthy Cup tie, but the match proved a big disappointment. Galway appeared to be in with a real chance when Frank Burke goaled after eighteen minutes to earn them a 1-3 to 0-3 lead. The westerners had lost the toss and were playing with a light breeze into the Canal end, and that Burke goal could not have come at a better time. But amazingly, the Connacht men failed to score again for 22 minutes while in the same period Kilkenny chalked up 1-8 to ensure a successful defence of their title. While the match was a disappointment, the confident approach and sheer skill of the Kilkenny men had to be admired. They made clever use of the hand pass and good off the ball running as they stamped their dominance on the match. The exchanges were keen enough in the opening quarter, but as the game progressed Kilkenny's superiority increased. They led 0-9 to 1-3 at the interval, and Liam O'Brien, who had a cracking game, and Frank Cummins were largely responsible for the match-winning display. They exerted an overwhelming advantage at midfield, where O'Brien was particularly impressive, as he exercised his many exciting skills to the best possible effect. Eddie Keher, after a quiet start, blossomed as the game progressed. He scored Kilkenny's first goal three minutes into the second half after being put through by a perfect pass from Mick Crotty. A quick Pat Delaney point left the defending champions comfortably ahead by 1-12 to 1-4.

Keher's second goal came from a penalty with twenty minutes of play remaining. Mick Crotty and Mick Brennan were other stars among the attack, while Phil Larkin had a superb game at right full back, his best performance in the black and amber in the opinion of many shrewd judges. Brian Cody was again masterly at left full back and Pat Lalor was another to stamp his personality on a win that earned Kilkenny a first successful defence of the MacCarthy Cup since 1933. Michael Conneely showed up very well in the Galway goal, and Niall McInerney, Frank Burke, and P. J. Molloy were the other top players for the westerners as they failed to complete a unique double of the National League title and the MacCarthy Cup. With that defeat, hopes receded greatly of an early break-through by Galway in their never ending quest for a first MacCarthy Cup triumph since their initial win in the third competition in 1923 (played in 1924).

1976 FINAL: THE MIGHTY PAT MOYLAN

5 September 1976   Cork 2-21, Wexford 4-11
Attendance: 62,684   Referee: P. Johnston (Kilkenny)
Top scorer: P. Moylan (Cork) 0-10

This was one of the great finals in hurling and one of Cork's most celebrated wins into the bargain. Cork could not have started more depressingly. Six minutes into the game they were, amazingly, in arrears by 2-2 to no score. But Cork rose superbly to that challenge. With Pat Moylan colouring the scene with a regal performance at midfield, they came back steadily into the reckoning and were on level terms at the interval. It was a perfect day for hurling with just a whisper of a breeze on a sunny after-noon, and Wexford played into the Railway end. Martin Quigley hit the Leinster champions' opening goal after five minutes from a Tony Doran pass, and a minute later Cork goalie Martin Coleman saved brilliantly from a Tony Doran drive, but the alert Martin Quigley was quickly on hand to smack the rebound to the Cork net for his second goal. Although the Munster men rallied strongly after that, it was not until the 30th minute that they got through for their first goal. Ray Cummins sent a rebound from a Jimmy Barry Murphy shot to the Wexford net. Moylan was the man who marshalled the Cork team with a series of long-range pointed frees. By half-time Cork had drawn level. Seánie O'Leary, who began the game with a heavily bandaged knee, was in trouble after fifteen minutes and was replaced by Eamonn O'Donoghue after the interval. Wexford started the second half with a flourish which resulted in a great Tony Doran goal. At that point it was obvious that a Cork goal was badly needed if the Wexford drive was to be halted. The important goal duly arrived, and with it Cork hopes soared. The diminutive Charlie McCarthy swooped from the right wing as a Brendan Cummins lob was dropping around the exclusion zone. McCarthy waited for it to hop, met the ball first time and drove it past a helpless John Nolan in the Wexford goal. Charlie's opportunist score put his team ahead by a point.

In those early exchanges the Cork team mentors were busy seeking a balance that was needed to get them back on track. John Horgan was introduced and replaced Pat Barry. And that allowed Martin O'Doherty to take over in the pivotal position with Horgan now in the corner. Jimmy Barry Murphy, normally a forward to be feared, had been closely watched by the Wexford defence, so once again the Cork mentors adjusted. Barry Murphy was switched to centre forward and celebrated with a quick point, and he was to add two more crucial points later to consolidate Cork's mastery at that stage. Goalie Martin Colemen was inspirational for Cork and brought off some marvellous saves to deny Wexford time and time again of scores that could have rescued their cause. This was a magnificent contest played in a commendable sporting fashion by two very committed sides. Both teams had periods of dominance during which many fines scores were recorded. It must be said that the ability of the Cork players to maintain their equilibrium and benefit from the team switches during the second half was to prove their lifeline to subsequent success. That meant capturing their 22nd All-Ireland title, level with Tipperary. While the Cork success was essentially a team victory, the work of Moylan at midfield stood out like a beacon, apart altogether from his superb point-taking accuracy. His standards never dropped from start to finish and all through that masterful display he remained cool, calm and collected. Credit must go also to the substitutes who were brought in to create their own star rating, Eamonn O'Donoghue and John Horgan. Once again the McCarthy brothers, Gerald and Charlie, filled their roles very capably, while Ray Cummins led the attack with his usual flair. Wexford came so close to causing an upset for three-quarters of the match, that their efforts should have been better rewarded. They still maintained Wexford's great tradition on All-Ireland occasions by playing to their full potential. Mick Jacob, Colm Doran and Willie Murphy were rock-like in the defence. Martin Quigley, with his two goals, Tony Doran and Johnny Murphy repeatedly caught the eye in a great attack.

1977 FINAL: MARTIN COLEMAN SAVES CORK

4 September 1977   Cork 1-17, Wexford 3-8
Attendance: 63,168   Referee: S. O'Grady (Limerick)
Top scorer: E. Buggy (Wexford) 1-4

Sadly, the game did not match the expectations raised by the 1976 thriller between the two counties, which was understandable in view of the exceptional quality of the first meeting. Ten thrilled-packed closing minutes saved this eagerly anticipated final from utter mediocrity, but the spirit of 98 flowed freely through the veins of Wexford's warriors. The pity was that it did so only in the closing stages. There was enough time to put a respectable gloss on the scoreboard, but it was too late to prevent Cork from gaining a record 23rd All-Ireland title and the coveted MacCarthy trophy.

It must be stressed that Cork were worthy winners on the day. Faster, fitter, better balanced and better able to master the tricky conditions, they won by a three point margin that might well have been three times as much. Yet there was only a goal between the teams at the finish, as compared with four years ago, and only a couple of fantastic saves by Cork goalie Martin Coleman from Ballinhassig foiled Wexford of at least a replay. It would have been an injustice, however, had Cork surrendered their claim to greatness and lost this confrontation. They were, on the day, nine or ten points a better hurling team than their off-key and often pedestrian opponents, and should have had victory safely tucked away long before Wexford came back at them. The slippy sod, drenched from heavy rain all through the morning, together with a stiffening wind, created major difficulties for the players from both sides. Naturally it also affected the standard of hurling on view. We had a lively and unfortunately brief opening flurry, and then for long, long periods the game appeared to die on its feet with far too much petty fouling, as Cork began to take control in almost every sector.

Undoubtedly, Martin Coleman brought a greater sense of realism to the contest because of his brilliance between the Cork posts, and this applied especially when, with only three points dividing the teams and when excitement was at its peak, Coleman really stamped his name on proceedings. He brought off a spectacular save from a blockbuster from right half forward Christy Keogh. Almost immediately afterwards Coleman had another excellent save from a fearsome effort by John Quigley.

Cork had won the toss and elected to play against the wind and into the Canal end goal. After Charlie McCarthy had neutralised a Wexford point within fifteen seconds by shooting over the bar from a free, Cork were never again headed. A heavy shower during the curtain raiser made the pitch very slippery and this did not help the hurlers to deliver top-class fare. Nevertheless, there were still bouts of hard grafting and hard tackles which led to only two bookings during the course of the game: Mick Jacob for an untypical indiscretion and Mick Butler for personal fouls. Only one player sustained anything more than a minor injury. That was Gerald McCarthy, who had to get stitches in his upper lip. Wexford were first on to the field and had been pucking about for several minutes before Cork arrived, and the champions promptly had a casualty when Seánie O'Leary got a blow of the ball in the face. The Youghal man had to go back to the dressing room for repairs and missed the pre-match parade but returned in time to take his place before the game commenced. There were still some fine passages of play in the opening period. Gerald McCarthy, who was appearing for the first time at centre half forward with the Leesiders, had such a fine performance in his new role that many rated him the man of the match. Denis Coughlan had an excellent game as well at left half back, Martin O'Doherty was outstanding at full back, and then there was Coleman who so superbly saved the day in more ways than one for Cork late in the match. John Nolan was safe in goal for Wexford, Teddy O'Connor, a tremendous competitor at right half back, and Christy Keogh and Ned Buggy in attack were the leading campaigners for the Model County. This was Cork's first successful defence of the MacCarthy Cup since the three in a row from 1952 to 54. In 1953 they were captained by a Glen Rovers man, Christy Ring, and Martin O'Doherty maintained that tradition as he filled the team captain's role in this success against Wexford.

1978 FINAL: MAJESTIC PERFORMANCE FROM O'DOHERTY

3 September 1978   Cork 1-15, Kilkenny 2-8
Attendance: 64,156   Referee: J. Rankins (Laois)
Top scorer: C. McCarthy (Cork) 0-7

A majestic display by Martin O'Doherty that many shrewd judges rated at the time as the best at full back seen in an All-Ireland final, was one of the top features of a contest that did not prove anything like the classic expected. Still, Cork chalked up their 4th three in a row, the first by a hurling county since they themselves did the trick in the seasons 1952 to 54. Cork thus captured their 24th All-Ireland crown, in all carving out a deserved four point victory over Kilkenny at a colourful Croke Park. Naturally the game was fiercely contested with the sides deadlocked on eight occasions, but in the heel of the hunt the greater hunger of Cork just about shaded the verdict in this contest. The reason, it was surmised, lay in the fact that the raw competitiveness of the rival selections was so great that tension led to many mistakes by both teams, while the hurling itself suffered from poor attempts at delivering the ball under pressure, despite the household names involved on the respective teams. That much said, it must also be stated that these two counties, the traditional stylists of the game, gave us far too little stylish hurling. Flashes of individual brilliance there were, but no sustained bouts of top-class hurling. The close marking throughout was, admittedly, too close for spectacular play, but that could not excuse some very scrappy passages or some misses and mess-ups by both teams that we did not expect to see in a senior All-Ireland final. Too many players seemed affected by the magnitude of the occasion. Nor was all the nervous tension confined to the younger men. Yet, though Kilkenny were four times ahead and eight times level, Cork were, in my estimation, deserving winners. Their forwards may have fallen well short of the standard that carried them to victory in 1976 and 77, but they were, as the scoreboard shows, more effective than a Kilkenny attack which received plenty of the ball but never looked capable of getting the scores that counted.

The defending champions won the toss and played into the sun and the Canal end. Jimmy Barry Murphy pointed after only 25 seconds. Kilkenny had the first real breakthrough, however, with a Kevin Fennelly goal in the fifth minute, but this final failed to get off the ground, and at the end of a not too memorable first half the score was Cork 0-7, Kilkenny 1-4. The issue appeared to be finely balanced for most of the opening stages of the second half, when Cork's Tim Crowley suddenly charted the winning way for the cup holders. He had been moved back from left half forward to midfield where Kilkenny's Frank Cummins was proving the outstanding player. Crowley in fact broke the Kilkenny dominance in the area. In the 50th minute he lashed over a superb point from an acute angle after a spectacular solo run along the Cusack Stand side of the park. Cork went ahead by 0-11 to 1-7 and seemed to gain new heart. They played with renewed spirit and assurance, and twelve minutes from time Jimmy Barry Murphy scored Cork's only goal of the match. But Kilkenny roused themselves with a great Billy Fitzpatrick goal to leave only two points between the teams. The Leesiders remained cool and unruffled and finished well for a deserved win and their first treble since the fifties.

Tim Crowley, apart from his spectacular point, made a strong impact overall on the scene after moving to midfield. Martin O'Doherty was a giant in every sense of the word at full back as he turned on the style in cool, competent fashion to thwart the Kilkenny attack time and time again and also got his own forward line moving with his lengthy clearances. Denis Coughlan was another stalwart at the back, where John Crowley showed up well. Charlie McCarthy and Jimmy Barry Murphy were important influences in the Cork attack. Joe Hennessy, a classy right half back, Pat Henderson, Frank Cummins and Brian Cody were the leading lights in the Kilkenny side. Incidentally, the final score of the game was fittingly slotted over the bar in injury time by the man who captained Cork—Charlie McCarthy.

1979 FINAL: GER HENDERSON BRINGS KILKENNY OF AGE

2 September 1979   Kilkenny 2-12, Galway 1-8
Attendance: 53,535   Referee: G. Ryan (Tipperary)
Top scorer: L. O'Brien (Kilkenny) 1-7

Kilkenny came of age with their 21st All-Ireland championship in the senior grade, and their fourteenth MacCarthy Cup win, but this was one of the least memorable finals in years. A heavy pre-match drizzle which carried on throughout the first twenty minutes of the game and a blustery wind into the Railway end did not make for good hurling. To sum up, Kilkenny took their chances of scores while Galway did not. A disappointing match attendance did not get value for their money as Kilkenny showed the power and tactical brilliance that has carried them through other All-Ireland tests.

The Noresiders won the toss and gave Galway the benefit of the wind, and as events transpired, it proved a tactical master stroke. It meant that the Leinster men could exercise a containment policy in the opening half against the Connacht men. They must also have felt that Galway would take a while to settle down and subsequently lose the early advantage of the wind. Having gained the psychological advantage of that move, they set about counteracting the major threat which John Connolly posed at midfield, and Frank Cummins provided the answer by taking over command of the centrefield area. It was a major blow to Galway. It emphasised the clear monopoly that Kilkenny held on the tactical front in other parts of the field as well. They pulled another stroke in bypassing their half forwards so as to minimise the effect of the powerful Galway half back line of Joe McDonagh, Seán Silke and Iggy Clarke. They then used Mick Brennan with cleverly placed long deliveries into the right corner of attack, and

Brennan revelled in the tactic. Galway erred in persisting with the pick-up of the ball, and more often than not were easy victims of the quick Kilkenny block which curtailed their scoring efforts to a degree. Kilkenny, with a strong rearguard powered by Ger Henderson and Nickey Brennan (the latter later became president of the GAA), the Leinster champions found themselves comfortably placed when they led at the break 1-7 to 0-5. The sorest blows to Galway's hopes were the complete anonymity of Bernie Forde and Frank Burke, their attacking heroes against Cork. Forde was completely blotted out by a brilliant Nickey Brennan, and Ger Henderson gave absolutely nothing away to Burke, who never came to grips with the wet sliothar. Galway did not help their cause by shooting eleven wides in that period.

The Kilkenny goal came after 31 minutes when Liam O'Brien steered a 70 all the way to the Galway net. Galway improved considerably on the changeover, and coming up to the tenth minute of the half were on equal terms. But once more Liam O'Brien stepped into the limelight as he flighted over a point. Within 30 seconds Galway were back in a big way as their full forward Noel Lane whipped home a fine goal. It was Kilkenny's turn to battle back, and O'Brien and Mick Brennan helped the revival with a point apiece. Two minutes after the Galway goal, Kilkenny were level and they began to turn their great skill and all round ability to good effect as they took charge of the exchanges. The westerners were on the defensive for much of the time after that, but 28 minutes into the half they were still two points adrift when they were awarded a penalty. It was a great chance for Galway and free-taker John Connolly. The Castlegar man's rocket-like shot was brilliantly saved and cleared, from which Kilkenny went downfield and a free was conceded which Liam O'Brien pointed. With just three minutes remaining a 45 yard shot from Mick Brennan was helped by the wind and dipped under the Galway crossbar and into the net to finally settle the issue. Ger Henderson, who had been ill on the previous Friday, proved the real star of the show. He was in tremendous form at centre half back and the rock on which many Galway attacks floundered, with great assistance from Nickey Brennan, who had his best ever display in the Kilkenny jersey at left wing back. Liam O'Brien's scoring flair and good leadership in attack made him another leading light, while Joe Hennessy, Frank Cummins and John Henderson provided excellent support. Joe McDonagh led the way for Galway with P. J. Molloy, Joe Connolly and Steve Mahon who did much to try and bridge a 56-year senior championship gap for Galway. The attendance was the lowest since 1958 but was undoubtedly affected by the rain and an unofficial train drivers' strike that prevented scheduled trains from leaving Galway.

Chapter 8 ～

THE EIGHTIES

The 1980 to 1989 All-Ireland hurling finals

The eighties brought a fresh wind of change to the MacCarthy Cup scene. Galway and Offaly emerged as the new aristocrats of senior hurling, and Antrim saw out the decade with a first All-Ireland final appearance in the top grade in 46 years. Galway took the trophy for the first time in the lives of many at Croke Park on the afternoon they beat Limerick for the 1980 All-Ireland title. When they lined out in that game, they had only one MacCarthy Cup win to their credit. That was as far back as 1924 (in what was in effect the 1923 final). As a result, only a minority at headquarters for the initial hurling final of the eighties could boast of having watched a western team win the game's most coveted trophy.

Galway were captained by Joe Connolly in a side that included his two brothers John and Michael. The 2-15 to 3-9 win made it a great year in more ways than one for the Connolly family. Earlier in the year the Castlegar club, with five Connolly brothers in action, beat Ballycastle of Antrim to take the All-Ireland club title for the first time. A double first then for Joe, John and Michael Connolly when the Shannonsiders were beaten in the MacCarthy Cup. A year after the Galway breakthrough came one of the most remarkable successes of all and a win that only a couple of seasons earlier would have been rated by most followers as wishful thinking. The 1981 success was forged out by a gallant crew from Offaly. It was only in the opening year of the eighties that the midland county won the Leinster senior championship for the first time. The newcomers lost their All-Ireland semi-final debut to Galway but bounced back in 1981 to dethrone their neighbours. When Offaly scaled the for so long unattainable peak by winning the 1981 championship, a new name went on the MacCarthy Cup for the first time in 26 years. An indication of the way in which the newcomers from Leinster helped to create new interest and appeal is the fact that the final attracted 71,384, the largest crowd at a decider in eighteen years, and the greatest at a MacCarthy Cup final in the eighties. One of the Offaly heroes was Liam Currams, who played at midfield and who also scored two valuable points. Just over a year later he held down the left back position as Offaly footballers beat Kerry in the All-Ireland final. Currams thus became the first dual player of the eighties to join the ranks of All-Ireland senior medal winners in hurling and football and the fourteenth member of this select club. He is also the only Leinster man to complete the double since the twenties. In view of Offaly's history-making achievement, it was fitting that they played a central role in the Centenary Year final in 1984. As the Association was founded in Hayes's Hotel on 1 November 1884, that game was arranged for Semple Stadium, Thurles, the birthplace of the GAA, as a central feature of the GAA celebrations to mark the 100th anniversary of the launching of the movement.

Offaly beat Wexford in the Leinster final and Galway at Semple Stadium in the All-Ireland semi-final, but lost the final to Cork. That game was the first in hurling played outside Croke Park since 1937, and the win strengthened Cork's status as the MacCarthy Cup specialists. The victory over Offaly gave them their eighteenth cup win. Kilkenny struck a blow for the traditional strongholds earlier in the decade when they beat Cork in the 'old firm' final in 1982. They retained the MacCarthy Cup the following year in another showdown with the men from the Banks of the Lee. The opening years of the eighties proved the least rewarding for Munster in the history of the cup. The province did not win a single title between 1980 and 1983, the first time the south was out of the rankings over a period as long as four campaigns in succession. The 1981 final was also the first in which Munster was not represented since Kilkenny beat Galway for the 1979 trophy. Munster missed out in two other finals in the decade. Offaly won their second title in 1985, beating Galway again, and Galway took their second crown of the decade in 1987 at the expense of Kilkenny. Galway proved the team of the decade with three titles—1980, 87 and 88. They recorded a famous first by retaining the title in 1988. That now ranks as their only double of MacCarthy Cup wins. Offaly, Kilkenny and Cork each won two titles, and Tipperary saw out the decade by beating Antrim for the 1989 title. The Tipperary win was of particular importance. The success was their first since 1971, surprisingly, and so ensured that the Premier County captured at least one All-Ireland senior championship title in every decade since the foundation of the GAA. A feature of their success was the scoring spectacular from left full forward Nicholas English. He banged in a remarkable 2-12 against the great-hearted Antrim men to establish a new Tipperary record for a MacCarthy Cup tie. Antrim helped to fan the wind of change when they beat Offaly at Croke Park in August 1989 to qualify for their first final since 1943, when they lost to Cork. They put up a brave bid in a most enjoyable and sporting final, even though well beaten at the end by eighteen points by Tipperary.

Statistics

Greatest Attendance	71,384 in 1981
Busiest referee	Noel O'Donoghue (Dublin) 1980, 82
Highest team score	4-24 (36 points) by Tipperary 1989
Highest score by losing team	2-15 (21 points) by Galway 1986
Highest winning margin	18 points by Tipperary 1989
Lowest winning margin	2 points by Kilkenny 1983 and Offaly 1985
Highest individual score	2-12 by Nicky English (Tipperary) 1989
Highest individual goals tally	2 by Eamonn Cregan (Limerick) 1980, C. Heffernan (Kilkenny) 1982, Seánie O'Leary (Cork) 1984, P. Cleary (Offaly) 1985, K. Hennessy (Cork) 1986, N. English (Tipperary) 1989
Goalless finals	None
Finals in which winning team failed to score a goal	None
Finals in which losing team failed to score a goal	1981 Galway; 1987 Kilkenny; 1988 Tipperary
Best points tally by winning team	24 by Tipperary 1989
Best points tally by losing team	21 by Galway 1986
Top scoring final on aggregate	1989: 7-33 (54 points)
Lowest scoring final on aggregate	1987: 1-21 (24 points)
Replays	None
Most successful captain	Conor Hayes (Galway)

1980 FINAL: CONNEELY INSPIRES RARE WIN

7 September 1980   Galway 2-15, Limerick 3-9
Attendance: 64,895   Referee: N. O'Donoghue (Dublin)
Top scorer: E. Cregan (Limerick) 2-7

Scenes of unbridled jubilation such as were ever seen at Croke Park at the end of a MacCarthy Cup tie greeted the first final win by Galway since the 1923 decider (which was played in 1924). Small wonder, after the many disappointments the Connacht stronghold endured over a 56-year wait for only the west's second cup triumph. The Galway victory was a splendid exhibition of polished, confident hurling, brilliant flashes of play and sparkling individual performances.

The Connacht men were firmly on their way after only three minutes. On an ideal day for hurling, with the sun warming Croke Park and a fresh breeze blowing into the Railway goal, Galway played against the breeze after losing the toss. Bernie Forde struck the first decisive blow when he collected a Joe Connolly centre and kicked home a splendid goal. The right full forward went on to prove one of the brightest stars of the Galway side. Eight minutes after the Forde goal, P. J. Molloy grabbed another for Galway. He soloed along the Limerick back line, inviting a foul which never came, but took advantage of a hesitatation by the Limerick defence and coolly blasted an unstoppable shot to the Limerick net. The westerners led at the interval 2-7 to 1-5.

On the restart, Galway looked set for a comfortable win as they pushed into a 2-10 to 1-6 lead with 25 minutes remaining. However, Limerick refused to give up, and but for splendid saves by Michael Conneely in the Galway net from Joe McKenna and Eamonn Cregan, Galway would have been in trouble. Limerick's pressure eventually paid off in the 61st minute. Cregan rifled a penalty to the Galway net, boosting the hopes of the Shannonsiders, with Galway's lead now cut to three points. Galway responded quickly, with the Connacht standard bearers now in no mood to allow a long-awaited crown to slip away again at that stage. The transfer of John Connolly from attack to midfield proved a master stroke by the Connacht selectors. His possession play kept the pressure on the Limerick defensive set-up and stopped the brief advantage Limerick held in the area. Indeed, Limerick had a problem at half forward where their line of Paudie Fitzmaurice, John Ryan and Willie Fitzmaurice came up against a solid brick wall in Galway's powerful trio of Sylvie Linnane, the masterful Seán Silke and Seamus Coen. Yet without detracting from the winners' performance, it must be said that Limerick never really attained the heights reached in their dismissal of Cork in the Munster final. They did not play with the same degree of fluency, cohesion or determination, and that was badly needed against a courageous Galway team. It must also be mentioned that the dominance of Galway's well-coordinated defence reduced the normal service the Limerick forwards needed or expected to survive such a mammoth test. The brilliance of Cregan's free-taking and general opportunism (he scored 2-7, 1-5 from frees) was exceptional while Joe McKenna with 1-1 and sub Brian Carroll 0-1 were Limerick's only marksmen. Limerick fought tenaciously throughout, and that was the reason why only three points separated the teams at the finish. Their most consistent performers were Len Enright, Liam O'Donoghue, Seán Foley and David Punch. The glory was Galway's, and never did a team deserve it more. The alleged curse, the hurling hoodoo, the psychological barrier which had separated this fine side from outright success had been shattered once and for all. There may have been lapses of concentration from time to time, but it was to the credit of Galway that they had the power, tenacity, determination and the fighting will to overcome all obstacles to attain hurling's top prize, the MacCarthy Cup. They produced a performance that will long remain in the memory of their supporters who had suffered the other side of the coin for many years. The emotions displayed at the final whistle made up for all those previous setbacks, because this was a team performance produced by men who gave their all and the honours rightly belonged to them on the day.

The Galway defensive cover was awesome at times. Michael Conneely in goal must surely have inspired the display of a very talented full back line of Conor Hayes, Niall McInerney and Joe Cooney. The half back line of Sylvie Linnane, Seán Silke and Seamus Coen played to such a high level of brilliance as to completely smother the opposing Limerick attacking force. The puck-outs from the respective goalkeepers were superb, bypassing the midfield areas and immediately instigating attacking action repeatedly for the forwards. The scorecard tells it all. Six players got their names on the scoresheet which was dominated by Bernie Forde and Joe Connolly. The others, P. J. Molloy, Noel Lane, John Connolly and John Ryan, all played massive roles with their contributing scores, not forgetting the soundness of Steve Mahon and Mick Connolly's midfield display. A final word. Noel O'Donoghue of Dublin deserved high praise for his exemplary refereeing. He did a first-class job. He was up with the play and his all round efficiency helped to make the day a thoroughly enjoyable occasion.

1981 FINAL: GOLDEN MEMORIES FROM FLAHERTY

6 September 1981   Offaly 2-12, Galway 0-15
Attendance: 71,384   Referee: F. Murphy (Cork)
Top scorer: Joe Connolly (Galway) 0-8

A great second half rally climaxed by a Johnny Flaherty goal three minutes from the end ensured a tremendous win for Offaly over the defending champions, and with the victory a new name went on the MacCarthy Cup for the first time since 1955. Offaly also became the first county since the concluding years of the last century to make a winning debut in the national senior championship decider. Conditions were good, with a hazy sun and a largely cross field wind which, however, favoured the team playing into the Canal end at Croke Park. The newcomers won the toss, giving Galway the wind advantage but still opened the scoring with a point in 45 seconds by Pat Delaney from a 70 yard free. After that Galway took charge and began to edge ahead. Offaly had a moment of joy when Pat Carroll put them two points clear with a great goal in the twelfth minute. The main credit belongs to Flaherty, who scythed past two defenders before setting up Carroll, whose smashing shot cannoned off the near upright and ended up in the opposite corner of the Galway net. Again the lead was short-lived, but Galway, while hurling well up to and including midfield, were slow and unsure in attack, apart from Joe Connolly and to a lesser extent P. J. Molloy. But the westerners were soon level. After that, the champions built up what many regarded as a winning lead as they went in at the interval leading by six points, 0-13 to 1-4.

Even though Offaly struggled to find their rhythm in some sectors, especially at midfield in the first half, they refused to accept defeat. The outlook appeared far from bright as they dropped a further point in arrears four minutes into the second half, but instead of wilting, the great-hearted Offaly men knuckled down to the task with new vigour.

Yet, the overall feeling was that two very talented teams had failed to produce the rich fare expected from such a meeting. Galway had, to be sure, hurled well and in a relaxed—sometimes over-relaxed—manner, while players such as Jimmy Cooney, Sylvie Linnane, Steve Mahon and Mick Connolly had actually succeeded in putting on the style. True, the losers' attacking play had improved with the transfer of Noel Lane to right half forward, but the penetration level remained disappointing. So too at the other end, where the cross field link-up of Johnny Flaherty and Pat

Carroll was cut off by Galway, who brilliantly blocked Brendan Bermingham when well placed, and forced Flaherty into an untypical wide from much closer range. Both sides reverted to their original positions for the second half, and within minutes Offaly's Galway-born Tom Donoghue was seen to be in distress, as blood from a head wound interfered his vision. He was replaced by Brendan Keesham, who went to left half back, and Ger Coughlan dropped back to the corner.

Joe Connolly put Galway double scores ahead within four minutes of the restart, 0-14 to 1-4, but their finish thereafter was to be a recipe for disaster, as in this period they ran up an untidy total of fourteen wides to Offaly's nine. Furthermore, the losers' failure to finish put a great deal of extra pressure, mental as well as physical, on their midfielders and defenders. All this was to have an accumulative effect as Offaly, gritty if disorganised, made changes which were to improve the side's firepower and ultimately its efficiency. The switches were made at half back where Pat Delaney and Aidan Fogarty swapped places, and in attack where Pádraig Horan and Paddy Flaherty likewise exchanged positions. Slowly the Galway lead was whittled down to manageable proportions, and when Delaney followed up another prodigious pointed free with another from play, one suddenly sensed that Galway were there for the taking. By the 61st minute the lead had been sliced to three points, 0-15 to 1-9. Four minutes later the Carroll-Flaherty link-up functioned once more for a Johnny Kinnitty point to leave just two points between the teams. Galway's anxiety was now apparent as Frank Burke came on for Finbarr Gantley and Steve Mahon, Mike Connolly, Sylvie Linnane and Jim Cooney tried desperately to turn the tide. The 'Sunday punch' came two minutes later when Joachim Kelly, strangely subdued up to then, Bermingham, Delaney and Flaherty shared in the shattering movement which Flaherty finished by palming the ball past a helpless Conneely. So shocked were the Tribesmen that within a minute the ball was fed along the right wing to Danny Owens who, unchallenged, from under the shadow of the Hogan Stand, was enabled to stretch the winners' lead with a magnificent point. A minute later skipper Padraic Horan secured the insurance point from a free, and rattled, spent and bewildered Galway could only fire wide with their last gasp effort. All praise to Offaly for their containment of the westerners and the great reserve displayed when suddenly all came right. Doubtless too they will find heroes among heroes. Among those surely were Damien Martin, Eugene Coughlan and Pat Delaney, who from defence accounted for five

points of their total, and Johnny Flaherty. Galway can blame only themselves for their failure to retain the title which they regained for the first
time in 57 years the previous season. Their outstanding players were
Jimmy Cooney, Sylvie Linnane, Mike and Joe Connolly and Steve Mahon,
while Niall McInerney, Mike Conneely and Seamus Coen also fared
particularly well.

1982 FINAL: VICTORY DUET FROM SKEHAN AND HEFFERNAN

5 September 1982   Kilkenny 3-18, Cork 1-13
Attendance: 59,550   Referee: N. O'Donoghue (Dublin)
Top scorer: C. Heffernan (Kilkenny) 2-3

Kilkenny started rank outsiders, but a brilliant save by Noel Skehan after
eighteen exciting minutes and a two goal burst late in the first half by
Christy Heffernan enabled the Leinster champions to not only upset the
odds but march on to a very convincing win for their 22nd crown. The
exchanges were even up until the moment that Skehan took a hand. Cork
bore down on the Kilkenny goal and Seánie O'Leary was in possession and
in full flight, but Skehan positioned himself perfectly to foil the Leesider
with a marvellous save, and suddenly Kilkenny were a transformed side.
They played like true champions and fourteen minutes later Heffernan,
who had not been making much of an impression until then, struck the
second decisive blow of the afternoon for the Noresiders. He flicked a
Frank Cummins shot to the Cork net for an opportunistic goal, and inside
a minute the tall full forward was back again. Taking a pass from midfielder Joe Hennessy, he rounded Cork full back Martin O'Doherty and
hand passed the ball to the net to give Kilkenny a 2-10 to 0-6 lead. Each
side added a point before the change of ends. Cork had played into the
Railway end, having won the toss, on a dry day where a cross field breeze
was of little consequence. Kilkenny were very much on top with Heffernan
having a successful time at full forward. Even so, Cork still had a good
quota of attacks and Skehan was called on to bring off some wonderful
saves—saves that helped break the Leesiders' resolve. Kilkenny's third goal
came after nine minutes of the second half, when Ger Fennelly was put
through by his brother Liam and cracked the sliothar wide of Ger
Cunningham to the net. That gave Kilkenny an unassailable lead of 3-14 to
0-9. Even so, Cork continued to battle with great heart and tested Skehan
time and time again before Eamonn O'Donoghue at last got through for

their only goal after nineteen minutes. The score was of little value to the Munster men though as Kilkenny finished very good winners. If Skehan and Heffernan dominated the scene for the black and amber brigade, Frank Cummins at midfield and Nickey Brennan, Ger Henderson and Paddy Prendergast in the half back line also played starring roles. Cork scored just 1-6 from play as compared to Kilkenny's 3-14. John Blake had an outstanding game for Cork at left full back. Tom Cashman showed up well at midfield but really found his best form when switched to the half back line. Tim Crowley worked hard at midfield, but the attack, of which much was expected, failed to get going against a very stubborn Kilkenny rearguard. In the post-match interviews, Kilkenny players were very much surprised at the manner in which Cork as a team failed to muster any real challenge after Heffernan's goal-scoring burst; nor was there any pity expressed in the winners' dressing room for the Leesiders, especially on the occasion of an All-Ireland final. Indeed, it was claimed that Pat Henderson was one of those who masterminded this Kilkenny victory, and his coaching of the side was acclaimed by the players afterwards. Certainly he knew from the victories over Cork in 1969 and 1972 when he was centre half back, what was required to bring about the downfall of the favourites.

Three men vied for the coveted man of the match award for Kilkenny, Noel Skehan in goal, Brian Cody the captain at full back and of course Christy Heffernan. There was that moment in the first half when Cork split the Kilkenny defence and Seánie O'Leary was left alone at the edge of the square with only Noel Skehan to beat. But Noel came off his goal line, thus narrowing the angle, and O'Leary's effort for a certain goal struck Skehan on the body. It was a crucial save at that stage of the match when Cork's forwards were moving dangerously. Captain Brian Cody, who cannot really relish the memory of the 1978 defeat by Cork when he was in the front line of attack, completely subdued Ray Cummins, and one glorious solo run down the touchline in front of the Hogan Stand should have resulted in a goal. But I would have to give the award to Christy Heffernan for the manner in which he turned the game around completely following his two dramatic goals before half-time. Cork captain, the great dual star and all-round sportsman, Jimmy Barry Murphy, was making no excuses for his side's defeat. He acknowledged frankly that while quite a number of the Cork team did not play up to their true form, Kilkenny surpassed themselves on the day. He said, 'It was one of the best prepared Cork sides ever. We just could not produce it on the day.'

1983 FINAL: DREAM FINAL FOR BILLY FITZPATRICK

4 September 1983   Kilkenny 2-14, Cork 2-12
Attendance: 58,381   Referee: N. Duggan (Limerick)
Top scorer: W. Fitzpatrick (Kilkenny) 0-10

Kilkenny staved off the doughty challenge of Cork to ring up a 23rd All-
Ireland hurling success—now just one short of the Leesiders—as well as
the first double-double (championship and league successes in successive
seasons) since Tipperary did the trick way back in 1964–65. A disappointing attendance of 58,381 watched a game sadly lacking the thrills of the big
occasion, but in fairness to both teams the day was spoiled because of a
whiplash wind which blew towards the Railway end. No doubt about the
verdict. Kilkenny fully deserved it because they adapted and applied themselves better in the prevailing conditions. But Kilkenny held the whip hand
too when it came to producing the key figures who dominated the crucial
areas of control. Billy Fitzpatrick, Kilkenny's left half forward, had an All-
Ireland final appearance that most players dream of but only a few realise.
He tormented the Cork defence with his skills and artistry, and his point-
scoring was on a par with anything seen in a MacCarthy Cup tie or a
national decider for that matter. Kilkenny definitely enjoyed the victory
over their old rivals, but they didn't make it easy on themselves either.
They built up a big lead but then had to experience a very stiff challenge
from Cork who very nearly pipped them to the post, and it took stern
defensive work to prevent Cork from snatching the laurels. Kilkenny were
ahead by 2-14 to 1-9 seventeen minutes from the end, playing against the
wind. They did not score a single point after that as Cork strove gallantly
to swing the match their way. Kilkenny's first goal was an opportunistic
one eight minutes from the break. That Liam Fennelly score sent the
Noresiders into a half-time lead of 1-10 to 0-7, but there were many who
felt that Cork, with that wind advantage in the second half, would prove
capable of overhauling the champions. However, Kilkenny struck quickly
and most decisively within seconds of the restart. Ritchie Power nipped in
smartly after good work by Ger Fennelly and Harry Doyle to snatch his
team's second goal. The score meant that Cork had a real mountain to
climb, but they went about their task with grit and determination, and
might have made it had the champions' defence, shrewdly generalled by a
magnificent Joe Hennessy and Ger Henderson, not stood firm. Cork had
no one to match Billy Fitzpatrick in the scoring line. He rifled over points

from left and right, with the wind and against it, an impressive performance by any standards. Fitzpatrick's showing and the high quality of the rear-guard's play were the main factors in the victory formula for the Noresiders. However, Frank Cummins played a vital part as well. He lined out at midfield where he contributed many important and invaluable touches, but he also found time to help out in defence and attack, as the need arose. Cork's fight back began five minutes into the second half when Tomas Mulcahy finished a Jimmy Barry Murphy cross to the net. Cork fell down badly when it came to turning good opportunities into scores. That second Cork goal for instance didn't come until five minutes from full time. Seánie O'Leary, who went in as a substitute, was the side's man of the match. The Cork stars were all in the defence. Tom Cashman, Dermot McCurtain and Donal O'Grady proved the guiding lights in that department. Undoubtedly both teams set about playing to their best standards, but the tricky wind changed that approach and it was to Kilkenny's credit that they conjured up the important scores when assisted by the elements in the first half. Kilkenny's ability to curtail Cork's scoring efforts in the second half was spectacularly sound and certainly proved a winning gambit. If Cork had taken a leaf out of Kilkenny's book and concentrated better on using the opportunities that cropped up in their wind-assisted second half, the story might well have been different. But Kilkenny were well aware of the consequences, had they slackened their grip when they faced Cork's second half charge. The order was strict man to man marking, and so it proved. The real turning point in the match was Ritchie Power's goal immediately after the restart, and with it Cork's small hill now grew into a towering mountain which they failed to climb.

1984 FINAL: JUBILEE TITLE FOR CORK

2 September 1984   Cork 3-16, Offaly 1-12
Attendance: 59,814   Referee: P. Long (Kilkenny)
Top scorers: J. Fenton (Cork) 0-7, S. O'Leary (Cork) 2-1

The final was played at a revamped Semple Stadium, Thurles, as a high point in the celebrations of the GAA Centenary Year. The occasion will be remembered as one in which everything went happily right except the match itself. That was the regrettable part as the meeting of Cork and Offaly did not catch fire at any stage, and long before the final whistle the issue was never in doubt as Cork swept convincingly to their Jubilee title.

Offaly started favourites after a sparkling performance when accounting for Wexford in an exhilarating Leinster final and an equally good showing against Galway in the All-Ireland semi-final at Thurles. However, they were on the losing end of the game right from the very first act—the toss. Cork won that, and in dry and humid conditions elected to play into the Killinan end. The Munster champions took only a minute to open the scoring, a pointed free from John Fenton, and by half-time the scoreboard showed Cork ahead 1-5 to 0-7. Then when the Cork men opened their shoulders after the resumption, scoring 1-6 without reply in fourteen minutes, Offaly's famed fighting spirit spluttered but never once caught fire. Maybe it was recognition of the fact that Cork on song, as they were at this stage, invariably call the tune. Yet, at the break there was a strong feeling among the Offaly supporters that the Leinster champions would turn on the style, being only a point in arrears. It was not to be. It was Cork who set about stamping their superiority on the proceedings. They took complete control and with high-class hurling and some excellent score-taking they chalked up a succession of scores from the eager beaver Cork forwards. The Cork goal in that particular sequence came in the thirteenth minute. Offaly goalie Damien Martin, who could not be blamed for the goals which passed him, had saved a blistering drive from Jimmy Barry Murphy, but the wily opportunist Timmy Crowley flicked the rebound to the Offaly net. Offaly were always fighting a losing battle after that, and Cork finished clear-cut winners after a disappointing match. Nevertheless, this historic All-Ireland final did have some memorable features. John Crowley was a master of the famed Thurles sod. Everything he did at centre half back for the Munster men bore the stamp of class. His was a remarkable individual performance after shouldering a lot of criticism over the previous two seasons. He silenced his critics with a display of rare grandeur. On top of his game from the word go, the brilliant Bishopstown defender hurled his heart out in a near classic exhibition of defensive skills, superb marshalling, covering and the time-honoured art of turning defence into attack. Offaly tried no fewer than three players in their attempts to curb him, but it was from another Crowley clearance that midfielder Pat Hartnett picked off the Leesiders' final point right on full time. Dermot MacCurtain also turned in a sizzling display, while behind him Denis Mulcahy, Donal O'Grady and John Hodgins were ice cool and solid with Ger Cunningham sound as a bell. John Fenton, who played a marvellous captain's role, and Pat Hartnett gained an early midfield edge and again, despite changes by the opposition, held it to the end. Fenton capped it all with seven points (three from play). Further upfield Tim Crowley, big, strong and ever willing, did a masterly job in containing the effectiveness of Paddy Delaney. Aidan Fogarty, Joachim Kelly, Padraic Horan, and to a lesser degree Pat Carroll were similarly pressured, thus severing Offaly's normal source of inspiration. The Offaly defence, in which Eugene Coughlan, Pat Fleury, Ger Coughlan and Damien Martin performed heroically, was also good enough to force Cork to make many changes. It has to be mentioned that not all the alterations were effective. There could be no doubt, however, that Cork's outstanding performer at this end was Tony O'Sullivan, who fully measured up to all the demands of the occasion. And what can be said about the bustling Youghal stalwart Seánie O'Leary that has not already been said. All one can now add is that he gloriously rifled in two great goals and a point. He would have had more, had his opponents been penalised for some blatant holding.

1985 FINAL: LONG SERVING HORAN SHOWS THE WAY

1 September 1985   Offaly 2-11, Galway 1-12
Attendance: 61,814   Referee: G. Ryan (Tipperary)
Top scorer: P.J. Molloy (Galway) 1-6

This will not be remembered as a great All-Ireland final but was always a keenly contested affair with the issue in doubt right until the final whistle. Galway did not help their cause by poor marksmanship. They had ten wides in the vital opening twenty minutes and nineteen in all over the game. Even so, Offaly deserved their success. They hurled with drive and determination all through, took their chances when they arose and had an inspirational figure in the oldest player on the field, Pádraig Horan, who at 35 provided the vital touches when they were needed most. He said in a pre-match comment, 'To be honest, I was rather worried coming up in the train this morning. The nerves started to hit me when we left Tullamore and I did not feel myself until I put over that first point. That took the pressure off me a little.' The genial Offaly full forward's three points proved invaluable to the winning cause. But it took character, craft, and above all experience to steer them through the choppy waters. It was those elements in their armoury which brought Offaly captain Pat Fleury on to the Hogan Stand to accept the coveted MacCarthy Cup after a dramatic and exciting finish.

Offaly scored first in each half. Mark Corrigan whipped over the opening point in three minutes, but Galway, playing into the Canal end and against a swirling breeze, enjoyed the better of the exchanges for a time after that. However, a Pat Cleary goal after 28 minutes revived Offaly hopes to give the midlanders a 1-3 to 0-4 lead. The exchanges were exciting after that and at the interval Offaly went into their dressing room with a two-point advantage, 1-6 to 0-7. Many felt that the margin would not be enough to set the Leinster champions on the road to success, but Offaly provided a dramatic answer to the doubters. Just 30 seconds after the throw-in, Pat Cleary sent a stinging ground shot to the Galway net and that score revitalised the Offaly men. The signs were briefly false, however. Galway stuck resolutely to their task and looked to be right back in contention when P. J. Molloy fielded a Michael McGrath lob and sent a cracking drive all the way to the Offaly net from twenty yards out. That left the score 2-8 to 1-8 for the Leinster champions after seven minutes of play. Two more points from Molloy had the final wide open again, but Offaly remained cool and collected, and with points from Paddy Corrigan in the seventeenth and 24th minutes, they maintained a steady grip on affairs. Still, the issue was in doubt coming up to the closing stages. Then came a classic touch from full forward Horan, who collected the ball 35 yards out from the Galway goal, turned under pressure and sent a peach of a shot straight between the Galway uprights to leave three points between the sides. But it fell to Galway's Tony Keady to close the curtain on a well-contested game with a smashing point from 65 yards—Horan's effort a minute before that, was to subsequently prove the match winner—to Galway's cost.

Horan had an outstanding game. Clever in his general play, accurate as well, he certainly led the Offaly attack by example, first at full forward and later when he moved to centre forward. Jim Troy kept a sound goal, Pat Fleury was an outstanding team leader and dependable left full back, while Pat Cleary showed his goal-scoring talent by grabbing two great goals at important stages of the match. Offaly struggled for long periods to get a grip on the game, their half backs and half forwards under extreme pressure by a no nonsense Connacht side. Offaly were often in trouble at midfield, but despite that they managed to stay in touch and early in the second half were seven points clear. When they needed inspiration, Pádraig Horan was there to provide it. Galway tried to reorganise their attack. Their marksmanship improved somewhat, but the good service they got from midfielder Steve Mahon was never properly utilised. They were never able to get far enough ahead to play to their strengths and that was a costly weakness. Indeed, the best goal of the game fell to 5' 8" P. J. Molloy, who leaped higher than Fogarty, Coughlan and Lane to grab a lob from Michael McGrath, turn and crack the ball to the roof of the Offaly net. Others to do well for the losers were Sylvie Linnane, Joe Cooney, the youngest on the team, Brendan Lynskey and Steve Mahon.

1986 FINAL: CROWLEY LEAVES INJURY WORRIES BEHIND

7 September 1986   Cork 4-13, Galway 2-15
Attendance: 63,451   Referee: J.F. Bailey (Dublin)
Top scorers: K. Hennessy (Cork) 2-1, J. Fenton (Cork) 1-4

Seldom if ever did Cork, the champion competitors of the game, start such outsiders for a national decider as for this clash with Galway. Seldom if ever did any team in such a role make the critics look as silly as Tom Cashman's crew did in this showpiece game. Galway had displayed skill and bold imaginative tactics with a two-man full forward line to trounce Kilkenny by eleven points in the All-Ireland semi-final at Thurles. They looked champions in waiting as they lined out in the MacCarthy Cup tie. But Cork turned on a quality performance inspired by left full back John Crowley to finish convincing winners in a dull decider. Crowley went into the game under an injury cloud. He was only passed fit from a thigh injury following a run-out just hours before the final but showed no ill effects at all. He was left on his own under Hill 16 in the opening minutes as Galway adopted the two-pronged full forward line that had worked so well against Kilkenny. They soon realised the move was not paying dividends and quickly reverted to the orthodox formation, only to find Crowley a tremendous stumbling block. He excelled in man to man marking and clever positional play, and his expertise and skill did much to set his team on a winning course.

Cork, playing against the wind, laid the foundation for success with a blistering opening quarter. They hit two goals, the first from a twenty yard free by John Fenton after only eight minutes, but to their credit Galway rallied strongly in the second quarter, so much so that Cork had just a point, 2-5 to 0-10, to spare at the break. The Connacht champions introduced wily P. J. Molloy to their attack for the restart and later called in Michael Connolly but failed to find the way through a tenacious Cork defence. The Leesiders lost their scoring midfielder, John Fenton, with an ankle injury early in the second half, but this did not upset their rhythm. Kevin Hennessy switched to the half forward line and had a great second half. He also contributed two cracking goals to the team's scoresheet. Tomas Mulcahy's second, probably the most spectacular of the day thirteen minutes into the second half, was truly brilliant. He collected a puck-out from goalie Ger Cunningham, ran 50 metres free and expertly rifled the sliothar to the back of the Galway net. Galway's first goal didn't come until eight minutes from full time. And it was a special one too. Galway goalkeeper John Commins made the long journey downfield to take a twenty metre free, and he expertly crashed the ball past a wall of Cork defenders to the net. The score came too late, however, to save the westerners, as just before that came Kevin Hennessy's second goal. P. J. Molloy got Galway's last goal a minute from time to boost interest, but it was all in vain. Teddy McCarthy, playing in his first senior championship game, impressed at right half forward for Cork, and Jimmy Barry Murphy with his deft touches was another who sparkled in attack for the winners. Tony Keady showed the way to his colleagues in the Galway attack by leading the county's scoring returns with five cracking long-range points. Peter Finnerty and Gerry McInerney were others in defence to show up well, while the pick of the forwards was Martin Naughton. Indeed, efforts by Galway to improve their attacking set-up failed, as they were never allowed to impose their will against a sound Cork defence. The task of the Galway defence was made more difficult because of the consistency and length of Ger Cunningham's puck-outs. Each time the half backs had to retreat to get under the ball and Cork's Mulcahy, O'Sullivan, Hennessy and Ger Fitzgerald won a lot of ball going forward. The loss of midfielder John Fenton with an injury in the second half was offset by the switch of Teddy McCarthy to midfield. Galway suffered from a number of ailments brought about by the sheer pressure on their defence by the very active Cork forwards. The Galway full back line was never assured as in previous deciders, and the moving of Sylvie Linnane to full back wasn't a wise move at the time. The use of the two-man full forward line, a tactical ploy that worked in the semi-final, came a cropper against a side that had already prepared for that gambit. Cork were clear-cut winners on the day. They outplayed Galway in most sectors of the field and deservedly captured their 26th MacCarthy Cup to confound all their critics.

1987 FINAL: MCINERNEY BACK FOR WINNING SHOW

6 September 1987   Galway 1-12, Kilkenny 0-9
Attendance: 65,586   Referee: T. Murray (Limerick)
Top scorer: G. Fennelly (Kilkenny) 0-7

Croke Park has never been the place for the faint-hearted on All-Ireland day, especially when two great hurling rivals, Galway and Kilkenny, provide the action. After losing the last two finals, the Galway team knew they had to win this time. Many of the Kilkenny players felt it would be their last chance to win a medal. The result was a final where marking was tight and uncompromising, thus denying players the space to operate in the quest for scores or back line clearances. The player in possession often found three or four adversaries bearing down on him. There was barely time to think, never mind act. It was a tough hard game, not helped by the conditions. Heavy rain which fell in the twelve hours before the match made matters difficult for both teams, as did the wind. Nevertheless, there were many bright moments with Gerry McInerney, Steve Mahon and John Commins providing the best in the Galway colours. McInerney returned from New York where he had been living for some months and had a very good first half, but he really exploded on to the scene in the second period. Wearing the Galway No. 7 jersey, McInerney was the key figure, clearly dominating the left wing, mopping up everything that came his way and setting his forwards in motion time after time. He was almost faultless in every facet of the game, positioning, tackling, fielding and striking. And the money invested in bringing him home from New York was money well spent. Behind him the full back line worked tirelessly, with Conor Hayes succeeding where few others had in keeping Kilkenny sharp-shooter Liam Fennelly scoreless from play. Peter Finnerty and Tony Keady also had their inspiring moments. In goal John Commins was being heralded as a hero. His two saves in quick succession from Liam Fennelly between the 21st and 23rd minutes of the second half were mind boggling. It was important too that Galway were the stronger unit in midfield. Steve Mahon was a powerful figure in this area and gave his best performance ever. Kilkenny's finishing was surprisingly poor considering the talent in their attacking force. In the first half they had nine bad wides, all from reasonable scoring positions, as Galway raced into an early 0-4 to 0-1 lead and stuck resolutely to their task. At the end of the first quarter that produced few scores, the westerners, who had won the National League earlier in the season, led by just 0-5 to 0-4. Galway started promisingly in the second half with a fine movement ending in an Anthony Cunningham point after two minutes. But Kilkenny began to get to grips with the exchanges, and thanks to the accuracy of Ger Fennelly had gained the lead for the first time after eight minutes. The westerners were in no mood, however, to finish second best for the third year in succession. They stormed back, and two points by Joe Cooney had them back in front again. Steve Mahon steadied Galway further with a fine point, but although they continued to play good solid hurling and worked ceaselessly, they could not shake off the Kilkenny challenge. Then into the picture stepped goalie Commins, and Noel Lane, who was brought on as a substitute five minutes after the restart, to seal the issue for Galway in the final fifteen minutes. In the 21st minute the Galway net minder Commins brought off the first of his two crucial saves from Liam Fennelly. He got his body firmly behind Fennelly's palmed effort and deflected away a second stinging shot with his hurley two minutes later. Had Fennelly scored from one of those efforts, the Noresiders might well have pulled away. Lane showed his qualities as a goal poacher when he popped up eight minutes from the end and hit the only goal of the match. Steve Mahon, Eanna Ryan and Joe Cooney were all involved in the build-up that eventually found Lane at an angle to the goal, and his shot was hard and true. There and then the MacCarthy Cup was won and lost, but Keady made doubly sure with an excellent point from 80 metres. Not all the heroes were on the Galway side. Seán Fennelly had an excellent game on the left flank for Kilkenny, and Ger Henderson shook off the effects of an early hand injury in the game to inspire his team with his determined and tireless hurling. The win earned Galway their first National League and MacCarthy Cup double in the same year.

1988 FINAL: COMMINS SAVES PROVE VITAL

5 September 1988	Galway 1-15, Tipperary 0-14
Attendance: 63,545	Referee: G. Kirwan (Offaly)
Top scorer: N. English (Tipperary) 0-6	

A historic day for Galway and Conor Hayes. The westerners retained the MacCarthy Cup for the first time ever, and Hayes became the first from the county to lead Galway to a brace of All-Ireland senior crowns. As Gaeilge, Conor Hayes in his victory speech told the delirious thousands that only in his sleep did he ever dream about a Galway man collecting the MacCarthy Cup on two successive years. The following morning he woke up to a glorious reality. Tipperary were giving everything away in experience, as the game marked the county's first outing at that stage since 1971. Nevertheless, they still played their part in providing an interesting and exciting match that was in doubt virtually until the closing minutes. The lessons learned the hard way over the last four years all bore fruit for the Galway hurlers at Croke Park. They knew what it was like to lose an All-Ireland final, even two. They also knew how to win and in this absorbing battle that knowledge proved invaluable.

Defences were on top. Tipperary looked in a special way to Nicholas English, their star marksman, but he was well contained by the holders' superb rearguard. The Galway forwards were a little more inventive and creative, and once more the attack had an ace in the pack in super sub Noel Lane, the man whose goal won the 1987 final. He again went into a final as a sub, and again scored the only goal of the match. Galway's half back line of Peter Finnerty, Tony Keady and Gerry McInerney was unyielding all through and proved a mighty stumbling block to the Tipperary attack. Michael Coleman and Pat Malone also exercised a vital edge at centrefield for Galway, with Malone proving one of the heroes of the day. Nevertheless, the challengers, after opting to play against the strong wind in the first half, looked well in contention as they trailed by only 0-10 to 0-6 at the interval.

Thirteen minutes into the second half Tipperary looked firmly on the road to victory as they trailed by just a single point, but Galway refused to panic. Their defence gave little away. Brendan Lynskey worked tirelessly and effectively and Joe Cooney produced his best hurling of the game. Then there was Lane. The forward with the goal-scoring touch was dropped for the final after having played in the two earlier championship ties but was sent in eventually in the second half. Near the end of the game he got in behind Conor O'Donovan, the Tipperary full back, to get a clear shot at goal, and the Ballindereen man was not found wanting in his finishing technique. That put Galway five points clear. The goals double for the long-serving Lane ensured that his name will be associated in a special way with Galway's history-making double of the late eighties. Paul Delaney had a cracking game for Tipperary, while Conor O'Donovan marked three different Galway men during the match and did really well against all three. John Commins brought off some great saves yet again for

Galway, with probably the most crucial a superb one from Pat Fox just before Lane got the solitary goal of the day. Galway were two points ahead when the Tipperary right full forward brought the best out of Commins with a blistering shot. A goal at that stage would have given Tipperary the lead and would probably have inspired them to victory. So the Commins save proved a vital moment in the destination of the MacCarthy Cup for 1988.

We may not have got the free flowing hurling that we had hoped, but the close marking and tension were factors which denied us that opportunity. It was also obvious that the tactics employed by both teams ensured that scores would be hard won. In Tipperary's case the isolation of their top star, Nicky English, left the Munster men without a leader in the scoring department. No other player could adopt the mantle of leader, though Declan Carr tried manfully in the second half. It was in defence that this title was won, and Galway had the stalwarts who fitted their roles to perfection, as did the rest of the team when the big challenge was offered. Glory then to the men from the west on a day when history was made.

1989 FINAL: SCORING SPREE FROM ENGLISH

3 September 1989   Tipperary 4-24, Antrim 3-9
Attendance: 65,496   Referee: P. Delaney (Laois)
Top scorer: N. English (Tipperary) 2-12

Tipperary were unbackable favourites to regain the MacCarthy Cup after a lapse of eighteen years at Croke Park. They easily overcame the challenge of a brave Antrim side in a rather one-sided contest which was over bar the shouting long before the final whistle. Antrim, appearing in their first decider since 1943 and rank outsiders on this occasion, still brought a huge colourful following as they battled against one of the major hurling forces in the game. Unfortunately they were well beaten in the end but still contributed to a very enjoyable and sporting occasion. Declan Carr and Nicholas English did much to ensure there was no fairytale ending to an Antrim Cinderella story that began in early August with a sensational but well-deserved semi-final win over Offaly. Carr was in terrific form in the centre of the field, ably assisted by Colm Bonnar, and the partnership dominated the area in spite of the efforts of the Antrim pairing of Paul McKillen and Dominic McMullan. Tipperary thus ensured that they had a very lucrative service going to their forward division. English, in the No. 15 jersey, led the attack with flair and imagination and displayed uncanny accuracy as he built up a new individual scoring record for a Tipperary hurler at 2-12, which was half his team's total. Antrim played into the Canal goal and matched their more fancied and much more experienced opponents in most scoring chances in that period, though they also missed chances that did not help them in the long run.

The match was firmly turned Tipperary's way after nineteen minutes. Declan Ryan, the Tipp centre forward, shot for a point. The sliothar deceived Niall Patterson in the Antrim goal and ended up in the net. That gave Tipperary a 1-4 to 0-1 advantage and they never looked back. It was to Antrim's credit that they continued to battle bravely, but at the interval they were well out of the hunt as they trailed 1-13 to 0-5. A moment of hope came for the northerners two minutes into the second half when they were awarded a penalty, but Aidan McCarry's shot was blocked. Three minutes later the door was finally closed on the gallant Ulster men as Nicky English collected his final goal. Even so, the Antrim men continued to try and improve matters. Aidan McCarry scored his side's first goal in a final after ten minutes of the half, and a fine one it was too. Brian Donnelly and Donal Armstrong also got on the scoresheet, but those scores only helped to earn the Glensmen a respectable tally. Tipperary collected their 23rd All-Ireland title and fourteenth MacCarthy Cup and never looked in danger at any stage. English used the occasion to display his undoubted hurling artistry and some of his scoring efforts were the work of a master's hands. There was no real pressure on a well-balanced and perfectly coordinated defensive set-up masterminded by Bobby Ryan. It was a spirited return to the final scene for Antrim, who had bright stars in Des Donnelly at left full back, Terence McNaughton at left full forward and hardworking midfielder Paul McKillen. No doubt about the input of the three Tipperary selectors, famous star hurlers Babs Keating, Donie Nealon and Theo English, who helped to atone for the previous year's failure against Galway.

Chapter 9 ~

THE NINETIES

The 1990 to 1999 All-Ireland hurling finals

The old Liam MacCarthy Cup was replaced by a new trophy, also known as the Liam MacCarthy Cup, for the 1992 All-Ireland senior final, in which Kilkenny, led by Liam Fennelly, beat Cork.

This addition to the GAA trophies is almost an exact replica of the original MacCarthy Cup but is heavier. A thicker gauge of silver was used to create the new trophy, and the handles were strengthened to allow for the inevitable wear and tear. Modifications raised the weight from two and a half kilos to nearly four kilos. The height remains at 33 cm and the diameter 22 cm. Master craftsman James Mary Kelly, a Kilkenny gold and silversmith, made the new trophy.

The opening years of the decade brought a new era in the All-Ireland senior hurling championship, and the second half of the nineties were enriched by Clare's entry into the MacCarthy Cup story.

The new era dawned in 1992 when a new MacCarthy Cup was presented for that year's final, and Liam Fennelly (Kilkenny) made his mark as captain in the history books. He became the first man to receive the new trophy, and completed a rare double. He also ranks as the last Kilkenny native to have been presented with the old MacCarthy Cup, having led the Noresiders to their last title of the eighties in 1983.

The decade opened on a high note for Cork. They caused something of an upset by beating Galway in 1990 to regain the All-Ireland title after four years. Their footballers later retained the Sam Maguire in September and earned Cork the first All-Ireland senior title double in the same year by any county since Tipperary completed that great double in 1920. Teddy McCarthy played in both the hurling and football finals to become the first to win senior All-Ireland medals in both codes in the same year.

It was a good decade for Offaly and Clare. The Faithful County joined the ranks of winners of the old and new trophies by capturing the All-Ireland crown of 1994, and went on to add another title four years later.

Clare brought a fresh and welcome wind of change in 1995. Starting that season one had to go back as far as 1914 to find their name on the All-Ireland senior hurling title rankings for the only time. Their last appearance in a final was in 1932 when they lost to Kilkenny. Adding to the novelty of Clare's return was the fact that their opponents were Offaly, then the defending champions. A gifted Clare side, led by Anthony Daly from left half back, made it a double glory day for the county by capturing the MacCarthy Cup. And, as if that was not enough to mark out the decade in a special way for the Banner County, they were back in the final again in 1997, with Daly once more as captain and left half back, and overcame the challenge of Tipperary.

Although Kilkenny did not win the old cup in the nineties, they still command an extra special place with that initial triumph of 1992. Moreover, Christy Heffernan, who went in as a substitute very early in the second half of the 1992 game, and Liam Fennelly rank as the first hurlers to win All-Ireland senior medals under the banners of the old and new MacCarthy cups.

It was a busy decade for referee Dickie Murphy of Wexford. He made his All-Ireland senior final debut in that special final of 1992 and went on to referee three more finals. Willie Horgan of Cork had charge of the last final under the old banner. Interestingly, that 1991 game also marked his first outing as the man with the whistle in a MacCarthy Cup tie. Tipperary beat Kilkenny in that 1991 final and they were captained by Declan Carr at midfield.

Statistics

Greatest attendance	65,848 in 1996
Busiest referee	Dickie Murphy (Wexford) 1992, 95, 97, 98
Highest team score	5-15 (30 points) by Cork 1990
Highest score by losing team	2-21 (27 points) by Galway 1990
Highest winning margin	6 points by Offaly 1994 and by Offaly 1998
Lowest winning margin	One point by Clare 1997 and by Cork 1990
Highest individual score	1-7 by Joe Cooney (Galway) 1990
Highest individual goals tally	2 by John Fitzgibbon (Cork) 1990 and by Damien Quigley (Limerick) 1995

Goalless finals	One, 1999
Finals in which winning team failed to score a goal	1997 Clare; 1999 Cork
Finals in which losing team failed to score a goal	1991 Kilkenny; 1996 Limerick; 1999 Kilkenny
Best points tally by winning team	20 by Clare 1997
Best points tally by losing team	21 by Galway 1990
Top scoring final on aggregate	1990: 7-36 (57 points)
Replays	None
Most successful captain	Anthony Daly (Clare) 1995, 97

1990 FINAL: TWO GOALS FROM FITZGIBBON

2 September 1990   Cork 5-15, Galway 2-21
Attendance: 63,954   Referee: J. Moore (Waterford)
Top scorer: J. Cooney (Galway) 1-7

Cork in the unusual role of outsiders and warm favourites Galway provided the best possible advertisement for hurling as an exciting spectator sport—a thrilling spectacle on a grand day weather-wise, some splendid individual performances, commitment, skill and all out effort, and all set off by an exhilarating and match-winning come-back by the Leesiders.

Forty-three scores including five goals coloured this superb game in which fortunes fluctuated. Cork had a dream start with a goal from full forward Kevin Hennessy a mere 40 seconds after the throw-in, but Galway dominated matters for the rest of the half to lead at the break by five points. Galway fielded eleven hurlers who helped fashion the county's only double of All-Ireland senior titles in 1987 and 88. With that rich vein of experience it was hardly surprising that the westerners took the setback of that early goal firmly in their stride and responded by setting the pace for the rest of the half. Their smart-moving and polished response was powered by Joe Cooney, who appeared to be on his way to the game of his life. He set a captain's example as he teased and tormented the Cork rearguard and helped himself to a splendid 1-6. All but a point came from play. Ollie Kilkenny, Peter Finnerty and Tony Keady also scaled the heights to mould the defence into a tight and unyielding rearguard, while Michael Coleman and Pat Malone also did well in midfield. As a result, the Connacht men were in no way flattered by their interval lead of 1-13 to 1-8.

Even though the wind would favour Cork in the second half, Galway looked to have laid the foundations of victory at the break. That opinion was strengthened as the westerners started the second half with a real flourish, chalking up three points as against one by the Munster champions in the first four minutes.

However, Cork are not renowned championship campaigners for nothing. They redoubled their efforts with flair and skill, aided in a big way by goalkeeper Ger Cunningham. He began to rain deliveries down behind the Galway half back line to create ideal opportunities for his forwards and add tremendously to the problems of the Galway defenders. In this period as well there was excellent stickwork and clever touches in attack from team captain Tomas Mulcahy, Tony O'Sullivan, Mark Foley and John Fitzgibbon for Cork.

Changes also improved the Leeside team. The transfer of Mulcahy from right full to centre half forward in the second half proved effective in turning the game the southerners' way. So too did the introduction from the substitutes of Cathal Casey to partner Tony O'Sullivan in midfield. The forwards received an improved supply as a result and came much more into the game. Mulcahy, who really sparkled after the change of ends, gave his colleagues a real boost when he goaled after seven minutes to reduce arrears to four points.

Cork maintained the pressure and hit two more points before Kevin Hennessy placed Mark Foley, and the Cork centre half forward scored an excellent goal to give his team a point lead. Eanna Ryan quickly levelled for Galway, but Cork were moving well and two goals inside a minute by John Fitzgibbon with about six minutes remaining had the Leesiders firmly on the road to a memorable win.

Twelve minutes into the second half, Ger Cunningham brought off a great save from Martin Naughton. He deserved great credit for his bravery and positional sense. Seán O'Gorman was formidable all through at left half back for the winners and Jim Cashman, after a trying opening half against Cooney, really came into his own in the second half to contribute richly to the fight back. Fitzgerald, with his two goals, was another of Cork's aces. Best for Galway were Cooney, Finnerty, Gerry McInerney and Keady at the back.

1991 FINAL: CLEARY GOAL DECISIVE

2 September 1991   Tipperary 1-16, Kilkenny 0-15
Attendance: 64,500   Referee: W. Horgan (Cork)
Top scorers: M. Cleary (Tipperary) 1-6, D. J. Carey (Kilkenny) 0-9

Tipperary returned to the final with much the same team that ended a long title famine by winning the 1989 crown and started favourites. They beat Cork, then reigning All-Ireland champions, in a replay in the Munster final and also further advertised their credentials with a resounding ten point semi-final win over Galway.

Kilkenny, in contrast, were generally rated somewhat unlucky to have triumphed in a high-scoring game against Antrim by two points. However, Kilkenny, not surprisingly with such a proud tradition in the game, were in no way daunted by their outsiders' ranking and lost no time in underlining that point.

They gook the game to the Munster champions right from the throw-in, played good hurling throughout and made Tipperary work all the way for their entry into the records as the last winners of the old MacCarthy Cup. The final held interest throughout and provided some fine passages of play and good individual displays, but overall did not rank with the great deciders of the past.

A vital and decisive moment came after 45 minutes. Tipperary won a twenty metre free and Michael Cleary's shot was deflected into the Kilkenny net for the only goal of the day. That was a key score, one that boosted the Munster champions' morale, and they responded well as a result.

The first half exchanges were fairly even with neither side capable of exercising a decisive influence on the game. Half forwards Christy Heffernan and John Power were to the forefront in helping Kilkenny get off to a bright start as they took the issue to their opponents in fine style. However, the Leinster champions failed to capitalise on some good scoring opportunities and Tipperary were three points to no score clear after nine minutes.

Undaunted, Kilkenny continued to play with drive and skill and two minutes from the interval were nicely placed with a three point advantage. Tipperary responded in electrifying fashion with a whirlwind finish that yielded a point from Pat Fox and two from Cleary to end the half on level terms at 0-9 each.

The southerners started the second half the way they ended the first, with Fox and Cleary keeping the onward charge moving with a point each. Kilkenny took up the challenge with enthusiasm and D. J. Carey opened their account in the second half with a point from a free after eight minutes. Then came that vital Cleary goal. Carey boosted Kilkenny's morale with a point from a free, but Tipperary came more into the picture after that. They pushed ahead to earn a five point lead with thirteen minutes remaining. However, Kilkenny did not flinch. They continued to strive with skill and determination and by the 63rd minute a Carey point, his ninth of the game, had them just a goal in arrears.

There followed then seven exciting though scoreless minutes before Fox stepped into the picture to settle the issue with a point from play. Tipperary, then, had many anxious moments before justifying their favouritism. However, they still well deserved the success that earned them their 24th All-Ireland senior title.

Cleary, who finished with 1-6, made a fine contribution, and a little behind him was Fox. John Leahy, who lined out at left half forward, was another commanding figure with his tireless play between his own half back line and midfield. Paul Delaney and Michael Ryan got through much valuable work at the back for the winners.

Kilkenny had their heroes too. John Henderson, who played with his hamstring heavily strapped, and Eddie O'Connor superbly marshalled a defence that made the opposing attack work hard for their scores. Michael Phelan did well in midfield, while Heffernan, Power and Carey provided many testing problems for the Tipperary rearguard. Declan Carr led Tipperary well from left midfield and earned his place in the record books as the last man presented with the old MacCarthy Cup.

1992 FINAL: CAREY AND O'NEILL VITALISE KILKENNY

6 September 1992   Kilkenny 3-10, Cork 1-12
Attendance: 64,534   Referee: D. Murphy (Wexford)
Top scorer: D. J. Carey 1-4

Rain which fell for most of the game and wind hampered the hurlers in their efforts to provide first-class fare, and understandably this was not a classic. Nevertheless, it was a keenly contested match with some spirited exchanges and impressive individual performances. The game also introduced a new era in hurling as it was the first final for the new MacCarthy Cup.

Kilkenny, runners-up for the title the previous year, had four points to spare over Galway in a splendid semi-final, while Cork booked their return to the showpiece game after two years with a nine point win over Down in their semi-final. The Leesiders lined out with eleven of the hurlers who fashioned their 1990 All-Ireland win and started slight favourites. However, Kilkenny, who won the toss and played against the wind, lost no time in showing they were in no mood to leave headquarters as the losers in a final for the second year in a row.

The game was only 40 seconds old when D. J. Carey had the Leinster men ahead with a fine point. However, Cork took control after that and with Tomas Mulcahy and Tony O'Sullivan setting the standard up front, sent over five points as against a solitary one for Kilkenny to lead by 0-5 to 0-2 after twenty minutes. Kilkenny got their game together much better after that and three minutes from the interval they were right back in the hunt following a penalty for a foul on corner forward Jamesie Brennan. Sharpshooter Carey rifled the ball expertly to the net and Kilkenny turned over at the interval just 0-7 to 1-2 in arrears and very much in the hunt. The Munster champions squandered some good chances in that half, but credit must still go to Kilkenny's backs, notably Eddie O'Connor, Pat Dwyer and Pat O'Neill, who generally made the opposing forwards work hard for scores.

Three minutes after the restart Kilkenny made an expected move by sending in wily Christy Heffernan from the substitutes' bench, just as happened in each of three earlier games. He brought a new sense of urgency and drive to the attack. Another boost around the three minute mark was a goal by centre half forward John Power. Both teams made switches, one of which was most beneficial for Kilkenny in sending Michael Phelan from midfield to full forward. He had played well at midfield, but brought added punch to the forward division. He also provided a long pass to Liam McCarthy that brought Kilkenny's third goal after 22 minutes. Phelan followed with two quick points to put Kilkenny ahead 3-7 to 0-11, and apparently coasting to their first title in nine years. However, Ger Manley, who had gone in as a substitute for Cork, had other ideas. The title was not yet won or lost as he set about reviving Leeside spirits with a kicked goal after 31 minutes.

Kilkenny did not lose their momentum after that setback and were rewarded when another substitute, Adrian Ronan, captured the spotlight. He had been very disappointed earlier in the week when he was omitted from the Noreside starting line-up, but he rewarded the selectors for their confidence in sending him in from the bench. He sent over a superb point from a difficult angle on the right wing to close the scoring. Heffernan had earlier collected a point, so the substitutes certainly were on target.

Pat O'Neill, who received a bloodied brow during the final, had a superb match at centre half back for Kilkenny. Eddie O'Connor, Dwyer and Liam Simpson were others who ensured that Michael Walsh was not overburdened in the Kilkenny goal. And, it was that defensive rampart which contributed richly in orchestrating the well-merited success.

Phelan and Carey, who was the top scorer for the easterners with 1-4, were others who made their mark in the Leinster champions' win. Liam Fennelly also led the team well from full forward to earn his place in history as the first man presented with the new MacCarthy Cup. Left full back Brian Corcoran was by far Cork's most consistent hurler. Midfielder Seán McCarthy, Tony O'Sullivan and Mulcahy up front caught the eye from time to time.

1993 FINAL: DELANEY GOAL KEEPS CUP IN KILKENNY

5 September 1993   Kilkenny 2-17, Galway 1-15
Attendance: 63,460   Referee: T. Murray (Limerick)
Top scorer: P. J. Delaney (Kilkenny) 1-4

Goals, it is often said, win games, and a well-taken one late in the game by P. J. Delaney sealed a successful defence of the MacCarthy Cup by Kilkenny against Galway in a final that was a splendid advertisement for all that is best in hurling.

Kilkenny, bidding for a first successful defence of the title since 1983, started favourites, but Galway rose to the challenge in great style to play their part in an exhibition of all the skills, artistry and speed of the ancient game.

The exchanges were very keen throughout an exciting first half, but the final really burst into full bloom after the interval. Thrilling exchanges and fine individual displays in a tension-laden atmosphere kept the bumper attendance in feverish excitement right until the final whistle.

Kilkenny, with a brilliant Pat O'Neill setting the standard at centre half back, had the better of the early exchanges and led by 1-5 to 0-3 after fifteen minutes. The goal was scored by Adrian Ronan, who went into the final the previous year and recorded the last score of the game—a point. Galway moved Liam Burke from left full forward to midfield, and Michael Coleman from there to No. 15. Soon afterwards Galway were buoyed up when a long ball from Burke in midfield finished in the Kilkenny net. Three minutes later Michael Walsh made a fine save from a penalty by Coleman. It was still everything to play for at the interval when the defending champions led 1-8 to 1-6.

Kilkenny were 1-11 to 1-8 ahead six minutes into the second half, but they did not score again for fifteen minutes. Galway came back strongly with some fine points and left half forward Joe Cooney sent a 65 over the bar in the 54th minute to put the challengers ahead by 1-12 to 1-11. They might have gone further ahead but for a splendid save by goalkeeper Walsh from Burke. Galway sent in Justin Campbell from the substitutes and he pepped up the forward division considerably. Two minutes later right half forward Liam McCarthy had Kilkenny level with a point from play. The game continued at a fast pace with neither side able to strike the decisive blow.

Then, with 67 minutes gone came that important goal by Delaney, who was appearing in his first senior final. Ronan floated the ball from the right under the Hogan Stand into the Galway goal area, and the then 20-year-old Fenians club man provided the final touch for the goal that put Kilkenny ahead 2-15 to 1-14 and really clinched the title double for Kilkenny. Michael McGrath in the No. 13 jersey gave Galway some hope with a point, but Kilkenny were back for points from Delaney and D. J. Carey.

This was a brave bid by Galway to regain the MacCarthy Cup after an interval of five years. However, they did not help their cause by failing to turn scoring chances to good account. On the Kilkenny side, Pat O'Neill scaled the heights at centre half back for the second successive year, two five-star performances to rank with the best in All-Ireland finals. Michael Walsh also made a fine contribution. Apart from that important penalty save from Coleman, he brought off another couple of vital saves in the second half.

Eddie O'Connor captained the side in great style from right full back, while Delaney, with his crucial goal and four points, Ronan and midfielders Bill Hennessy and Michael Phelan were other commanding figures for the winners. However, the man of the match was Galway defender Pádraig Kelly, who celebrated his All-Ireland senior final debut with the type of display every player dreams of. Kilkenny tried five different forwards on Kelly, but the Sarsfields club man reigned supreme. He marshalled his skills to the best possible effect and at the end of the day deserved his award. Pat Malone, who had been doubtful before the game but lined out with a heavily strapped right leg, did well at midfield. Tom Helebert and Gerry McInerney in the half back line, Richard Burke in goal and Joe Rabbitte, who hit four points, were others to show up well for Galway.

1994 FINAL: DOOLEY TURNS THE TIDE

5 September 1994   Offaly 3-16, Limerick 2-13
Attendance: 56,458   Referee: W. Barrett (Tipperary)
Top scorer: D. Quigley (Limerick) 2-3

In a most extraordinary turnaround in All-Ireland final history, new champions Offaly stunned Limerick with a last five minute explosion of scoring power which yielded the staggering total of 2-5. The victory, Offaly's third senior hurling crown, was the result of a miracle of such magnitude that it beggared belief. What made it all the more incredible was that Limerick were enjoying the fruits of a memorable performance at the time and appeared safely on the road to All-Ireland greatness. A game which had flowed Limerick's way for 65 minutes was to be transformed with such rapidity that it left supporters of both teams gasping. The outcome was proof, if proof were needed, to explain the cruelty of sport, where a team had reached the top rung of the ladder, only for it to be pulled from under them in brutal fashion.

While Limerick supporters were left speechless, ecstatic Offaly fans were pinching themselves as they awoke to the startling truth that they had won a game which appeared to have deserted them midway through the second half. The occasion appeared to affect both sides as they bungled a number of chances from good scoring positions. In Limerick's case they failed to utilise the possession they enjoyed. Had they done so they would have been out of reach at the interval. Undoubtedly, their cause was not helped by the tricky wind and a total of twelve wides in the first half. The Shannonsiders looked very much the dominant team, even though they had periods when a few shrewd switches would have helped their morale. Offaly manager Eamon Cregan, former Limerick star hurler, was disgusted with the performance of the Offaly team. They were in tatters due to the tension of the occasion, which did play a part in the concession of the bulk of the twelve wides recorded against them. Joe Dooley's goal, when he pushed home a rebound in the fourth minute of the match, acted as a valuable prop as they stumbled through the first half, at the end of which Limerick led 2-8 to 1-5.

It was no surprise that Offaly reshaped the team for the restart. Brian Whelehan went to centre back in a switch with Hubert Rigney, Declan Pilkington moved to wing forward and Joe Dooley moved to the corner of the attack. They also moved Johnny Pilkington off Limerick dynamo Ciaran Carey at midfield on to Mike Houlihan in an effort to break the tight grip the two Limerick men held in the centre of the field. Offaly came more into the picture as Johnny Pilkington began to be far more effective and forthright in his approach. The other alterations were also beginning to show results as Offaly suddenly began to strengthen their opposition. Limerick shrugged off the challenge and kept playing to their own strengths. The Offaly team mentors went into a huddle and made two further changes. Michael Duignan replaced Daithí Regan at midfield; Leo O'Connor took over from Joe Dooley in attack, and pointed with his first touch of the ball. Duignan was quickly into his stride at midfield, proving the worth of his inclusion. But Limerick appeared untroubled as they measured up to the new challenge being posed by the midlanders. A superb Gary Kirby point put the Shannonsiders 2-13 to 1-11 in front in the 30th minute as All-Ireland glory beckoned.

The gods were in wicked mood at that stage. Billy Dooley had his jersey pulled by Joe O'Connor and it proved costly when a free was awarded. Offaly didn't take a quick free. Johnny Dooley lined up as if to go for a point. Instead, he cracked the ball low and hard past a packed Limerick goal line to the net. Limerick 2-13 Offaly 2-11. Forty seconds later, Johnny Pilkington drove the ball from ten yards inside his own half towards the Limerick goal posts. As Leo O'Connor broke away, the ball hopped twice before he struck it sharply to the Limerick net. Limerick 2-13 Offaly 3-11 now. Limerick were gobsmacked and totally unprepared for the disasters which struck them so cruelly, as Offaly now went on a scoring rampage with a series of marvellous points. Everything the Offaly players did turned to gold, and when referee Willie Barrett blew the final whistle, all the pent up emotions of the stunned Offaly supporters were finally released as they ran on to the pitch to acclaim their heroes.

In my report of the game in the *Evening Press* the following day, I wrote: 'Unbelievable, mind boggling, sensational, incredible, unforgettable. Trot out all the descriptive tags that might spring to mind, and they still wouldn't do justice to one of the most amazing All-Ireland hurling finals witnessed at Croke Park. The heroes were Offaly and their luckless victims Limerick, who must be wondering how they allowed a match, which they dominated and controlled for virtually 65 minutes, slip away from their grasp, in an unforgettable closing five minutes. Not for many, many years has one team dominated an All-Ireland occasion as Limerick did, and still walked away empty handed. There was no denying that Limerick looked a team of all the talents from an early stage, and while they were not allowed to perform to the heights achieved against Antrim in the semi-final, they appeared to be in command in all sectors. The rest will go down in hurling history as a gallant Offaly side committed grand larceny in defying all the odds to bring off the greatest recovery operation ever seen on a hurling pitch on an All-Ireland occasion.'

1995 FINAL: CLARE REACH PROMISED LAND

4 September 1995   Clare 1-13, Offaly 2-8
Attendance: 65,092   Referee: D. Murphy (Wexford)
Top scorer: Johnny Dooley (Offaly) 0-5

It was undoubtedly one of the greatest moments in Irish sport as Clare captain Anthony Daly accepted the MacCarthy Cup from GAA President Jack Boothman to underline for all Clare men that an All-Ireland hurling final win after all of 81 years made this an occasion to savour and remember. And it was remarkable that the victims of Clare's win – Offaly—had the previous year stolen the title from a gallant Limerick side, who looked out and out winners until a late Offaly resurgence won the day for the Leinster men.

It was a game where the hand of fate played a major role assisted by the decision of Clare team manager Ger Loughnane to make a late change. With twenty minutes to go, Offaly seemed set to acquire a coveted back to back run of All-Ireland successes. They had withstood a remarkable series of Clare pressure periods and were about to savour the thrill of All-Ireland glory once again when Loughnane and his selectors acted. Eamonn Taffe, on the substitutes' bench and still suffering from a hamstring problem, was told by Loughnane, as the story goes, to get on the field and score the winning goal, and if he did, he would take him off again, so he wouldn't be too wrecked after his labours. With twelve minutes remaining Offaly led 2-7 to 0-11 and hanging on desperately despite the pressure being applied by Clare to overtake them. With five minutes remaining Eamonn Taffe, hovering around the Offaly square, reacted quickest to a long free taken by Daly. When the incoming ball was batted down by Offaly goalie David Hughes, Taffe whipped it to the net. Clare 1-11, Offaly 2-7. Offaly, undaunted, fought back with a Johnny Dooley pointed free. Scores were then level with four minutes remaining. Two minutes later, Clare star and captain, Daly, fired over a prodigious pointed free. Clare 1-13, Offaly 2-8. A very dubious free for a foul on Cyril Lyons was tapped over the bar by Jamesie O'Connor, much to the relief of the Clare fans, on the call of full time with the final score Clare 1-13 to Offaly's 2-8.

It must be said that the Banner men had played the more consistent hurling even though the defending champions' level of performance failed to reach the height of the previous year's shock win over Limerick. Loughnane was true to his word with his promise to take Taffe off after scoring his crucial goal. That inspirational decision must surely go down in Clare hurling history as the match-winning move. And Taffe's goal certainly ignited the Clare hurling spirit at the time and altered the destination of the MacCarthy Cup. It was not to be Offaly's year. Surprisingly, the Offaly challenge was never powerful enough to conquer the Banner. In the first place, the Clare defensive set-up was too well marshalled, and that gave Clare goalie Davy Fitzgerald all the cover he needed to keep the Offaly forwards at bay.

I would say that the performance of the Clare defence was the real key to the outcome of this clash and all that was to follow in the succeeding seasons. The Lohan brothers, Brian and Frank, were powerful figures in the Clare back line, ably assisted by the consistent Michael O'Halloran. There was no denying the role played by a truly magnificent half back line of Liam Doyle, Seán McMahon and Anthony Daly, which exercised power, control and the necessary authority to minimise the threat of the Offaly attackers. Another factor which added immensely to the team performance was the contribution made by Ollie Baker, who recovered from a subdued first half display to give a commanding one in the second half when creating scoring chances. The Clare forwards collectively owed a lot to the ability of their outfield players to pick off points from long-range frees and 65s. Fergus Touhy, by his own admission a low-scoring forward, produced the display he was craving for on the big occasion, and his well-taken four points tally was crucial to the team's victory.

It was easy to pick out Offaly's best players. The laurels go to Kevin Kinahan, Brian Whelehan and Martin Hanamy. There were good performances too from Michael Duignan, Daithí Regan, Johnny Dooley, Kevin Martin and Shane McGuckin. But the former champions, from whom much was expected, never seemed to fire on all cylinders to enable them to upset the better balanced Clare team. There was the odd flash followed by periods of obscurity, which was the direct opposite to Clare who had the greater passion during long spells when the game hung in the balance. The arrival of Eamonn Taffe on the scene brought the rich reward of the goal and inevitably the MacCarthy Cup. Overall, it wasn't the most thrilling of All-Ireland matches, though the finale did help to keep both sets of supporters on a knife edge until the final whistle.

1996 FINAL: JOY FOR WEXFORD HURLERS

1 September 1996   Wexford 1-13, Limerick 0-14
Attendance: 65,849   Referee: P. Horan (Offaly)
Top scorer: T. Dempsey (Wexford) 1-3

Wexford strode the scene at Croke Park displaying power, courage and determination to capture their first All-Ireland senior hurling title since their previous success in 1968. Their victims, Limerick, lost their second title challenge in three years, a rather cold statistic that revived memories of their 1994 defeat at the hands of Offaly. Wexford's win was uncannily reminiscent of Clare's last-gasp victory over Offaly the previous year, a sequence of events that crop up occasionally at All-Ireland final level.

The question could be posed: did Limerick's decision to shorten their pre-match parade march at the Canal end upset their equilibrium? The Wexford team continued their march up to Hill 16 where, with hurleys raised aloft, they acknowledged the cheers of their delirious supporters. The ways of some men can be strange indeed. The Shannonsiders were hell bent on regaining the coveted MacCarthy Cup which they had last won in 1973 when they were captained by Eamonn Grimes and bolstered by a fabulous display at centre back by Eamonn Cregan.

In Wexford's case, a transformed team under new manager Liam Griffin had built up an unparalleled pre-match eminence that boded no good for all other championship contenders, Limerick included. They had a tougher road to travel to reach the final in comparison with their Munster opponents. But with each obstacle the stature of Wexford grew and the final bonding was completed when they disposed of Galway in the All-Ireland semi-final. Limerick had a facile win against Antrim in their semi-final test, and perhaps a stiffer game would have prepared them better for what lay ahead. Griffin had instilled the necessary belief in his charges that the winning of an All-Ireland crown was in the hands of the players themselves. He had added one extra ingredient to the match preparations that would fire them to unprecedented heights—passion with a capital P. It was one facet of this final that was lacking in Limerick's battle armour, and they really needed it at crucial periods. Wexford also benefited from the game against Galway. It was, as Wexford liked it, tough and uncompromising, and no weaknesses were exposed, so Griffin and his team selectors were feeling very confident that their match plan would stand the test of whatever Limerick had to offer. Limerick, on the other hand, needed to take all the chances that were offered to them, but sadly they never reached the desired standard, and as the game advanced their performance level dropped alarmingly. The quick, relentless Wexford marking did untold damage as the Limerick forwards struggled to get their shooting properly focused. This had not been a problem in earlier matches, but when it came to the crunch and against such formidable opponents as Wexford, there was no relief. The Leinster men dictated the play and their standards were never allowed to drop, even when corner forward Eamonn Scallan was sent off in the 34th minute, reducing Wexford to fourteen men. Scores were level at the time, Wexford 1-7, Limerick 0-10.

Limerick were thrown a lifeline for the second half as they were going to enjoy a numerical advantage, but that dream was to get its comeuppance. The margin was to remain static as Limerick battled bravely to get the scores that might bring them salvation, but there was no way through a rock-like Wexford defensive set-up unwilling to bend. That apart, Limerick adopted a very cautious approach and were not willing to match Wexford's passion in their quest for match-winning scores, efforts that were needed more by the Munster champions if their cause was to succeed.

It was a glorious occasion for Wexford instead. It was a complete team performance in which every player filled a vital role and lived up to its name, the Model County. The full back line of Colm Kehoe, who was brilliant, Ger Cush and John O'Connor ruled fearlessly and revelled in the pressure of the occasion. Liam Dunne and Larry O'Gorman did not treat the Limerick half forwards with kid gloves. The hurling was hard, and it was no place for the faint hearted. The dismissal of Eamonn Scallan appeared to bring a bigger response from the Wexford men and Limerick's numerical advantage was never allowed to blossom. However, the Wexford attack found the going tough against a resolute Limerick defence which was never overrun. But Larry Murphy, Martin Storey, Tom Dempsey and Garry Laffan took their chances of scores brilliantly. Limerick goalkeeper Joe Quaid enhanced his reputation with a very impressive display between the posts and could not be faulted for the Wexford goal. The best triers on the Limerick side were Stephen McDonagh, Dermot Clarke, Ciaran Carey, Mark Foley, Barry Foley, and to a lesser extent Mike Houlihan and T. J. Ryan.

After the game Liam Griffin paid a special tribute to his opposite number, Tom Ryan. 'He is a man who has done much for hurling and Limerick and I hope he will not be judged on this defeat. He will be feeling deep disappointment, especially for his players, but I know he will not take this defeat lying down. We need men like him to remain in hurling.' Griffin will always be revered in Wexford for his phenomenal achievement that led to Wexford gaining their sixth All-Ireland crown and the coveted MacCarthy Cup.

1997 FINAL: CLARE ARE TRUE CHAMPIONS

14 September 1997   Clare 0-20, Tipperary 2-13
Attendance: 65,575   Referee: D. Murphy (Wexford)
Top scorer: J. O'Connor (Clare) 0-7

It was the first all-Munster All-Ireland hurling final and it was truly a magnificent occasion in which Clare had their greatness as a hurling force well and truly affirmed in a heart-palpitating one point win over Tipperary at Croke Park. It was as close as that, but a touch of controversy over a disallowed Tipperary point left thousands of Tipperary supporters very angry at the final whistle. As matters transpired, the point that Tipperary claimed was valid but which was ruled out by the umpires, was a major talking point when the match ended. Tipperary got the final chance to save the day a minute from full time. A point would have equalised the match when Conor Gleeson's long-range effort came sailing towards the Clare posts. But sadly for Tipp it went the wrong side of the posts. A minute before that, Tipperary, who were still battling away with great fervour as the tension was rising, created another scoring opportunity. Clare were leading 0-20 to 2-13 at the time. Brian O'Meara picked out the unmarked John Leahy. He was near enough to the Clare goal area but far enough out to go a bit further if he so wished. The Mullinahone man opted for swift action and let fly a cracking shot, aimed for the left corner of the Clare net. The eagle eyed Clare goalie David Fitzgerald waited and watched Leahy's effort all the way and pounced. A goal would have won the game at that stage. He moved swiftly and turned the ball around the posts for a 65 from which Gleeson failed to score. That brought proceedings to a close as thousands of Clare supporters invaded the pitch to congratulate their heroes.

The controversial Aidan Ryan point came in the fourteenth minute of the first half. He struck the ball high from the left wing towards the Clare posts, and one of the umpires raised his hand to signify a score. Clare players swarmed around to protest and the umpire then signalled a wide. Furious Tipperary players complained about the decision to disallow the score. When referee Dickie Murphy ran in and spoke to the umpires, a wide was again signalled. It was an important match incident in view of the final outcome, which unfortunately went against Tipperary. No further action followed.

The blueprint for Clare's victory was drawn up by the Banner County's midfield partnership of Colin Lynch and Ollie Baker, who formed the firm foundation for Clare's thrilling one point success. While other areas were suffering from unease as the Tipperary forwards fought and secured telling scores, Baker and Lynch kept their poise at midfield. Tipperary were leading 0-9 to 0-3, but Clare got into a scoring mood following points from Jamesie O'Connor. Niall Gilligan, enjoying a new role at right corner forward, opened his shoulders and casually knocked over a point. Ollie Baker fired in a long delivery and found a willing Gilligan waiting to collect and score another point. Tipperary's lead was now down to three points coming up to the interval before John Leahy added a further point to leave the Premier County ahead 0-10 to 0-6.

The Clare dressing room was the happier one facing into the second period. Manager Ger Loughnane told his squad that a four point deficit could be quickly wiped out and their patience and hunger would be rewarded.

The first half was brimful of high-class hurling by both teams The exchanges lived up to expectations, hip to hip tussles, exciting bouts of play and a fervour that belongs exclusively to the Munster scene on a good day. Both sets of forwards could point to a number of scoring chances missed because of the tension—due mainly to the very tight marking imposed by the respective defenders. It was Clare who finally broke the mould. But for Tommy Dunne's excellent work in creating Tipperary's scoring total in the first half (he pointed six frees), the Premier County could have been in trouble. The Munster champions set to work on manager Loughnane's words of wisdom from the start of the second half. Liam Doyle pointed from the middle of the field in the opening minute, followed by another from Conor Clancy and one from Ger O'Loughlin. The wind of change had suddenly arrived for Clare and was now reflected in their whole approach as confidence replaced anxiety and a more positive mood was evident in all their players. There was a noticeable change in Tipperary's demeanour as their half-time lead was reduced to a single point, 0-10 to 0-9. The Tipp defenders paid the price for conceding frees, which Jamsesie O'Connor enjoyed popping between the Tipperary posts. Clare pressure began to pay off and their scoring total increased. They now led 0-17 to 0-13, but Tipperary hung on tenaciously. Their cause was not yet lost. John Leahy floated a ball in from the left wing. Dinny Cahill, the smallest player in the area, somehow caught it cleanly and fired it to the Clare net. The Clare defenders rounded on the umpire and pleaded for a square ball. Referee Dickie Murphy was having none of it, and signalled that it was a goal—new hope for Tipperary. O'Connor cashed in on a Tipperary fluff and added a point, 0-18 to 1-13. But the issue was far from settled. The excitement was at fever pitch when Tommy Dunne sent a 65 into the Clare square, where Eugene O'Neill met it first time straight to the Clare net. Tipperary 2-13, Clare 0-18. Five minutes remained in the game. It was in that closing period that the destination of the 1997 All-Ireland title was finally decided, and the men from Clare were the worthy recipients. Ollie Baker levelled for Clare, who had seen their five point lead turned into a one point deficit. Colin Lynch went to work again for Clare and managed to play a ball out to the unmarked Jamesie O'Connor, who had the noted distinction of firing over the all-important winning point.

It is safe to say that when Tipperary sat down to analyse the team performance, they must have asked, how could their solid attacking force have failed to score a single point in those final closing minutes. Clare did, and they were now the MacCarthy Cup winners and All-Ireland champions. Tipperary bravely battled all the way up but went away empty-handed—the cruelty of modern day sport.

1998 FINAL: OFFALY KEEP THE FAITH

14 September 1998   Offaly 2-16, Kilkenny 1-13
Attendance: 65,491   Referee: D. Murphy (Wexford)
Top scorer: Brian Whelehan (Offaly) 1-6

Offaly, winners of two All-Ireland titles, one National League crown and two All-Ireland club awards to date, added a third MacCarthy Cup to their growing honours list when they defeated one of their keenest rivals, Kilkenny, to capture a third All-Ireland senior hurling crown in a thriller at Croke Park. Shrewd tactical switches by their team manager Michael Bond and his selectors helped the midlanders to achieve a sensational result against a highly fancied Kilkenny side. Offaly's success was all the more meritorious in view of the fact that they had come through the qualifiers to achieve All-Ireland glory. It must also be mentioned that Offaly were held to a draw by Clare in their All-Ireland semi-final and the replay of that match ended when the referee played short time with Clare leading 1-16 to Offaly's 2-10. A replay was ordered, which took place on 29 August, with Offaly emerging as winners on an 0-16 to 0-13 scoreline. So history will record that Offaly are the only team to date to have played eight matches to win the coveted All-Ireland crown. Even their presence as All-Ireland qualifiers brought them plenty of criticism, but they had the last laugh.

The big talking point arising from the pre-match rumours about Brian Whelehan proved to be true. The truth of the matter was that big Brian was sniffling and sneezing all day on Friday and Saturday. He worked in a bar on Friday night. Sunday morning brought no relief and his participation in the All-Ireland that day was in grave doubt. The selectors were in a quandary, but the decision was taken to play him as his presence was essential on such an important occasion. After fourteen minutes the alarm bells were ringing. Whelehan was not making any headway against Kilkenny's Brian McEvoy, who had picked off two points and created another for Andy Comerford. Whelehan was switched to right half forward in the hope that he might rediscover his form. A further shift saw him at full forward in the second half, in which period he totted up the magnificent tally of 1-4 against Kilkenny full back Pat O'Neill, who had lorded it over all opposition in the opening half. The impact on the other Offaly team players was dramatic. Instead of being the hunted, they were now the hunters as the opening for All-Ireland success looked very positive. More important still was the effect Whelehan's scoring feats were having in other areas of the team. Kevin Martin, who had brilliant displays in the earlier rounds at wing back, had the measure of Kilkenny dynamic star forward D. J. Carey, whom he shadowed and confined to four points from frees.

The exchanges in the first half were very routine and no positive picture was emerging. Kilkenny led 1-7 to 0-8 at the interval, a lead which didn't flatter them. Whelehan and Carey were the free-takers for the respective teams and the match was tied at 0-12 to 1-9 at the 47th minute. But the first half was a hurried affair, and Charlie Carter's goal for Kilkenny, courtesy of a slackness on the part of the Offaly defenders, didn't bring any great change in the game's trend or the pursuit of the objective. Offaly were to change that situation very rapidly. The game needed an uplift and it was provided by Whelehan's point two minutes into the second half and another from a free two minutes later. Kilkenny maintained their usual doggedness and Charlie Carter and D. J. Carey kept in touch with points to steady the ship. Five minutes later, Offaly's John Troy pointed a free, to which D. J. Carey replied. Whelehan was on target again from a placed ball to level the match. After taming Jamesie O'Connor of Clare last time out, Kevin Martin kept the shackles on the dangerous D. J.

With Kilkenny's danger man held, there was an upsurge in the Offaly approach following a well-taken Joe Errity goal. The spell was broken and Offaly were immediately roused in most parts of the field. This applied particularly to their defensive set-up which very much curtailed the efforts of the Kilkenny forwards. The foundation had been put in place by the brilliance of Michael Duignan, reborn under the managerial skills of Michael Bond, who came speeding out of defence, ball in hand, shrugged off a couple of stiff challenges and shot over the bar. The Offaly supporters were now in full cry as the Kilkenny spirit appeared shattered. But more important still was the effect the game was having on the Offaly players. They sensed that the door to All-Ireland greatness was already open to them. Kevin Martin, who had already made an unmistakeable impact, produced a stupendous piece of hurling skill on the left wing by tapping the ball over a Kilkenny opponent, rounding him, collecting the ball and dropping it into space at the other end of the play. The magnificence of Martin, Duignan and team captain Hubert Rigney's efforts helped to bring out the best in the other Offaly defenders, Simon Whelehan, Kevin Kinahan and Martin Hanamy. Brian Whelehan's crucial 65th minute goal was masterminded by a whole series of attacking play when Offaly were in the ascendancy. John Troy got a touch to a loose ball and played it away to John Ryan. He fed it to Joe Errity on the left, who coolly flicked the ball to Brian Whelehan, who finished to the net. Offaly then led 2-15 to 1-13. Kilkenny failed to produce a score in the closing five minutes. So ended a very remarkable contest which, at the halfway stage, appeared wide open, but the value of the shrewd switching of players and its immediate effect weighed heavily in Offaly's favour. For once, a fancied Kilkenny failed to impose their will on proceedings, nor were they able to find the means of halting Offaly's indefatigable spirit. Kilkenny's title hopes started to slide in the second half.

While Offaly's All-Ireland victory was duly celebrated, one of the men primarily responsible was team manager Michael Bond. He was an unknown quantity in the history of hurling and took over the job on 10 July. When asked by the media after the All-Ireland success would he continue on as manager, Michael Bond said (much to the amusement of his audience): 'I have achieved what I wanted to achieve with Offaly hurling. I had a job to do in a very short period of time. That was nine weeks ago and that is long enough for anyone to get a team right for the All-Ireland.' But when asked what his response would be if the Offaly County Board asked the Galway man to stay on in the manager's job, he replied, 'Perhaps when I retire from the job of principal of St Brigid's Vocational School in Loughrea I will be able to come back.' Michael Bond stayed on as Offaly team manager for 1999, but Offaly were beaten in the Leinster final that year by Kilkenny 5-14 to 1-16 and were subsequently beaten by Cork in the 1999 All-Ireland semi-final.

1999 FINAL: CORK WIN WITH FINAL FLOURISH

13 September 1999   Cork 0-13, Kilkenny 0-12
Attendance: 62,989   Referee: P. O'Connor (Limerick)
Top scorer: H. Shefflin (Kilkenny) 0-5

Cork edged this All-Ireland senior hurling final winning verdict over great rivals Kilkenny in what was one of the least stirring confrontations between the two hurling forces seen at Croke Park. The outcome was a personal triumph for Cork manager Jimmy Barry Murphy, who had experienced the entire gamut of emotions associated with the game as a player and now as manager. He braved the consequences of fielding a team with an average age of 22 while adding the necessary element of experienced players as well. The net result was an astounding victory over a formidable Kilkenny side who were firm favourites with the bookmakers. It was billed as a final to outdo all others to date, but sadly it fell far below expectations. Some might blame the conditions (a tally of 34 wides was shared by the combatants). At the close, Cork deservedly emerged with the honours, capturing their 28th All-Ireland crown and the coveted MacCarthy Cup.

For the hurling purist viewing the contest, it simply did not rank with some of the great epics of former years. Cork would undoubtedly gain more from the outcome because of the inclusion of so many new faces to senior inter-county fare—a tribute to Barry Murphy and his selectors. The Cork players had great faith and respect for their manager and left no stone unturned in their efforts to ensure that success would repay his confidence in them. It goes without saying that the work of the better known Cork stars who played in this decider proved a formidable factor in the outcome. The only area where the Leesiders had problems for a spell was at midfield, where the dominance of Kilkenny's Andy Comerford and Denis Byrne remained unchallenged for a very long period before the penny dropped and a change was made. Cork's Timmy McCarthy was switched from right half forward to midfield, and the gap was closed. McCarthy's move came a minute before half-time, but his surging runs and point-taking had the Kilkenny defence on tenterhooks every time he gained possession. It is fair to say that McCarthy's move to the centre of the field was a very obvious priority, and it turned out to be one of the match-winning Cork moves. At half-time Kilkenny led 0-5 to 0-4, but the extraordinary aspect of the scoring was that at no stage were there more than four points separating the teams at any given time. There was tension and alarm in evidence in one of the lowest-scoring games at All-Ireland level. On Kilkenny's side was the accomplished and noteworthy D. J. Carey, who invariably left an imprint on the exchanges, but not on this occasion. The free-taker was Henry Shefflin (0-5, four from frees), which meant that

Carey failed to find the range and produce a score for the game's entirety. He did have a goaling chance in the 66th minute when placed by sub P. J. Delaney. Surrounded by Cork backs, the Kilkenny star was unable to swing his hurley and his kicked effort hit the side netting. It was another disappointing day for the black and amber brigade. Only two points separated the teams at the time, Cork 0-13, Kilkenny 0-11, and Carey's attempt at a goal proved to be his last chance for glory with time running out. He found no salvation either in the various positions he tried to fill when opposed by Seán Óg Ó hAilpín, Brian Corcoran, Diarmuid O'Sullivan and John Browne, who kept clean sheets against his efforts for badly needed scores. There was no joy either for the other accepted Kilkenny sharpshooters John Power, Charlie Carter and Brian McEvoy, who were never allowed to express their talents in the scoring department, much to the chagrin of the Kilkenny supporters. The game's honours must go to the Cork defensive set-up who kept a tight rein on the Kilkenny attack, rendering them impotent for long periods, a crucial factor in the end result. It must be stressed that in any analysis of the game the effect of the torrential rain, which fell all through the match, had a distinct bearing on the scoring efforts of the teams. When the scores were needed, it fell to the Cork forwards to provide them, and that was the prime difference between the two sides. It was perhaps fitting that Cork should win that particular All-Ireland final because it was the last final of the 1990s and will be best remembered by the gallant Leesiders and the men who achieved it.

Chapter 10 ↶

THE NEW CENTURY

The 2000 to 2008 All-Ireland hurling finals

A new name was not added to the list of MacCarthy Cup winners during the first nine seasons of this new century, 2000 to 2008 inclusive. However, the appeal of hurling and the increased accommodation at Croke Park following the completion of the major developments there resulted in 80,000-plus attendances over four successive finals in the latter years of the decade.

The 2006 final, in which Cork's hopes of a third successive title were ended by Kilkenny, drew the largest attendance at 82,275. This now ranks as the third highest attendance at a MacCarthy Cup tie.

A feature of the decade was Kilkenny's achievement in recording their first-ever treble of MacCarthy Cup wins—2006, 07 and 08. That was also their first All-Ireland senior treble since 1911, 12 and 13. Kilkenny gave what many regarded as the best-ever display in any final when completing their MacCarthy Cup treble with a resounding win over Waterford in 2008. Whether or not the performance merited ranking as the greatest ever is a debatable point, but what is beyond dispute is that the Noresiders produced a sparkling array of skills, craft, teamwork and scoring that was as close to the perfect performance as made little difference. Three goals, 30 points, a whopping winning margin of 23 points and so many superb individual displays that it was almost impossible to select a man of the match, added up to a display to cherish. Great credit for Kilkenny's achievements of late must go to Brian Cody, a former All-Ireland title winning captain and top-class hurler. His latest success was his sixth time managing a MacCarthy Cup winning team in this new decade.

Another noteworthy feature of the early years of the decade was D. J. Carey's achievement in earning the only major honour that until then was missing from his great range of distinctions. One of the outstanding hurlers of any era, he joined the ranks of All-Ireland title winning captains when he led Kilkenny to a successful defence of the MacCarthy Cup in

2003 at the expense of Cork. The success earned the gifted Carey his fifth senior medal since 1992.

The decade also saw Limerick and Waterford achieve rare appearances in the showpiece game of the year. In 2007 the Shannonsiders qualified for their first MacCarthy Cup appearance since 2006 when they went down to Wexford. However, their hopes of a first cup win since 1973 were ended by Kilkenny. Waterford returned to final action in 2008 for the first time since losing to Kilkenny in 1963, only to find the Cats in such dynamic form.

Only three counties—Kilkenny, Cork and Tipperary—inscribed their names on the Roll of Honour in the opening years of this new decade. Although Eoin Kelly did not win an All-Ireland senior medal with Waterford, he still earned a special place in the review by scoring a splendid 1-9 in the unsuccessful outing against Kilkenny in 2008. That not only ranked as the top individual match return of the period under review, but it also earned Kelly a place well up in the rankings of leading individual scoring achievements in the MacCarthy Cup story.

On the refereeing front, Barry Kelly stepped into the history books when he took charge of the 2006 senior final. He became the first Westmeath native to referee the top hurling match of the year. A member of the St Oliver Plunkett's hurling club in Mullingar, Kelly refereed his second final in 2008. He was one of three referees who took control of two finals in the decade.

Clare, with Davy Fitzgerald in goal, unsuccessfully contested the 2002 final against Kilkenny. He was back on All-Ireland final duty in 2008 as the Waterford manager, having taken up that position only a few months earlier—his first appointment in that role.

Galway unsuccessfully contested two finals, 2001 and 05.

Statistics

Greatest attendance	82,186 in 2008
Busiest referee	P. O'Connor (Limerick) 2001, 03; A. MacSuibhne (Dublin) 2002, 04; B. Kelly (Westmeath) 2006, 08
Highest team score	3-30 (39 points) by Kilkenny 2008
Highest score by losing team	2-15 (21 points) 2001
Highest winning margin	23 points by Kilkenny 2008
Lowest winning margin	3 points by Tipperary 2001, Kilkenny 2003 and Kilkenny 2006

Tony Doran of Wexford was one of the finest full forwards of the 1970s, a bustling, physical threat to every defence he faced.

Cork and Kilkenny in 1978, as one of the great Cork teams marches to a three in a row. (*RTÉ*)

The Limerick championship winning side of 1973. (*Cork Examiner*)

Cork and Wexford fight for possession in the 1976 final. (*RTÉ*)

The Galway team of 1980 that ended a drought which had lasted since 1923. (*Sportsfile*)

The Galway goalkeeper
Michael Connolly blocks
the ball to frustrate another
Limerick attack in the 1980
final. (*Sportsfile*)

Brian Cody led Kilkenny to
their championship triumph
in 1982. Twenty years later he
went on to become the most
successful manager in the
history of the modern game.

A historic victory for Offaly in 1981 as Pádraig Horan lifts the Liam MacCarthy Cup after their victory against Galway. (*Sportsfile*)

A general view of Hill 16 during the 1987 final between Galway and Kilkenny. (*Sportsfile*)

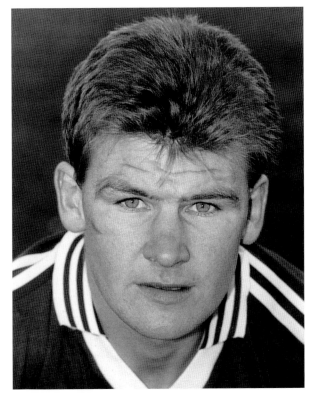

Peter Finnerty, a key member of the Galway sides that won in 1987 and 1988, later became a respected media pundit on the game.

Pat Fox of Tipperary
is tackled by Galway's
Ollie Kilkenny in the
1988 final. (*Sportsfile*)

Ken Hogan was a key member of the
Tipperary teams that ended the long
drought in 1989 and 1991. He was
one of the great goalkeepers of the
modern era.

The talisman of these Tipperary teams of 1989 and 1991 was Nicholas English, shown here celebrating one of his side's goals against Antrim in the 1989 final. (*Sportsfile*)

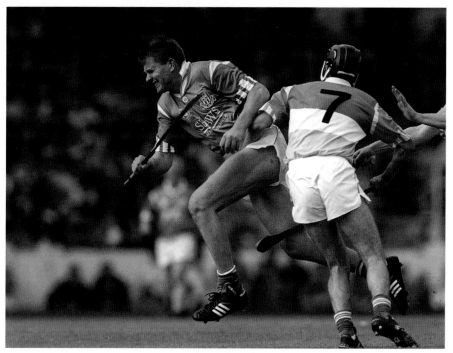

1994 saw the greatest smash and grab in the history of the modern championship, as Offaly scored 2-5 in the last six minutes to snatch a game that Limerick seemed to have won. (*Sportsfile*)

Ger Loughnane: not always loved
but always respected, he was
indispensable to the great romance
that was Clare hurling in the second
half of the 1990s. (*Sportsfile*)

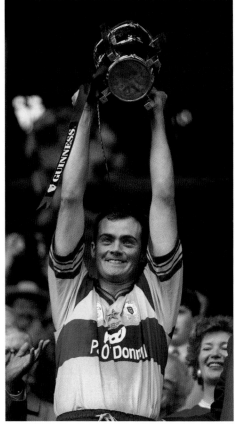

They had waited since 1914 for this
moment: the Clare captain Anthony Daly
lifts the Liam MacCarthy Cup after
Clare's victory over Offaly in the 1995
final. (*Sportsfile*)

Another long wait ended in 1996 when Wexford won their first championship for 28 years. Once again Limerick were the runners-up. This photograph shows one of the Wexford stalwarts, Larry O'Gorman, in action. (*Sportsfile*)

In 1999 a young and inexperienced Cork team surprised everyone by winning the championship. Their manager, former playing legend Jimmy Barry Murphy, brings the cup to their fans on Hill 16. (*Sportsfile*)

Wexford supporters at the 1996 final. (*Sportsfile*)

Ben O'Connor of Cork in action against Canice Brennan of Kilkenny in the 1999 final. (*Sportsfile*)

The Cork team of the early 2000s was one of the most controversial in the history of the game, twice going on strike in disputes with the county board. But they proved their point on the pitch, winning back-to-back All-Irelands in 2004 and 2005. In this photograph their 2005 captain Seán Óg Ó hAilpín lifts the trophy. (*Sportsfile*)

Most celebrated hurler of the modern era, D. J. Carey of Kilkenny. (*Sportsfile*)

Brian Corcoran of Cork runs past the Liam MacCarthy Cup at the start of the 2005 final. (*Sportsfile*)

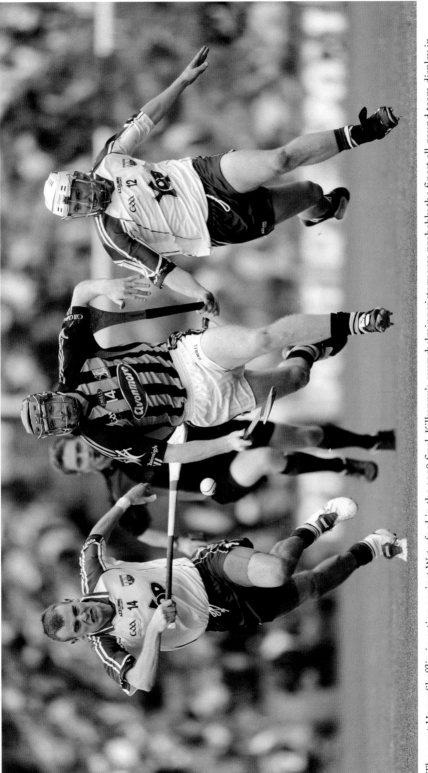

The great Henry Shefflin in action against Waterford in the 2008 final. Kilkenny's overwhelming victory was probably the finest all-round team display in modern Irish sporting history. Kilkenny completed a historic three in a row with a performance that approached perfection. (*Sportsfile*)

The great Kilkenny squad of 2008. (*Sportsfile*)

Highest individual score	1-9 by Eoin Kelly (Waterford) 2008
Highest individual goals tally	2 by D. J. Carey (Kilkenny) 2000; M. O'Leary (Tipperary) 2002 and E. Brennan (Kilkenny) 2008
Goalless finals	One, 2004
Finals in which winning team failed to score a goal	2004
Finals in which losing team failed to score a goal	2002, 04
Best points tally by winning team	30 by Kilkenny 2008
Best points tally by losing team	19 by Clare 2002
Top scoring final on aggregate	2008
Lowest scoring final on aggregate	2004
Replays	None
Most successful captain	No hurler captained more than one title winning team

2000 FINAL: D. J. STAMPS HIS CLASS

11 September 2000   Kilkenny 5-15, Offaly 1-14
Attendance: 61,493   Referee: W. Barrett (Tipperary)
Top scorer: D. J. Carey (Kilkenny) 2-4

Displaying power, pace and poise, Kilkenny simply annihilated Offaly in one of the most disappointing All-Ireland contests between the two counties in recent years. Kilkenny took the field fully bent on reversing the setback experienced two years previously when they were one point losers to an Offaly team that fully deserved the honours. Kilkenny showed a far different face on this occasion. They were brimming with confidence and possessed with an unstoppable determination to avoid chalking up a three-in-a-row run of defeats at All-Ireland final level. They signalled their intentions right from the start that only a clear-cut victory would ease the humiliation of that defeat suffered two years before. There was a new focus on matters, a very understandable approach, that was inevitably going to destroy the hopes of an Offaly team totally unprepared for the fire and brimstone which was to follow. This was to be Kilkenny's day and it depended on the ability of three of their formidable full forwards, D. J. Carey, Charlie Carter and Henry Shefflin, whose combined scoring total on the day added up to 4-10—a crushing blow to Offaly's prospects. Carter scored 1-3, Carey 2-4 and Shefflin 1-3, a very positive exhibition of marks-manship and quick thinking all round. And remarkably, that combined scoring total was two points more than their combined totals scored in their last two All-Ireland finals. The predatory finishing of the trio was one of the highlights of a game. Carey, held scoreless from play against Cork the previous year, unleashed all the power and hurling expertise which has made him a phenomenon in the game. His opening goal after six minutes was an opportunistic one. Capitalising on a silly error by an Offaly defender, he grabbed possession, soloed through a hesitant defence and whipped the ball to the Offaly net. The significance of that goal, and the manner in which it was finished, set the agenda for the rest of the match. Offaly's prospects looked beyond redemption when they trailed 3-8 to 0-7 at the break. The switch of Brian Whelehan from defence to attack the year before proved a master stroke for Offaly, but the rich result then was not to be repeated. The midlanders were now facing a very different Kilkenny defensive set-up which was not given to making errors. Indeed, the number of Offaly scoring chances were very much restricted. It took great pride and very hard work from the Offaly forwards to cut Kilkenny's lead to eight points, 3-10 to 0-11, after 45 minutes, but a goal was badly needed to ease their plight and create a possible revival. That dream quickly faded and it was Kilkenny who broke through to achieve it instead. Canice Brennan floated in an outfield lob to the Offaly square and the very alert Henry Shefflin was on hand to stab it home. It was panic stations for the Offaly defenders. Kilkenny midfielder, the polished Denis Byrne, fired over a point to put his team four goals clear and on their way to the easiest All-Ireland win in their hallowed history. Friends and foes began the trek to the exits now, firmly convinced that the MacCarthy Cup was well on its way to the banks of the Suir.

It was a sad occasion for Offaly who had to battle courageously to avoid total humiliation, in comparison to their sterling display some weeks previously when they put paid to a formidable Cork challenge in the semi-final. They did launch several belated attacks and in the 59th minute Johnny Pilkington worked his way through for a goal. Two more points followed to give the scoreboard a more respectable look. But Kilkenny finished with a flourish. Substitute Eddie Brennan whipped home a goal, and in injury time Carey and Carter knocked over pressure points to crown a masterful performance. Offaly had a number of problems which they were not given time to rectify. The defence leaked like a sieve and the changes tried never looked like succeeding. Kilkenny always held a grip at midfield and the Offaly forwards were mostly restricted to single points. The three Kilkenny 'terrorists', Carter, Carey and Shefflin, with their impressive individual tallies made it all too easy for the Cats. Backed by that scoreline, their confidence grew rapidly and everything they attempted appeared to bear fruit. Kilkenny gave a magnificent team performance, something Offaly just couldn't match on the day. But perhaps more important still was the fact that, having lost the two previous finals, they made doubly sure there would not be a third setback. Hunger for success and patience while earning it are mighty weapons when the need arises.

2001 FINAL: DUNNE SHOOTS TIPP INTO ALL-IRELAND ORBIT

10 September 2001   Tipperary 2-18, Galway 2-15
Attendance: 68,512   Referee: P. O'Connor (Limerick)
Top scorer: E. Cloonan (Galway) 1-5

Tommy Dunne from Toomevara, a stylish midfielder, delivered a man-of-the-match display when he captained Tipperary to a majestic victory over Galway in the All-Ireland hurling final at Croke Park, and in so doing brought the MacCarthy Cup back to the Premier County for the first time since 1991. The little village of Toomevara had another hero, Matt Hassett, who had also become a legendary figure when he captained Tipperary to All-Ireland glory in 1961 against Dublin. Dunne's performance against Galway measured up in every way to some of the best served up by other illustrious figures of the past. He gave his side an early lead with a marvellous point from the left-hand side of the field after only three minutes, and leading by example he added four more points to his tally in an awe-inspiring display of point-taking. Dunne's commanding presence in centrefield proved a rare morale booster and gave Tipp an edge that they never relinquished. It was a game that was going to be won the hard way, thanks to the spirited resistance mounted by Galway, who had the capacity to make the Munster men fight for every score in a most entertaining contest. But Tipperary were blessed with accomplished marksmen, which proved essential in their quest for match-winning scores. A goal from Mark O'Leary in the 23rd minute helped the Munster champions to a 1-6 to 0-3 lead. Galway quickly responded with Eugene Cloonan whipping home a goal after Brendan Cummins had saved brilliantly from an Alan Kerins shot. That should have energised the Connacht men to put more pressure on Tipperary. But Tipp were unfazed by the westerners, who were playing against the wind at the time, and showed plenty of composure in defence while their forwards fired over three unanswered points to stretch their lead to six points. Galway's reply was very emphatic and, displaying equal conviction, they slammed over four points to leave the half-time position, Tipp 1-9 Galway 1-7. It was Galway's most rewarding spell and provided the Munster team with plenty of food for thought at the midway break.

Galway fans were hoping for a repeat of that late first half splurge of scores to boost their chances of success as the teams came out for the second half. But it was Tipperary who took over the initiative instead. Mark O'Leary, ever vigilant for a scoring opening, chased in after a lobbed delivery to the Galway square and shot past Michael Cummins to the net in the 39th minute. That gift score really stabilised Tipperary as they faced into the second half wind now five points clear. It was a firm base on which to launch a winning surge. Tipperary tried doggedly to keep Galway at bay, and to their credit the westerners did not submit to Tipperary rule for long periods in the second half. Galway mounted plenty of pressure charges but they could never break down the strong Tipperary defensive cover, manned by goalie Brendan Cummins. Brilliant between the posts and brave in some of his uncanny advances, Cummins frustrated the Galway attack, along with Thomas Costello, who bore the brunt of Galway's penetrating sorties, aided by Philip Maher, who adopted a man-marking role with Galway danger man Eugene Cloonan, while Tommy Dunne always seemed destined to give a massive performance on the biggest stage. Eoin Kelly was a brilliant free-taker, while Mark Healy's opportunistic goals proved match-winners. Aidan Ryan's ball-winning expertise made up for some shooting misses, while Lar Corbett enjoyed good work when moved to the wing. The experience gained by Tipperary over the past three seasons stood to them when it was needed most on this important occasion. Sadly for Galway, they never appeared to have the intuitive survival instinct when it came to breaking Tipperary's stranglehold from the outset. It must be pointed out though in Galway's favour, that they did at least score more than Clare, Limerick or Wexford against Tipperary, but their giveaway rate was also the highest. When Galway would sit down and analyse their performance, they might have considered their relatively slow start, some poor first half shooting and an inability to raise momentum levels sufficiently in the closing stages.

2002 FINAL: CLASSY CATS CREAM CLARE

9 September 2002   Kilkenny 2-20, Clare 0-19
Attendance: 76,254   Referee: A. MacSuibhne (Dublin)
Top scorer: H. Shefflin (Kilkenny) 1-7

Dublin referee Aodan MacSuibhne, who gave an excellent performance, raised his hand and blew the final whistle, which allowed Kilkenny to celebrate their 27th All-Ireland senior hurling success in a manner befitting very worthy champions. Opponents Clare had their hopes of a fourth crown well and truly dashed under the heavy weight of forward failure. So, Kilkenny moved to within one title of Cork in the Guinness All-Ireland honours table after a game in which so much that was predicted just failed to ignite. It wasn't Kilkenny's fault; they were really a class apart on this occasion, winning the senior and minor finals by a combined total of 21 points. Clare unfortunately were never allowed to produce a semblance of their true ability by opponents who were fully geared to meet all contingencies. It was all so impressive for the black and amber brigade, whose supremacy manifested itself when one hero, D. J. Carey, finished off a goal from a diagonal pass from another hero, Henry Shefflin, after three minutes. The signs were beginning to look ominous even at that early stage that luck was not going to attend Clare's efforts when a couple of good scoring opportunities were allowed to slip away. In a game of such importance chances of goals can never be ignored and the Munster men were to pay a dear price for that failure factor. Facts speak louder than words. Clare's nineteen points provided the perfect illustration of their attacking weakness. Six points came from their centre back; four came from Jamesie O'Connor frees; midfielders Lynch and Baker landed three between them, as did substitutes Gearoid Considine and Andrew Quinn. That leaves just three points from play between the six starting forwards, a miserable tally. Kilkenny by comparison can show that 2-19 was compiled from play by the original starting forward division. Henry Shefflin and D. J. Carey fired over 1-6 each from play, while they were also in punishing mood from frees, adding another 0-7 between them. It can be truly said that the whole purpose of having scoring forwards is to win matches. The Cats fulfilled that maxim very adequately, but Clare missed out.

At 1-2 to 0-0 after six minutes, Kilkenny were in a happy frame of mind and that feeling grew as the game progressed. Kilkenny's tactical plan of straight down the middle attacks by Martin Comerford and Henry Shefflin appeared to lessen the power of formidable Clare stars of other occasions, Seán McMahon and Brian Lohan, who were unable to cope with problems constantly popping up in other berths around them. Likewise at midfield where Colin Lynch was fighting a lone battle on two fronts against Kilkenny's very powerful pairing of Andy Comerford and Derek Lyng. D. J. Carey, who had a very disappointing performance against Cork in the 1999 All-Ireland final when he failed to score from play, declared that they would be back. But it was Clare who were to feel the awesome power of Carey this time as he produced all the class and hurling skills that had made him one of the most feared forwards in the game. He was brought back prior to the semi-final by the very astute team manager Brian Cody, a former star defender, a decision that was to pay rich dividends. Not alone did Carey show his proficiencies when picking off crucial scores, but he also created openings for others to get on the scoresheet, a tribute to his unselfish nature. With such talented and elegant players as Shefflin and Carey spearheading Kilkenny's All-Ireland bid, there was little room for error, though Clare, who could not be faulted for lack of effort, did make them sweat on some occasions.

One of Clare's best periods came just after half-time when the Banner men set about cutting back an interval deficit of 1-11 to 0-8. They outscored Kilkenny by 0-4 to 0-1 in the first thirteen minutes to trail by 1-12 to 0-12 and could have been closer but for misses by Markham and Lynch. It was perhaps the only time that Brian Cody's heart beat that degree quicker. The balance of power was restored in a matter of minutes when Kilkenny regained their composure. They fired over six great points between the 50th and 59th minutes to crush any further resistance. Clare's failure to score a goal could be attributed to the magnificence of the power-packed display served up by the Kilkenny full back line of Michael Kavanagh, Noel Hickey and my man of the match, Philip Larkin, who was simply brilliant for his consistency, tenacity and perseverance. Clare will not remember the match kindly, if only for the reason that they had no plan to break down the defensive wall erected by the Leinster champions. However, there were individual performances of note from Davy Fitzgerald, Gerry Quinn, Frank Lohan, Colin Lynch and Jamesie O'Connor.

2003 FINAL: KILKENNY SURVIVE REBEL RALLY

15 September 2003   Kilkenny 1-14, Cork 1-11
Attendance: 79,3630   Referee: P. O'Connor (Limerick)
Top scorer: M. Comerford (Kilkenny) 1-4

Kilkenny collected their 28th All-Ireland hurling crown at the expense of great rivals Cork at Croke Park, highlighted by the fact that D. J. Carey, who had been such a commanding figure in hurling for some time, earned the one major honour that until then was missing from his great range of distinctions. He joined the ranks of All-Ireland senior winning captains when he led Kilkenny to the successful defence of the MacCarthy Cup. The win earned him his fifth All-Ireland senior medal. His first was won in 1992. It may not have been Carey's most gratifying All-Ireland display, but there was a reason which impinged on his duty as team leader. A shameful intrusion into his private life in the days preceding the final must have made it difficult for him to concentrate, so it was scarcely surprising that his influence on the game was less than normal. He failed to score for only the second time in a thirteen year championship career—ironically the previous occasion was in 1999, also against Cork. However, he was spared any embarrassment as his colleagues in attack made up for him. One such player was Martin Comerford, who served up a brilliant performance, grabbing 1-4, starting at full forward and later at right half forward. He shot two points in a Kilkenny dominated first half, but even more significantly hit 1-2 in a second period when the going was toughest and most competitive. Comerford's display earned him man of the match. It was he who held his nerve best when the Cats were wavering under strong Cork pressure when Kilkenny's half-time lead of 0-9 to 0-3 at the interval was wiped out. That change of events followed a marvellous Cork rallying surge which saw them outscore the champions 1-6 to 0-2 in the opening minutes of the second half. Setanta Ó hAilpín's fifth minute goal, finished with confidence after Joe Deane poked the ball to him, levelled the match 1-8 to 0-11. Niall McCarthy put Cork ahead with a point for the first and only time a minute later. Four tense minutes followed during which Niall McCarthy blazed wide from good scoring ground to deny Cork an addition to their lead. The next score was going to be the crucial one and Lady Luck smiled on Kilkenny's Martin Comerford, who grabbed a loose ball and angled it over the bar to level the game in the 59th minute. The atmosphere was electric and tension gripped both sides. It was the champions who proved the braver at the closing stages. The very polished Henry Shefflin put his team ahead with a neat point in the 62nd minute, much to the relief of the Kilkenny supporters. Their spirits were to get a major boost when Shefflin squeezed the ball to Comerford, whose finish was crisp and mighty as he blasted the ball to the Cork net. True to their nature, Cork were not prepared to concede and battled bravely for a goal to earn a second chance. Cork had outscored Kilkenny 0-2 to 0-1 in the closing minutes, but they just couldn't break through an unyielding Kilkenny defence. Cork could ill afford to complain anyway after they had produced an abysmal display in the first half with only a miserable three points to show for their labours, regrettable on such an important occasion and one of the prime causes for their defeat. They failed to score between the fourth and 31st minutes during which Kilkenny amassed seven points. As a wiseacre opined after the game, had Cork players spent time practising their shooting in the pre-match workout instead of the training drills, they might have improved their marksmanship during the game itself. In sharp contrast, Kilkenny were plugged in to the power from the start as Tommy Walsh fired over the first Kilkenny point after ten seconds and by the fifteenth minute he had added another three points. While the Cork defence had the shackles on Carey and Brennan, the failure of the Cork forwards to raise flags led to their defeat. If Kilkenny were not all that convincing in the scoring department at times, they were made to look good by Cork's self-destructive streak. But then again Kilkenny had a real power horse in Noel Hickey at full back, one of their top stars. To their credit, Cork did make a few tactical changes which helped their team performance in the latter stages of the game. It took a brilliant James McGarry save to foil Cork of a crucial goal, which, if it had found the target could well have changed the final outcome—that's how close Cork came to realising their game plan. Outfield, Cork also made sure that the forward bursts of Kilkenny's centre back Peter Barry were curtailed. But the very shrewd Brian Cody, Kilkenny's team manager, had his course of action well and truly thought out as well. He brought in experienced Andy Comerford in the 60th minute for Ryall, with J. J. Delaney moving into the No. 4 slot. The effect was dramatic. Delaney mopped up the defensive charges willingly while Comerford used his great positional craft and good anticipation to win possession around the mid-field area. Henry Shefflin enjoyed a new supply of the ball as a result and he picked off two priceless points in the last eight minutes before creating the opportunity for Comerford to slam home the all important goal that crushed Cork's late recovery ambitions. Brian Cody said after the game, 'All-Ireland finals are won by men, men with character, heart and guts. If we had lost, our skill level was never going to be questioned, but our heart for the battle and our ability to fight our corner would. You do what it takes when your back is to the wall.' On a question about D. J. Carey, Cody said, 'The rest of the squad, the young lads, would openly say that they idolise D. J. They all wanted to be D. J. and then suddenly they discovered that they were hurling with him. They found a superstar who doesn't behave like one.'

2004 FINAL: FIRED-UP REBELS SHOCK THE CHAMPIONS
13 September 2004   Cork 0-17, Kilkenny 0-9
Attendance: 78,212   Referee: A. MacSuibhne (Dublin)
Top scorers: J. Deane (Cork) 0-5, H. Shefflin (Kilkenny) 0-5

Kilkenny's dream of a three in a row was well and truly shattered at Croke Park at the hands of a fired-up Cork, who atoned for their defeat at the hands of Kilkenny twelve months previously. On this occasion the circumstances were different. Kilkenny had their hearts set on winning a coveted three in a row and topping the honours roll, but that wasn't allowed to happen. Cork saw to that in spectacular fashion on a day that was spoiled by the vagaries of the wind and a slippery sod. Certainly those two aristocrats of hurling, Cork and Kilkenny, were never allowed to parade their normal artistry and hurling know-how on this very important occasion. Twelve months before, Cork had wilted with the finishing line in sight in the second half, but this time the rewards were much greater and more gratifying. The chance to take a 29th All-Ireland crown, top the honours roll and deny Kilkenny that grandiose prize was now within their grasp and there for the taking. It was achieved simply because Cork applied themselves to the task with a far greater measure of tenacity, courage and energy, and their objective was not going to be denied this time. Time and space had turned matters around. They won the final 23 minutes by 0-9 to 0-0, which reflected a level of dominance that didn't appear possible. Kilkenny on the other hand, and amazingly so, scored just two points—a 65 and a free by Henry Shefflin—in the entire second half to finish on 0-9, their lowest total in an All-Ireland final since Galway beat them 1-12 to 0-9 in the 1987 decider. The outcome of this epic tussle brought a remarkable change in the fortunes of both teams. Once Cork had stamped their class on proceedings, attitudes changed rapidly. Cork's newly found forward dominance spread to other areas of contention, leaving the defending champions reeling under the pressure. Even Kilkenny's young stars who had shone last year found themselves isolated and unable to contribute to the scoreline. Cork on the other hand had a splendid second half where they were able to pick off some delightful points. Henry Shefflin managed one point from play for Kilkenny, while D. J. Carey drew a blank for the third time in an All-Ireland against Cork. Eddie Brennan shot four wides and no scores; John Hoyne grafted but failed to score; Martin Comerford hit 0-2 which was 1-2 short of his 2003 final return; while James 'Chah' Fitzpatrick lacked the experience to get back into the picture. So manager Brian Cody was in a pickle. His attacking formation, which had served him so well in the past, was no longer a potent force despite the wealth of talent they represented. He knew he hadn't the replacements on the bench and retained the starting fifteen until the 62nd minute before bringing in Conor Phelan for Fitzpatrick. Cork had no problems at that stage. They were sitting on a five point lead and looking comfortable winners on the way to an All-Ireland crown for the first time since 1999.

Kilkenny's last chance of a face-saving goal disappeared when Cork goalie Donal Óg Cusack saved a stinging shot from Shefflin. It was one of the few occasions that the Cork goalie was called upon to avert danger as their defensive set-up fronting Cusack was impregnable. Cork team captain Ben O'Connor played a stormer in the second half, even though he was off target at times from frees. Joe Deane gave the Kilkenny defence a torrid time and emerged with five points from frees. Cork's second quarter revival cut Kilkenny's lead to a single point 0-7 to 0-6 at the break, a position which gladdened the heart of Cork manager Donal O'Grady. Seán Óg Ó hAilpín, John Gardiner and Diarmuid O'Sullivan proved a massive force, doing most to keep Kilkenny's scoring efforts at a minimum. Niall McCarthy was again Cork's biggest driving force in attack in the second half when Cork outscored the Cats 0-11 to 0-2. The return to form of Kieran Murphy and Brian Corcoran with Joe Deane proved very important in the scoring department when it mattered. But the Cork defence was the real key to the Munster champions' success story and that applied to the hard work of Wayne Sherlock, Diarmuid O'Sullivan and sub John Brown. They held the highly vaunted Kilkenny attack in a vice-like grip. It was fitting that the final score of the match should fall to one of Cork's long-serving stars, Brian Corcoran. He took a big gamble coming back to inter-county hurling after a three year retirement spell. He chased a ball that was dropping at the Canal end with two defenders on his tail. A quick lay-off appeared a sensible course of action, but not for Corcoran. He made a better angle for himself on his left side and shot for the posts. The ball was steered correctly between James McGarry's goal posts for one of the best points scored that day. Brian dropped to his knees and raised his arms in supplication to the darkening clouds, knowing full well that the MacCarthy Cup was on its way south to the Rebel County for the first time since 1999.

2005 FINAL: CORK CLAIM 30TH TITLE

12 September 2005   Cork 1-21, Galway 1-16
Attendance: 81,136   Referee: S. Roche (Tipperary)
Top scorer: B. O'Connor (Cork) 1-7

Cork rightly claimed their 30th All-Ireland senior hurling crown at Croke Park after an exhilarating contest against a very competitive Galway team who fought the issue to the last stroke. It was an excellent contest in which the greater experience of the Munster champions paved the way for their success. But Galway took many positives from this display, and the fact that they saw off the challenge of Limerick, Tipperary and Kilkenny. No doubt Cork were very much influenced by the splendid marksmanship of Ben O'Connor, who accounted for 1-7 of his team's scoring returns—his man-of-the-match performance assisted Cork in maintaining a tight grip on the exchanges. In Galway's case, they provided tangible evidence that they had the ability to match Cork in many facets of the play, if not all. Cork had that natural gift of being able to quickly retaliate to every score by the westerners, an essential ingredient in a championship test. To illustrate that comment, I can recall an incident in the second half. After three minutes Alan Kerins slotted over a Galway point to cut their deficit to a point, 1-9 to 0-11; again when Damian Hayes smacked in Galway's goal in the nineteenth minute, 1-14 to 1-13; and finally when Ger Farragher pointed in the 52nd minute, 1-15 to 1-14. On all three occasions the Galway supporters' response was magnificent, urging their team to greater deeds, but Cork remained cool, calm and confident to deny Galway any hope of denting their armour.

Cork had learned valuable lessons during their trials and tribulations in the All-Ireland finals of 2003 and 04. Vital scores had to be created and the Leesiders had the ability to do just that. Another factor which may not have helped Galway's bid was their failure to get length on their clearances from the defence, especially with Cork's young stars waiting like hawks to grab the loose ones and pick off scores. It also helped Cork's game plan to have active forwards operating around the midfield area where the pickings were rich. Cork had three such players in Ben O'Connor, Tom Kenny and Jerry O'Connor, who between them accounted for 1-10 from play, ably assisted by a lot of hard work by their half backs Ronan Curran and Seán Óg Ó hAilpín. John Gardiner had his hands full curbing Galway's best forward Alan Kerins. In a game where defences took the laurels, Cork could point to the effectiveness of their full back line of Murphy, O'Sullivan and Mulcahy, who saw to it that Galway's Ger Farragher, Niall Healy and Damien Hayes were restricted to a combined scoring total of 1-3. The goal came from Healy who cashed in on a good save from Cusack in the Cork goal in the 49th minute. It looked for a time that Healy's goal might inspire Galway to shake off the Cork shackles and open up the play that was still being dominated by the red jerseys. Ger Farragher, a renowned free-taker, was unhappy about missing a close in free which he sent wide a minute before Healy shot to the Cork net. Galway did produce a masterly movement which ended in a score. Liam Donoghue's puck-out in the thirteenth minute reached Derick Hardiman, who swiftly laid the ball off to Farragher. He made no mistake with a slick point. Had Galway produced a few more similar scores, they would have worried the Cork men more. The bulwark of the Cork defence was undoubtedly Diarmuid O'Sullivan. He was a commanding figure and his fearless approach was instrumental in minimising the effectiveness of the Galway attackers.

While the hurling content was generally pleasing and Galway matched Cork during various spells of pressure, the Leesiders always appeared to have that sharper edge. I have seen better displays from Cork in the past, but on this occasion they played at a level that was sufficient to gain them their 30th All-Ireland crown.

2006 FINAL: PERSONAL TRIUMPH FOR CODY

4 September 2006   Kilkenny 1-16, Cork 1-13
Attendance: 82,275   Referee: B. Kelly (Westmeath)
Top scorer: H. Shefflin (Kilkenny) 0-8

It was a personal triumph for Kilkenny manager Brian Cody when he strode across Croke Park clutching the MacCarthy Cup after his superstar team had shattered the dreams of Cork by denying them the coveted three in a row. Cork were firm favourites to win this one, but Kilkenny's game plan was viable and purposeful enough to dethrone the defending champions. It was a year which brought Kilkenny all the hurling honours, All-Ireland, National League, Leinster Championship, Walsh Cup and unbeaten all year. The smile on Cody's face as he watched Kilkenny captain Jackie Tyrrell raise the MacCarthy Cup to a tumultuous roar said it all. Mission accomplished. It was an All-Ireland final that had been given a monster build-up by the media. Indeed, in some quarters Kilkenny's prospects were totally written off and surprisingly so. True, Cork were the reigning champions and their form in winning two finals in a row convinced a lot of people that a third garland was befitting the best team to come out of the Rebel County. But Kilkenny had a game plan which was going to prove infallible. Some of the pre-match comments relegating Kilkenny to a secondary role infuriated the Cats—and their manager. He said after the game: 'There was a lot said and written at the start of the year that wasn't exactly genuine. There were cowardly things said. Some of our players were written off; some of our set-up was written off; the usual rubbish that goes on from the start of the year. I was supposed to retire and resign; Noel Hickey was too slow to play in Croke Park. Noel Hickey hasn't forgotten that he is too slow. The people who were writing us off up to a short time ago can change their tune now. The thing had a momentum and there is just massive, massive honesty in our panel.'

Kilkenny won the 2006 All-Ireland title because they imposed such an overwhelming sense of aggression on Cork that even the powerful three-in-row ambition wasn't enough to sustain the defending champions. Cork were three points in arrears at the end of the game and were beaten more comprehensively than the score suggests. More importantly, Kilkenny regarded this game as a test of themselves as individuals and as a county, and they worked so hard at getting things right that nothing was left to chance. The Kilkenny defence was brilliantly marshalled and James

McGarry had little to worry him except the odd thrust at his goal. James 'Cha' Fitzpatrick and Derek Lyng were the midfield masters of Cork's Tom Kenny and Jerry O'Connor, while their attack took the Cork defence into dark caves before stealing their torches. The highly vaunted Cork half back line suffered their worst day for a considerable time against a variety of Kilkenny opponents. Centre back Ronan Curran was the best of the line, but John Gardiner and Seán Óg Ó hAilpín never reached their normal performance levels on the day. Henry Shefflin, Ritchie Power and Martin Comerford displayed slickness and style and the accuracy that went with it. The real match-winner was undoubtedly left corner forward Aidan Fogarty, who chose All-Ireland day to deliver his best performance in a Kilkenny senior jersey. He scored a very valuable 1-3 from play and collected a few frees which were safely put away by Henry Shefflin. His marker, Cork captain Pat Mulcahy, never got to grips with Fogarty's threat, and it was surprising that the Cork team mentors didn't resolve the situation early on in the game.

The pressure was telling in other areas as well. In the 29th minute Diarmuid O'Sullivan allowed a dropping ball to fall from his grasp, only for the ever vigilant Aidan Fogarty to whip the ball to the Cork net. It was a grievous defensive error at the time. It turned out to be the match-defining score, as it gave Kilkenny a three point cushion that sustained them all the way to the final whistle. Kilkenny led 1-8 to 0-8 at the interval. While the Munster men did cut the lead to two points in the early stages of the second half, they were unable to sustain the desired momentum and forward thrust. The number of errors committed by the Leesiders was far and away more than that experienced in other campaigns. Even the ever accurate Joe Deane failed with a close in free in the 41st minute, much to the horror of the Cork fans. Another example of Cork ill luck on the day was when Jerry O'Connor, their midfielder, went on one of his spectacular solo runs towards the Kilkenny defensive wall, only for James Ryall to knock the ball off his hurley and deny Cork a probable score. It was all part and parcel of the harrying and hustling tactics pursued by Kilkenny that completely upset the Cork game plan. Under the circumstances the Cork players were constantly being pressured whenever Donal Óg Cusack's goal deliveries reached his forwards. They were speedily dealt with by a very composed Kilkenny defence not given to handing out scoring presents to the opposition. Manager Brian Cody had primed his men very well and they in turn repaid him with the MacCarthy Cup and another All-Ireland senior hurling crown.

2007 FINAL: BUSINESS AS USUAL FOR KILKENNY

3 September 2007   Kilkenny 2-19, Limerick 1-15
Attendance: 82,127   Referee: D. Kirwan (Cork)
Top scorer: E. Brennan (Kilkenny) 1-5

Under Brian Cody, Kilkenny have played in eight of the last ten All-Ireland finals and have won five of them. They launched themselves into this one against Limerick at Croke Park and to a victory which steered them to the top of the honours roll with 30 titles, now level with Cork. Their victory was virtually sealed after they had knocked up a 2-3 to 0-0 lead in the opening ten minutes. Limerick showed tremendous heart and passion and never dropped their heads, but the concession of those early Kilkenny scores left the Munster champions with too great a mountain to climb.

To their credit, Limerick managed to claw their way back into the match, but they were always chasing the Cats from a distance. The Kilkenny defence was magnificent on the day and consequently Limerick's Andrew O'Shaughnessy and Brian Begley, their two main attacking forces, were never allowed to display the power and accuracy which had helped them over other obstacles. With O'Shaughnessy and Begley isolated, the Limerick attack was never allowed to create scoring chances to any degree.

When Kilkenny lost their star full back Noel Hickey with a pulled hamstring after seventeen minutes, a door might have opened for Limerick, and when Henry Shefflin had to retire with a serious knee injury, Brian Cody looked to have major problems. But no panic. The back-up talent was waiting to be called in. John Tennyson replaced Hickey with Brian Hogan switching to full back, while Michael Fennelly came in for Shefflin. The ease with which two important berths were capably filled underlined the strength of Cody's replacement panel. If that wasn't enough, Ritchie Power was summoned into the action from the subs bench as a replacement free-taker for the peerless Shefflin.

Limerick needed a spark to lift the gloom which prevailed at the time, and it came in the 45th minute when Ollie Moran raised hopes of a Limerick upsurge after cutting the Kilkenny lead to five points. Limerick had chances of making further inroads into the Kilkenny lead, but weak marksmanship from easy scoring ground proved the team's undoing. By contrast, Kilkenny moved away with great authority and points were marked up with ease from a composed attacking unit. The marksmen were Ritchie Power and Eddie Brennan.

That was enough to clinch the All-Ireland title for Kilkenny for the fifth time this decade. Without doubt Brennan revelled in this epic clash, which enabled him to walk away with the man-of-the-match award after serving up a performance of brilliance with his pace, anticipation and above all his accuracy from scoring opportunities. He ended up top scorer with 1-5.

The concession of those two early goals was a staggering blow to Limerick's morale, a deficit from which they never fully recovered. But they displayed a rare fighting spirit against a side that always appeared to hold the whip hand. They battled gamely in the second half, and won the last hour by outscoring the champions 1-15 to 0-16. Unfortunately, they still couldn't establish a foothold long enough to rattle the confidence and unwavering spirit which motivated the Leinster champions throughout the game.

Eoin Larkin, who hit four points in the first half, sub Ritchie Power, Tommy Walsh, J. D. Delaney and Jackie Tyrrell supplemented Brennan's wonderful contribution to such a degree that Martin Comerford and Aidan Fogarty who starred the previous year had a much easier ride this time. With the exception of Ollie Moran, who shot 1-3 from play, the rest of the Limerick contenders were outfoxed by a vigilant Kilkenny side too well focused on victory. The winners were never in danger of losing the initiative at any stage.

2008 FINAL: HIGH KINGS OF HURLING

7 September 2008   Kilkenny 3-30, Waterford 1-13
Attendance: 82,186   Referee: B. Kelly (Westmeath)
Top scorer: E. Kelly (Waterford) 1-9

Some of the morning after newspaper headlines told it all: 'Awesome', 'Cats maul Deise to land three in a row', 'Cody's Weapons of Mass Destruction Level Deise', 'Kilkenny One of the Greatest Teams Ever', 'This is Greatness. This is Kilkenny.' Never before had a winning All-Ireland team been lauded to this extent. Following their demolition of luckless Waterford at Croke Park in the 2008 All-Ireland senior hurling final. Waterford's failure to measure up to a very demanding challenge was difficult to quantify. Their resultant defeat at the hands of the reigning champions was proof positive that Kilkenny were a team apart and there was nothing Waterford could do. It must be said that Waterford were a better team than that which collapsed in their bid for greatness on All-Ireland day. They joined the ranks of other counties who inexplicably failed to come up with the necessary formula on similar missions in the past. Kilkenny's performance in the 2008 All-Ireland final was stunning and set standards that will take a long time for future contenders to emulate. The record books will show that Kilkenny sit higher than any of the other hurling strongholds with 31 All-Ireland crowns. If measured on the basis of this performance, it is not beyond reason to assume that a four in a row to match that of Cork (1941 to 44) will be theirs for the taking in 2009. That observation is based solely on the evidence of the power, skill and the zestful approach adopted by a young band of hurlers that really beggars description. The result was a first three in a row since the last in 1913 that will serve as an objective to be bettered in 2009. After that the sky is the limit and the target of a historic five in a row, not achieved to date, will appear quite feasible.

This 2008 All-Ireland hurling final was best remembered for the style, commitment, hurling artistry and, above all else, the effort and accuracy of a very complete attacking forward division. Adding immeasurably to a great team performance was the fact that four of the Kilkenny stars, Michael Kavanagh, Noel Hickey, Eddie Brennan and Henry Shefflin, now have six All-Ireland medals, just two short of the record held by John Doyle and Christy Ring. Waterford may have been the underdogs going into this final, but they were never given the time or space to exercise any degree of authority or lay down any markers to offset the power of the formidable Kilkenny opposition. That was reflected in the fact that for the first time in the history of the All-Ireland championship a competing team managed to score a record 30 points. There was no real turning point in the game. From the throw-in all the focus was on Kilkenny. The body language of the black and amber men was clearly in evidence on the field. It was marked by their ability to gain possession whether from high catching or low pick-ups. That helped produce waves of Kilkenny attacking sorties and, more importantly, crucial scores. There were times when the Kilkenny forwards vied with one another for the chance to score, and if not, to create the opening for a colleague better placed. That was unselfish teamwork in every sense of the word.

At the other end of the field the Waterford forwards were struggling to find an opening in a Kilkenny defence unwilling to share space and light with the opposing forwards. After ten minutes of hard battling Waterford could only record two pointed frees from Eoin Kelly as Kilkenny weaved their magic, firing over points from all angles and distances. By half-time this final was as good as over.

Leading 0-10 to 0-4, Kilkenny's Eddie Brennan shot the first of his two crushing goals when Eoin Larkin sent him a slick pass and he buried the ball in the Waterford net. One minute later the roof fell in again when Eddie Brennan arrived on the scene to pulverise the stricken Deise defenders. Aidan Fogarty shot for a goal, but the Waterford goalkeeper Clinton Hennessy saved bravely, only for Brennan to nip in on cue to finish the loose clearance to the Waterford net. The half-time scoreline read 2-16 to 0-6—game over as a contest.

There was no respite for the Munster men. They just couldn't exert the sort of pressure necessary to unlatch the hold the Kilkenny backs held all through the game and even the highly reputable Dan Shanahan never posed the expected threat as he was pitted against the unflappable J. J. Delaney, who mopped up every ball that fell between the two players. Perhaps one of the game's many features, from a Kilkenny viewpoint at least, was that the high standard set by the black and amber brigade never wilted and, more surprisingly, the intensity of the exchanges from the out-set was never allowed to flag in the second period, when the defending champions left no room for Waterford to mount a possible recovery plan. It was clearly the mass destruction of a Deise side that lacked the fire and bravery of earlier outings in that they were not allowed to express them-selves against a team that held all the answers to every question. The paucity of the Waterford scoring machine was due mainly to the strict man to man marking indulged in by the Kilkenny defensive set-up who were prepared for all contingencies. Candidly, Waterford were unfortunately devoid of plans to offset the brilliance of Cody's men, and if there were such tactics drawn up by Davy Fitzgerald, they never saw the light of day once the Kilkenny machine went into action from the outset. Many of the game's skills were on display which team coaches will have noted: shielding the ball from opponents during solo runs; shortening the grip on the hurley to prevent a hooking before striking the ball. And there were more. It was a disastrous day for Waterford and their players. They lost all the personal duels from an early stage and were unable to raise their game as Kilkenny moved up a gear. They briefly managed parity in the opening ten minutes, but by the half-time break the figures show that seven different Kilkenny players had contributed 2-16 while Waterford's 0-5 had come from Eoin Kelly frees. The sheer perfection and mastery employed by Kilkenny made this All-Ireland the one that hurling fans will remember best. Waterford were forced to juggle their team placings for a second half in which the champions showed them little or no mercy. Indeed, they were ruthless in every aspect of the game. And while Waterford pared four points off the embarrassing deficit in the remaining minutes, it still left Waterford facing their biggest defeat in an All-Ireland final for 65 years. In a disappointing Waterford attack only John Mullane battled on bravely, while Eoin Kelly picked off his points well from frees.

To win an All-Ireland title at top hurling level demands complete dedication to the task on hand and many sacrifices as well. It was obvious watching this game that a strong bond had been established a long time ago between this Kilkenny panel of players for them to serve up such a brilliant performance on the day. There were no weaknesses, no blank spots, only a driving ambition which ensured that no obstacle would stand in their way of achieving immortality and the rewards that go with it. It would not have been achieved but for the genius of manager Brian Cody, under whose tutelage the greatest Kilkenny team ever has now emerged from the county to stand proudly and magnificently on top of the leaderboard as the kings of hurling. For that we salute them.

APPENDIXES

Appendix 1 ～

FACTS AND FIGURES

Radio and TV

The first radio commentary on a MacCarthy Cup tie—and also on an All-Ireland senior hurling final—was by Paddy Mehigan, who wrote under the pen-name, 'Carbery', in 1926 on the clash of Cork and Kilkenny for that season's trophy.

Mehigan was then well established as a writer and commentator on Gaelic games, and was also a former inter-county hurler. He was a native of Cork. He also wrote for years under the pen-name, 'Pato'.

He was the commentator on the 1926 All-Ireland senior hurling semifinal between Kilkenny and Galway on 29 August 1926 at Croke Park, which game made history as the live broadcast was the first on an outdoor sporting event outside the US. Those commentaries went out on 2RN, forerunner of Radio Éireann and now, of course, RTÉ Radio.

The MacCarthy Cup final joined the colour age on television in 1971 when Tipperary and Kilkenny ushered in the new era. Francis Loughnane, Tipperary's left half forward, pointed after three minutes for the first score in colour. That final produced a feast of goals, ten in all, and Tipperary led the way in this regard as well with their centre half forward Noel O'Dwyer scoring a goal in the nineteenth minute.

Points only wins

The first year a county won the trophy without scoring a single goal was in 1947. Kilkenny had one of their memorable one point wins over Cork, 0-14 to 2-7.

Then there was a long wait until 1961 for the next final in which the winning team failed to beat the net-minder—Tipperary 0-16, Dublin 1-12. That was the last time that a decider with the old MacCarthy Cup as the prize failed to produce a goal.

Since the new cup was awarded for the first time in 1992, the finals of

1997 (Clare 0-20), 1999 (Cork 0-13) and 2004 (Cork 0-17) were all won without the successful county finding the net.

Winning debut

Offaly became the twelfth county to contest a MacCarthy Cup tie when they made a winning debut in 1981, seeing off Galway in the show-down. The list was not added to after that and no county has made a debut in the annals of the new trophy so far.

Jersey numbers

Players' jerseys were numbered for the first time in a MacCarthy Cup tie in the 1922 final between Kilkenny and Tipperary, which was not played until September 1923. The Noresiders won that match.

Playing time

The All-Ireland final of 1970 was noteworthy for more than the fact that the game provided eleven goals. That was also the first final over 80 minutes. Cork beat Wexford 6-21 to 5-10. Later in the seventies the playing time for finals was reduced to 70 minutes. Kilkenny and Galway contested the first such match over that playing period for the 1975 title, and the Leinster standard-bearers came out on top.

Finals outside Croke Park

Only two MacCarthy Cup ties have been played outside Croke Park. The 1937 final was switched to Fitzgerald Stadium in Killarney because of construction work on what was then the new Cusack Stand at headquarters. Tipperary beat Kilkenny. The GAA celebrated its Centenary Year in 1984 and, as part of the celebrations, the All-Ireland senior hurling final was staged at Semple Stadium, Thurles. It was also a unique final in another way as it brought together Cork and Offaly in opposition at that stage for the first time. The Leesiders proved the superior team.

Referee—then medal

Generally, it is a case of enthusiasts refereeing All-Ireland finals after their playing days are over. However, Vincent Baston refereed an All-Ireland senior final before he played on a winning side. He had charge of the 1945 encounter when Tipperary overcame old rivals Kilkenny. Then in 1948 he was centre half back as Waterford put their name on the trophy for the first time with a win over Dublin.

Northern counties

Ulster were represented in a MacCarthy Cup tie for the first time in 1943. Antrim caused a major upset by beating Kilkenny in an All-Ireland semi-final at Corrigan Park in Belfast, but they lost the final heavily to a strong Cork outfit that went on in 1944 to complete the only sequence of four All-Ireland senior title wins by any county in hurling. The North had to wait until 1989 for representation again in the show-down match. Antrim surprised Offaly in a Croke Park semi-final and put up a gallant display when losing out to a Nicky English inspired Tipperary.

Highest scores

The initial MacCarthy Cup tie set a superb standard in goals by a winning team. Limerick hit eight and no county has equalled that since.

The second highest goals return stands at seven, scored by Galway, amazingly enough against Limerick in 1923, by Cork in their 1946 win over Kilkenny, and by Tipperary in 1951 in their victory over Wexford.

The best return, goals and points combined by a MacCarthy Cup winning team is Cork's 6-21 (39 points) in their 1970 success at the expense of Wexford in the first 80 minute game.

Waterford recorded the highest goals tally by an unsuccessful team in a clash for the trophy when they found their way through to Kilkenny's net six times in 1963. The Munster team also hit eight points, an overall tally well above that which many of the returns that won deciders over the years, but was still not enough to offset Kilkenny's 4-17.

Interestingly, Waterford's combined total of goals and points of 26 is by no means the highest recorded by a losing team. Kilkenny helped themselves to 5-14, with marksman supreme Eddie Keher in lethal finishing form with a splendid 2-11 in their 1971 defeat by Tipperary.

Galway ushered in the nineties by scoring 2-21 (27 points) as they inflicted a shock defeat on Cork, while in 1972 Kilkenny were on the receiving end of a 5-11 (26 points) barrage from Cork but still scored enough to capture the trophy.

Unusual switches

Positional switches are common enough in Gaelic games, and many were made over the years as well in MacCarthy Cup ties. But one of the most unusual and spectacularly successful was in the 1998 meeting of Offaly and Kilkenny. Brian Whelehan was unwell on the days immediately before the game, but still took his place at right half back. However, not surprisingly he did not come up to his usual high standard of play and was moved to the half forward line after eighteen minutes. Another move sent him to full forward for the second half—and what a match-winning transfer that proved! Whelehan struck it rich in a manner few could have expected. He exerted new pressure on the Kilkenny rearguard, and proved so target conscious that he pioneered the way to victory by scoring 1-6 (1-3 from play) to end the game not only as the Faithful County's ace marksman but top scorer as well. Offaly won 2-16 to 1-13.

Another unusual change took place in the 1958 All-Ireland senior final between Tipperary and Galway. Mike Sweeney lined out in goal for the westerners and Fergus Benson took his place at the start at left half back. However, during the game Sweeney moved outfield and Benson took his place between the posts. And both showed up well in their new positions. Another change of goalkeepers came in 1963 when E. Power was replaced during the match in Waterford's goal by Percy Flynn.

Scoring goalkeeper
And what of goalkeepers scoring goals? Rare enough, but John Commins did just that in the 1986 final. He made the long trip up from the Galway goal with eight minutes remaining to take a 20 metre free and expertly rifled the ball to the Cork net.

Appendix 2 ∿

SCORERS AND TEAMS: 1921–2008

1921
SCORERS:
Limerick: B. McConkey 4-0, W. Gleeson 2-2, T. McGrath 2-1, W. Hough 0-1, G. Howard 0-1.
Dublin: B. Mockler 1-1, M. Neville 1-0, T. Hayes 0-1. The other Dublin goal was scored in a mêlée.
Limerick: B. McConkey (capt), M. Murphy (goal), T. Mangan, D. Murnane, P. McInerney, J. Keane, W. Hough, D. Lanigan, W. Gleeson, J. Humphries, W. Ryan, G. Howard, M. Mullane, C. Ryan, T. McGrath.
Dublin: R. Mockler (capt), Martin Hayes, Tom Hayes, M. Neville, Tom Moore, Jas Walsh, R. Doherty, J. Clune, F. Burke, J. J. Callanan, T. Daly (goal), E. Tobin, M. Darcy, J. Cleary, Jos Bannon. *Sub*: J. Kennedy for Tom Hayes.

1922
SCORERS:
Kilkenny: R. Grace 2-0, P. Donoghue 1-0, R. Tobin 1-0, J. Roberts 0-1, M. Lalor 0-1.
Tipperary: P. Power 2-0, J. J. Hayes 0-4, J. Cleary 0-1, W. Dwan 0-1.
Kilkenny: M. McDonald (goal), J. Tobin, J. Holohan, P. Glendon, T. Carroll, Wattie Dunphy (capt), R. Grace, P. Aylward, B. Kenny, M. Lalor, Eddie Dunphy, P. Donoghue, R. Tobin, J. Roberts, M. Power.
Tipperary: J. Leahy (capt), J. Power, A. O'Donnell, P. Power, P. Browne, J. Cleary, M. Kennedy, S. Hackett, J. O'Meara (goal), J. J. Hayes, P. Spillane, J. Fitzpatrick, T. Dwan, W. Dwan, J. Darcy.

1923
SCORERS:
Galway: L. McGrath 3-0, B. Gibbs 2-1, M. Kenny 1-0, R. Morrissey 1-0, M. Gill 0-1, A. Kelly 0-1.

Limerick: W. Gleeson 1-2, D. Lanigan 1-0, T. McGrath 1-0, M. Neville 1-0, J. Humphries 0-2, J. O'Grady 0-1.

Galway: M. Kenny (capt), J. Mahony (goal), M. Derivan, I. Harney, J. Power, A. Kelly, B. Gibbs, E. Gilmartin, J. Morris, M. King, T. Fleming, R. Morrissey, L. McGrath, M. Gill, J. Garvey.

Limerick: P. McInerney (capt), D. Lanigan, J. Keane, B. McConkey, M. Fitzgibbon, J. Hanley (goal), D. Murnane, W. Gleeson, W. Hough, M. Newville, J. Humphries. J. J. Kinnane, M. Cross, T. McGrath, J. O'Grady.

1924

SCORERS:

Dublin: G. Howard 2-0, M. Holland 2-0, W. Banim 1-1, P. Aylward 0-1, T. Barry 0-1.

Galway: B. Gibbs 2-1, I. Harney 0-2, A. Kelly 0-1, J. Morris 0-1, R. Morrissey 0-1.

Dublin: T. Daly (goal), J. Bannon, W. Small, T. Kelly, M. Gill, Jas Walsh, R. Mockler, P. Aylward, R. Doherty, M. Holland, D. O'Neill, G. Howard, Tom Barry, W. Banim, T. Finlay. Non playing captain: Frank Wall.

Galway: M. Kenny (capt), J. Mahony (goal), M. Derivan, Ignatius Harney, J. Power, A. Kelly, B. Gibbs, E. Gilmartin, J. Morris, M. King, T. Fleming, R. Morrissey, L. McGrath, J. Garvey, J. Keogh.

1925

SCORERS:

Tipperary: T. Duffy 2-1, J. D'Arcy 1-1, J. J. Hayes 1-0, P. Power 1-0, Leahy 0-1. There are confused reports as to how the other scores were compiled.

Galway: R. Morrissey 1-2, M. King 0-2, J. Shaughnessy 0-1.

Tipperary: J. Leahy (capt), A. O'Donnell (goal), M. Mockler, M. D'Arcy, J. J. Hayes, M. Kennedy, S. Hackett, J. Power, P. Leahy, P. Cahill, T. Duffy, J. D'Arcy, W. Ryan, P. Power, P. O'Dwyer. *Sub*: S. Kenny for Mockler.

Galway: A. Kelly (capt), J. Mahony (goal), J. Stanford, J. Fallon, M. Derivan, M. Broderick, P. J. Morrissey, I. Harney, M. King, P. O'Donnell, M. Connaire, M. Houlihan, Richard Morrissey, J. Shaughnessy, P. Rooney. *Sub*: J. Finn for Shaughnessy.

1926

SCORERS:

Cork: P. Ahearne 2-2, E. Coughlan 1-1, M. Ahearne 1-0, W. Higgins 0-1, P. Delea 0-1. No record of Cork's other point scorer.

Kilkenny: J. Roberts 1-0, E. Dunphy 1-0.

Cork: S. Óg Murphy (capt), J. Coughlan (goal), Maurice Murphy, E. O'Connell, D. Barry-Murphy, Ml Murphy, J. O'Regan, J. Hurley, E. Coughlan, W. Higgins, P. Delea, J. Kearney, Matt Murphy, M. Ahearne, P. Ahearne.

Kilkenny: R. Grace (capt), R. Cantwell (goal), W. Meagher, P. O'Reilly, T. Carroll, E. Doyle, W. Barry, W. Dunphy, M. Power, L. Meagher, J. Carroll, M. Brennan, E. Dunphy, H. Meagher, J. Roberts.

1927

SCORERS:

Dublin: T. Barry 2-1, M. Gill 0-4, M. Power 1-1, N. Fahy 1-0, J. Walsh 0-1, J. Gleeson 0-1.

Cork: E. Coughlan 1-1, M. Murphy 0-1, J. Hurley 0-1.

Dublin: M. Gill (capt), T. Daly (goal), P. McInerney, W. Phelan, E. Tobin, J. Gleeson, T. O'Rourke, G. Howard, M. Power, E. Fahy, T. Barry, J. Walsh, D. O'Neill, J. Bannon, M. Hayes.

Cork: S. Óg Murphy (capt), J. Burke (goal), E. O'Connell, D. Barry-Murphy, M. Murphy, J. Hurley, E. Coughlan, M. Leahy, P. Ahearne, M. Ahearne, P. Delea, J. O'Regan, P. Daly, Maurice Murphy, W. Higgins.

1928

SCORERS:

Cork: M. Ahearne 5-4, P. Ahearne 1-0, P. Delea 0-3, J. Hurley 0-3, E. Coughlan 0-1, D. Barry-Murphy 0-1.

Galway: P. Greene 1-0.

Cork: S. Óg Murphy (capt), E. O'Connell, J. Hurley, E. Coughlan, P. Ahearne, P. Delea, M. Ahearne, M. Leahy, M. Burke, M. Madden, D. Barry-Murphy, J. O'Regan, T. Barry, P. O'Grady, M. O'Connell.

Galway: J. Power (capt), M. Derivan, I. Harney, J. Mahony, P. Greene, R. McCann, J. Shaughnessy, R. Morrissey, P. Gilligan, M. Broderick, F. Kealy, M. Cunningham, W. Curran, M. King, T. Mullins. *Sub*: J. Deely for King.

1929

SCORERS:

Cork: J. Kenneally 2-1, P. Delea 2-0, M. Ahearne 0-3, J. Hurley 0-3, E. Coughlan 0-2.

Galway: R. Morrissey 1-0, J. Deely 0-1, I. Harney 0-1, C. Cooney 0-1.
Cork: D. Barry-Murphy (capt), J. Burke (goal), M. Madden, P. Collins, T. Barry, J. O'Regan, M. O'Connell, J. Kenneally, M. Ahearne, P. 'Balty' Ahearne, P. Delea, J. Hurley, E. Coughlan, P. O'Grady, E. O'Connell. *Sub*: D. McCarthy for P. Ahearne.
Galway: J. Mahon (goal), P. Clarke, T. Fleming, J. Shaughnessy, W. Keane, L. Geoghegan, F. Feely. M. Cunningham (capt), I. Harney, C. Cooney, P. Corcoran, J. Derivan, R. Morrissey, W. Derivan, J. Deely. *Subs*: M. Broderick for Shaughnessy, W. Furey for W. Derivan.

1930
SCORERS:
Tipperary: M. Kennedy 1-1, J. J. Callanan 1-1, P. Cahill 0-4, T. Treacy 0-1.
Dublin: M. Power 1-0, T. Burke 0-1, M. Gill 0-1, T. Teehan 0-1.
Tipperary: J. J. Callanan (capt), J. O'Loughlin, J. Maher, M. Ryan, J. Harney, J. Lanigan, T. O'Meara (goal), M. Kennedy, P. McKenna, P. Purcell, P. Cahill, M. F. Cronin, T. Butler, T. Leahy, T. Treacy. *Sub*: J. Heeney.
Dublin: J. Walsh (capt), John Dwyer (goal), T. O'Meara, E. Campion, M. Gill, C. Griffin, C. McMahon, P. McInerney, M. Finn, T. Quinlan, T. Burke, Matty Power, E. Byrne, T. Teehan, J. Gleeson. *Subs*: H. Quirke, M. Daniels.

1931 Draw
SCORERS:
Cork: M. Ahearne 1-0, E. Coughlan 0-2, M. O'Connell 0-1, W. Clancy 0-1, P. Ahearne 0-1, P. O'Grady 0-1.
Kilkenny: D. Dunne 1-1, L. Meagher 0-3, M. Power 0-1, M. Larkin 0-1.
Cork: J. Coughlan (goal), M. Madden, E. O'Connell, P. Collins, D. Barry-Murphy, J. O'Regan, T. Barry, J. Hurley, M. O'Connell, E. Coughlan (capt), M. 'Gah' Ahearne, P. O'Grady, P. Delea, P. 'Balty' Ahearne, W. Clancy. *Sub*: G. Garrett.
Kilkenny: J. Dermody (goal), P. Larkin, P. O'Reilly, W. Dalton, T. Carroll, P. Byrne, E. Doyle, L. Meagher (capt), E. Byrne, P. Phelan, M. White, R. Morrissey, D. Dunne, M. Larkin, M. Power. *Sub*: J. Duggan for Morrissey.

1931 First Replay
SCORERS:
Cork: E. Coughlan 1-2, W. Clancy 1-0, J. Hurley 0-1, M. Ahearne 0-1, P. Delea 0-1.

Kilkenny: L. Meagher 0-4, D. Dunne 1-0, P. Walsh 1-0, P. Phelan 0-1.
Cork: J. Coughlan, M. Madden, P. Collins, E. O'Connell, D. Barry-Murphy, J. O'Regan, T. Barry, J. Hurley, M. O'Connell, E. Coughlan, P. O'Grady, P. Ahearne, M. Ahearne, W. Clancy, P. Delea. *Sub*: G. Garrett for Madden.
Kilkenny: J. Dermody, P. Phelan, P. Walsh, E. Doyle, T. Carroll, J. Duggan, P. Reilly, L. Meagher, P. Byrne, E. Byrne, D. Dunne, M. Power, Paddy Larkin, M. Larkin, W. Dalton. *Sub*: T. Leahy for Paddy Larkin.

1931 **Second Replay**

SCORERS:
Cork: P. Delea 2-0, W. Clancy 1-3, M. Ahearne 1-1, P. Ahearne 1-0, J. Hurley 0-3, D. Barry-Murphy 0-1.
Kilkenny: D. Dunne 1-0, P. Walsh 1-0, J. Leahy 1-0, M. Power 0-3, E. Byrne 0-1.
Cork: J. Coughlan, M. Madden, P. Collins, E. O'Connell, D. Barry-Murphy, J. O'Regan, T. Barry, J. Hurley, M. O'Connell, E. Coughlan (capt), P. O'Grady, P. Ahearne, M. Ahearne, W. Clancy, P. Delea. *Sub:* G. Garrett for O'Grady.
Kilkenny: J. Dermody, P. Phelan, P. O'Reilly, D. Treacy, T. Carroll, P. Byrne, E. Doyle, T. Leahy, E. Byrne J. Duggan, J. Leahy, R. Morrissey, D. Dunne, M. Larkin, M. Power. *Sub:* M. Murphy for Duggan.

1932

SCORERS:
Kilkenny: M. White 2-1, Matty Power 1-1, E. Doyle 0-1.
Clare: T. Considine 2-1, J. Holohan 0-1, J. Gleeson 0-1.
Kilkenny: J. Dermody, P. Larkin, P. O'Reilly, J. 'Sag' Carroll, P. Phelan, P. Byrne, E. Doyle, E. Byrne, L. Meagher, J. Walsh (capt), M. Power, T. Leahy, D. Dunne, M. White, Matty Power.
Clare: T. Daly, J. Higgins, P. 'Fowler' McInerney, J. J. Doyle (capt), J. Houlihan, J. Hogan, L. Blake, J. Gleeson, T. McInerney, M. Falvey, M. Connery, M. O'Rourke, J. Mullane, T. Burnell, T. Considine.

1933

SCORERS:
Kilkenny: J. Dunne 1-1, Martin Power 0-2, Matty Power 0-2, L. Meagher 0-1, J. Duggan 0-1.
Limerick: M. Mackey 0-3, C. O'Brien 0-1, W. O'Donoghue 0-1, T. Ryan 0-1.

Kilkenny: J. Dermody, P. Larkin, P. O'Reilly, E. Doyle (capt), P. Phelan, P. Byrne, T. Leahy, E. Byrne, L. Meagher, J. Walsh, Martin Power, M. White, J. Fitzpatrick, J. Dunne, Matty Power. *Subs*: J. O'Connell for Dermody, J. Duggan for White.

Limerick: P. Scanlan, N. Creggan, T. McCarthy, M. Fitzgibbon (capt), M. Cross, P. Clohossy, G. Howard, T. Ryan, M. Ryan, J. Mackey, M. Mackey, J. Roche, D. Clohossy, P. Ryan, C. O'Brien. *Sub*: W. O'Donoghue.

1934

SCORERS:

Limerick: D. Clohossy 2-2, T. Ryan 0-2, J. Roche 0-2, M. Close 0-1.

Dublin: D. O'Neill 2-0, D. Canniffe 1-0, M. Daniels 0-1, T. Treacy 0-1, E. Wade 0-1, S. Hegarty 0-1.

Limerick: P. Scanlan, N. Cregan, T. McCarthy, M. Kennedy, M. Cross, P. Clohossy, G. Howard, T. Ryan (capt), M. Ryan, J. Mackey, M. Mackey, J. Roche, J. Close, R. McConkey, D. Clohossy. *Sub*: M. Condon for Howard.

Dublin: C. Forde, A. Murphy, J. Bannon, T. Teehan, J. Walsh, D. Canniffe, P. Roche, E. Wade, M. Daniels, S. Hegarty, T. Treacy, S. Muldowney, C. Boland (capt), D. O'Neill, J. O'Connell. *Subs*: F. McCormack for Teehan, J. Cullerton for Daniels.

1934 Replay

SCORERS:

Limerick: D. Clohossy 4-0, M. Mackey 1-1, G. O'Connell 0-1.

Dublin: D. O'Neill 2-2, T. Treacy 0-3, D. O'Connell 0-1.

Limerick: T. Shinny, E. Cregan, T. McCarthy, M. Kennedy, M. Cross, P. Clohossy, G. Howard, T. Ryan (capt), M. Ryan, J. Mackey, M. Mackey, J. Roche, J. O'Connell, D. Clohossy, J. Close.

Dublin: C. Forde, A. Murphy, J. Bannon, T. Teehan, J. Walsh, D. Cunniffe, P. Roche, E. Wade, M. Daniels, S. Hegarty, T. Treacy, S. Muldowney, S. Feeney (capt), D. O'Neill, G. O'Connell. *Subs*: C. McMahon for Murphy, J. Cullerton for Forde.

1935

SCORERS:

Kilkenny: J. Duggan 1-0, M. White 1-0, J. Walsh 0-2, M. Power 0-2, L. Meagher 0-1.

Limerick: P. McMahon 2-0, M. Mackey 0-2, J. O'Connell 0-1, M. Cross 0-1.

Kilkenny: J. O'Connell, P. Larkin, P. O'Reilly, P. Blanchfield, E. Byrne, Podge Byrne, P. Phelan, L. Meagher (capt), T. Leahy, J. Walsh, J. Duggan, M. White, J. Dunne, L. Byrne, M. Power. *Subs*: L. Duggan for Dunne, Dunne for Duggan.

Limerick: P. Scanlan, N. Cregan, T. McCarthy, M. Kennedy, M. Cross, P. Clohossy, G. Howard, T. Ryan (capt), M. Ryan, J. Mackey, M. Mackey, J. Roche, J. O'Connell, P. McMahon, J. Close.

1936

SCORERS:

Limerick: P. McMahon 2-0, D. Clohossy 2-0, M. Mackey 0-4, J. Power 1-0, P. Clohossy 0-1, J. Mackey 0-1.

Kilkenny: J. Dunne 1-0, L. Meagher 0-2, E. Byrne 0-2, J. Duggan 0-1.

Limerick: P. Scanlan, P. O'Carroll, T. McCarthy, M. Kennedy, M. Cross, P. Clohossy, G. Howard, T. Ryan, M. Ryan, J. Mackey, M. Mackey (capt), J. Roche, D. Clohossy, P. McMahon, J. Power.

Kilkenny: J. O'Connell, P. Larkin (capt), P. O'Reilly, P. Blanchfield, E. Byrne, P. Byrne, P. Phelan, L. Meagher, T. Leahy, J. Walsh, J. Duggan, M. White, J. Dunne, L. Byrne, M. Power. *Sub*: W. Burke for Blanchfield.

1937

SCORERS:

Tipperary: D. Murphy 2-1, J. Coffey 1-3, T. Doyle 0-2, J. Cooney 0-2, T. Treacy 0-1, D. Mackey 0-1, P. Ryan 0-1.

Kilkenny: P. Phelan 0-1, J. Morrissey 0-1, L. Meagher 0-1.

Tipperary: T. Butler, D. O'Gorman, J. Cornally, J. Lanigan (capt), J. Ryan, J. Maher, W. Wall, J. Cooney, J. Gleeson, J. Coffey, T. Treacy, T. Doyle, W. O'Donnell, D. Murphy, P. Ryan. *Subs*: D. Mackey for Gleeson, T. Kennedy for Wall.

Kilkenny: J. O'Connell, P. Larkin, P. Byrne, P. Blanchfield, E. Byrne, W. Burke, P. Phelan, T. Leahy, V. Madigan, J. Morrissey, P. Obbins, J. Duggan (capt), L. Duggan, M. White, M. Power. *Sub*: L. Meagher for Leahy.

1938

SCORERS:

Dublin: M. Flynn 1-0, W. Loughman 1-0, M. McDonnell 0-3, H. Gray 0-1, P. Doody 0-1.

Waterford: J. Keane 0-4, D. Goode 1-0, L. Byrne 0-2.

Dublin: C. Forde, T. Teehan, M. Butler, C. McMahon, M. Gill, P. Farrell, J. Byrne, M. Daniels (capt), H. Gray, R. Ryan, M. McDonnell, P. Doody, M. Brophy, M. Flynn, W. Loughman. *Sub*: J. Gilmartin for Daniels.

Waterford: M. Curley, M. Hickey (capt), C. Ware, J. Fanning, W. Walshe, J. Keane, J. Mountain, C. Moylan, S. Feeney, W. Barron, T. Greaney, P. Sheehan, J. Halpin, L. Byrne, D. Goode.

1939

SCORERS:

Kilkenny: J. Phelan 2-1, J. Langton 0-3, S. O'Brien 0-1, T. Leahy 0-1, J. Kelly 0-1.

Cork: J. Lynch 1-2, T. O'Sullivan 1-1, W. Campbell 1-0.

Kilkenny: J. O'Connell, P. Grace, P. Larkin, P. Blanchfield, R. Hinks, W. Burke, P. Phelan, J. Walsh (capt), J. Kelly, J. Langton, T. Leahy, J. Gargan, J. Mulcahy, S. O'Brien, J. Phelan. *Sub*: R. Brannigan for Gargan.

Cork: J. Buttimer, A. Lotty, W. Thornhill, W. Murphy, W. Campbell, J. Quirke, J. Young, J. Lynch (capt), J. Barrett, C. Buckley, R. Dinneen, W. Tabb, J. Ryng, T. O'Sullivan, M. Brennan.

1940

SCORERS:

Limerick: J. Power 1-2, John Mackey 1-0, R. Stokes 1-0, Mick Mackey 0-3, P. Clohossy 0-1, T. Ryan 0-1.

Kilkenny: T. Leahy 1-2, J. Phelan 0-1, J. Langton 0-1, J. Mulcahy 0-1, S. O'Brien 0-1, J. Walsh 0-1.

Limerick: P. Scanlan, J. McCarthy, M. Hickey, M. Kennedy, T. Cooke, P. Clohossy, P. Cregan, T. Ryan, J. Roche, J. Mackey, M. Mackey (capt), R. Stokes, E. Chawke, P. McMahon, J. Power. *Sub*: A. Herbert for Clohossy.

Kilkenny: J. O'Connell, P. Grace, P. Larkin, P. Blanchfield, R. Hinks, W. Burke, P. Phelan, J. Walsh, J. Kelly, J. Langton (capt), T. Leahy, J. Gargan, J. Mulcahy, J. O'Brien, Jas Phelan.

1941

SCORERS:

Cork: T. O'Sullivan 2-2, J. Quirke 2-0, C. Ring 0-5, M. Brennan 1-0, J. Barrett 0-2, J. Lynch 0-1, C. Buckley 0-1.

Dublin: E. Wade 0-2, H. Gray 0-1, C. Downes 0-1, J. Byrne 0-1, J. White 0-1.

Cork: J. Buttimer, W. Murphy, B. Thornhill, A. Lotty, W. Campbell, C. Cottrell, D. J. Buckley, J. Barrett, J. Lynch, C. Ring, C. Buckley (capt), J. Young, J. Quirke, T. O'Sullivan, M. Brennan.

Dublin: C. Forde, D. Nicholls, M. Connolly, C. McMahon, M. Gill Jnr, P. Farrell, J. Byrne, H. Gray, F. White, M. McDonnell, E. Wade (capt), G. Glenn, E. O'Boyle, P. McSweeney, C. Downes.

1942

SCORERS:

Cork: J. Quirke 1-2, C. Ring 0-3, J. Lynch 0-3, D. Beckett 1-0, S. Condon 0-2, M. Kennefick 0-2, D. J. Buckley 0-1, C. Tobin 0-1.

Dublin: M. McDonnell 1-1, D. Davitt 1-0, E. O'Brien 1-0, E. Wade 0-2, S. Skehal 0-1.

Cork: E. Porter, W. Murphy, B. Thornhill, C. Murphy, A. Lotty, D. J. Buckley, J. Young, J. Lynch (capt), P. O'Donovan, C. Ring, S. Condon, M. Kennefick, C. Tobin, J. Quirke, D. Beckett. *Sub*: J. Buttimer for Porter.

Dublin: J. Donegan, C. O'Dwyer, M. Butler, P. McCormack, E. O'Brien, F. White (capt), J. Byrne, E. Wade, H. Gray, M. Ryan, M. McDonnell, J. Roche, D. Davitt, P. Kennedy, J. Mullan. *Subs*: S. Skehal for Roche, M. Griffin for Skehal.

1943

SCORERS:

Cork: J. Quirke 2-2, T. O'Sullivan 1-2, M. Brennan 1-1, C. Ring 0-4, M. Kennefick 1-0, S. Condon 0-3, J. Lynch 0-2, C. Cottrell 0-2.

Antrim: N. Campbell 0-2, S. Mulholland 0-2.

Cork: T. Mulcahy, W. Murphy, B. Thornhill, C. Murphy, A. Lotty, D. J. Buckley, J. Young, J. Lynch, C. Cottrell, S. Condon, C. Ring, M. Kennefick (capt), J. Quirke, T. O'Sullivan, M. Brennan.

Antrim: J. Hurl, J. Currie, K. Murphy, W. Graham, P. McGarry, J. Walsh (capt), P. McKeown, J. Bateson, N. Campbell, D. McKillop, J. Butler, J. Mullan, K. Armstrong, D. McAllister, S. Mulholland. *Subs*: S. McNeill for Walsh.

1944

SCORERS:

Cork: J. Kelly 2-3, S. Condon 0-3, J. Lynch 0-3, C. Ring 0-1, C. Cottrell 0-1, J. Quirke 0-1, J. Morrison 0-1.

Dublin: H. Gray 1-0, T. Leahy 0-2.

Cork: T. Mulcahy, W. Murphy, B. Thornhill, D. J. Buckley, P. O'Donovan, C. Murphy, A. Lotty, J. Lynch, C. Cottrell, C. Ring, S. Condon (capt), J. Young, J. Quirke, J. Morrison, J. Kelly. *Sub*: P. Healy for C. Murphy.

Dublin: J. Donegan, J. O'Neill, M. Butler (capt), P. McCormack, F. White, C. Flanagan, J. Egan, M. Hassett, H. Gray, T. Leahy, E. Wade, J. Byrne, P. Maher, C. Downes, M. Ryan. *Sub*: M. Gill for Egan.

1945

SCORERS:

Tipperary: E. Gleeson 2-0, A. Brennan 1-2, J. Coffey 1-0, M. Ryan 1-0, H. Goldsboro 0-1, T. Wall 0-1, P. Ryan 0-1, T. Doyle 0-1.

Kilkenny: T. Maher 1-1, T. Walton 1-0, S. O'Brien 1-0, J. Mulcahy 0-2, J. Langton 0-2, T. Murphy 0-1.

Tipperary: James Maher, J. Devitt, G. Cornally, F. Coffey, M. Murphy, John Maher (capt), T. Purcell, H. Goldsboro, T. Wall, M. Ryan, T. Doyle, E. Gleeson, J. Coffey, A. Brennan, P. Ryan.

Kilkenny: J. Walsh, P. Grace, M. Kelly, P. Blanchfield (capt), J. Heffernan, W. Burke, S. Maher, D. Kennedy, T. Murphy, J. Gargan, J. Langton, T. Maher, T. Walton, S. O'Brien, J. Mulcahy. *Subs*: W. Walsh for Burke, J. Kelly for Kennedy.

1946

SCORERS:

Cork: C. Ring 1-3, M. O'Riordan 2-0, C. Murphy 2-0, G. O'Riordan 1-0, J. Kelly 1-0, B. Murphy 0-1, J. Lynch 0-1.

Kilkenny: T. Leahy 2-0, J. Langton 0-5, P. O'Brien 1-0, T. Walton 0-2, S. O'Brien 0-1.

Cork: T. Mulcahy, W. Murphy, C. Murphy, D. J. Buckley, P. O'Donovan, A. Lotty, J. Young, J. Lynch, C. Cottrell, P. Healy, C. Ring (capt), C. Murphy, M. O'Riordan, G. O'Riordan, J. Kelly.

Kilkenny: J. Donegan, P. Grace, M. Butler, W. Walsh, J. Kelly, S. Downey, J. Mulcahy (capt), D. Kennedy, T. Leahy, J. Gargan, J. Langton, L. Reidy, T. Walton, P. O'Brien, Seán O'Brien. *Subs*: T. Murphy for S. O'Brien, M. Kelly for Butler.

1947

SCORERS:

Kilkenny: T. Leahy 0-6, J. Langton 0-3, T. Walton 0-2, S. Downey 0-1, J. Mulcahy 0-1, L. Reidy 0-1.

Cork: J. Kelly 1-1, S. Condon 0-4, M. O'Riordan 1-0, J. Lynch 0-1, C. Ring 0-1.

Kilkenny: J. Donegan, P. Grace, P. Hayden, M. Marnell, J. Kelly, P. Prendergast, J. Mulcahy, D. Kennedy (capt), J. Heffernan, T. Walton, T. Leahy, J. Langton, S. Downey, W. Cahill, L. Reidy. *Sub*: E. Kavanagh for Prendergast.

Cork: T. Mulcahy, W. Murphy, C. Murphy, D. J. Buckley, P. Donovan, A. Lotty, J. Young, J. Lynch, C. Cottrell, S. Condon (capt), C. Ring, C. Murphy, M. O'Riordan, J. O'Riordan, J. Kelly.

1948

SCORERS:

Waterford: J. Keane 3-2, C. Moylan 1-2, W. Galvin 1-1, E. Daly 1-0, V. Baston 0-1, E. Carew 0-1.

Dublin: J. Kennedy 2-2, F. Cummins 1-0, S. Óg Ó Ceallacháin 1-0.

Waterford: J. Ware (capt), A. Fleming, J. Cusack, J. Goode, M. Hickey, V. Baston, M. Hayes, J. O'Connor, E. Carew, K. O'Connor, J. Keane, C. Moylan, W. Galvin, E. Daly, T. Curran.

Dublin: K. Matthews, E. Dunphy, D. Walsh, S. Cronin, A. Herbert, J. Butler, P. Donnelly, M. Hasset, L. Donnelly, J. Kennedy, D. Cantwell, S. Óg Ó Ceallacháin, M. Williams, J. Prior, F. Cummins (capt).

1949

SCORERS:

Tipperary: J. Kennedy 2-4, P. Kenny 1-2, S. Kenny 0-2, P. Stakelum 0-1, P. Shanahan 0-1, T. Ryan 0-1.

Laois: J. Styles 0-2, W. Dargan 0-1.

Tipperary: A. Reddan, M. Byrne, A. Brennan, J. Doyle, P. Stakelum (capt), F. Coffey, T. Doyle, S. Kenny, P. Shanahan, T. Ryan, M. Ryan, J. Kennedy, J. Ryan, S. Maher, S. Bannon. *Sub*: P. Kenny for Coffey.

Laois: T. Fitzpatrick, L. White, J. Bergin, P. McCormack, J. Murray, T. Byrne, P. Rustchitzko (capt), J. Styles, W. Bohane, P. Hogan, H. Gray, P. O'Brien, P. Lawlor, D. Forde, P. Kelly. *Subs*: W. Dargan for O'Brien, A. Dunne for Rustchitzko.

1950

SCORERS:

Tipperary: P. Kenny 1-2, J. Kennedy 0-2, S. Kenny 0-2, S. Bannon 0-2, M. Ryan 0-1.

Kilkenny: J. Langton 0-6, J. Kelly 1-0, J. Heffernan 0-1, D. Kennedy 0-1.

Tipperary: A. Reddan, M. Byrne, A. Brennan, J. Doyle, J. Finn, P. Stakelum, T. Doyle, S. Bannon, P. Shanahan, E. Ryan, M. Ryan, S. Kenny (capt), P. Kenny, M. Maher, J. Kennedy. *Sub*: T. Ryan for Maher.

Kilkenny: R. Dowling, J. Hogan, P. Hayden, M. Marnell, J. Kelly, P. Prendergast, W. Walsh, D. Kennedy, S. Downey, J. Heffernan, M. Kenny (capt), J. Langton, W. Costigan, J. Mulcahy, L. Reidy. *Sub*: T. Walton for Costigan.

1951

SCORERS:

Tipperary: P. Kenny 0-7, S. Bannon 2-0, Tim Ryan 2-0, Ned Ryan 1-0, Mick Ryan 1-0, M. Maher 1-0.

Wexford: N. Rackard 3-2, T. Russell 0-3, Padge Kehoe 0-2, Paddy Kehoe 0-1, E. Wheeler 0-1.

Tipperary: A. Reddan. M. Byrne, A. Brennan, J. Doyle, J. Finn (capt), P. Stakelum, T. Doyle, P. Shanahan, J. Hough, E. Ryan, M. Ryan, T. Ryan, P. Kenny, M. Maher, S. Bannon. *Sub*: S. Kenny for P. Kenny.

Wexford: R. Brennan, M. Byrne, N. O'Donnell, M. O'Hanlon, S. Thorpe, R. Rackard, W. Rackard, E. Wheeler, J. Morrissey, Padge Kehoe, J. Cummins, T. Russell, T. Flood, N. Rackard (capt), Paddy Kehoe.

1952

SCORERS:

Cork: L. Dowling 2-0, C. Ring 0-6, P. Barry 0-2, W. J. Daly 0-2, J. Twomey 0-2, W. Griffin 0-1, G. Murphy 0-1.

Dublin: N. Allen 0-2, C. Murphy 0-2, G. Kelly 0-2, R. McCarthy 0-1.

Cork: D. Creedon, G. O'Riordan, J. Lyons, A. O'Shaughnessy, M. Fouhy, V. Twomey, S. O'Brien, J. Twomey, G. Murphy, W. Griffin, W. J. Daly. C. Ring, L. Abernethy, L. Dowling, P. Barry (capt). *Subs*: M. O'Riordan for Griffin, J. Lynam for Abernethy.

Dublin: K. Matthews, S. Cronin, P. Ryan, J. O'Callaghan, D. Ferguson, J. Prior (capt), T. Fahy, C. Murphy, N. Allen, G. Kelly, R. McCarthy, S. Kennedy, J. Finan, A. O'Brien, A. Herbert. *Subs*: M. Wilson for Finan, M. Williams for Kennedy.

1953

SCORERS:

Cork: C. Ring 1-1, J. Hartnett 1-0, T. O'Sullivan 1-0, W. J. Daly 0-1, P. Barry 0-1.

Galway: W. Duffy 0-2, J. Molloy 0-2, J. Gallagher 0-1, J. Duggan 0-1, J. Killeen 0-1, H. Gordon 0-1.

Cork: D. Creedon, G. O'Riordan, J. Lyons, A. O'Shaughnessy, M. Fouhy, D. Hayes, V. Twomey, J. Twomey, G. Murphy, W. J. Daly, J. Hartnett, C. Ring (capt), T. O'Sullivan, L. Dowling, P. Barry.

Galway: S. Duggan, C. Corless, W. O'Neill, J. Brophy, M. Burke (capt), J. Molloy, E. Quinn, J. Salmon, W. Duffy, J. Duggan, H. Gordon, J. Killeen, M. McInerney, J. Gallagher, P. Nolan. *Subs*: M. J. Flaherty for Nolan, P. Duggan for J. Duggan.

1954

SCORERS:

Cork: C. Ring 0-5, J. Clifford 1-0, E. Goulding 0-1, W. J. Daly 0-1, V. Twomey 0-1, J. Hartnett 0-1.

Wexford: T. Ryan 1-0, N. Rackard 0-3, T. Flood 0-2, Padge Kehoe 0-1.

Cork: D. Creedon, G. O'Riordan, J. Lyons, A. O'Shaughnessy, M. Fouhy, V. Twomey, D. Hayes, G. Murphy, W. Moore, W. J. Daly, J. Hartnett, C. Ring (capt), J. Clifford, E. Goulding, P. Barry. *Sub*: T. O'Sullivan for Barry.

Wexford: A. Foley, W. Rackard, N. O'Donnell, M. O'Hanlon, J. English, R. Rackard, E. Wheeler, J. Morrissey, S. Hearne, Paddy Kehoe, T. Flood, Padge Kehoe (capt), T. Ryan, N. Rackard, R. Donovan. *Subs*: T. Bolger for O'Donnell, D. Hearne for Paddy Kehoe.

1955

SCORERS:

Wexford: N. Rackard 1-3, T. Flood 1-2, E. Wheeler 1-2, Paddy Kehoe 0-2, Padge Kehoe 0-1, S. Hearne 0-1, T. Ryan 0-1, J. Morrissey 0-1.

Galway: W. Duffy 0-4, P. Duggan 0-3, J. Burke 1-0, P. Egan 1-0, J. Salmon 0-1.

Wexford: A. Foley, R. Rackard, N. O'Donnell (capt), M. O'Hanlon, J. English, W. Rackard, M. Morrissey, J. Morrissey, S. Hearne, Paddy Kehoe, E. Wheeler, Padge Kehoe, T. Ryan, N. Rackard, T. Flood. *Subs*: O. Gough for Wheeler, Wheeler for Gough, D. Aherne for Ryan.

Galway: T. Boland, J. Fives, B. Power, W. O'Neill, M. Burke, J. Molloy,

T. Kelly, J. Salmon, W. Duffy, J. Duggan (capt), J. Young, P. Duggan, P. Egan, J. Burke, T. Sweeney. *Subs*: H. Gordon for Power, M. Elwood for Sweeney.

1956
SCORERS:
Wexford: N. Rackard 1-5, Padge Kehoe 1-1, T. Flood 0-3, T. Dixon 0-2, M. Codd 0-2, W. Rackard 0-1.
Cork: C. Ring 1-5, P. Barry 1-1, M. Regan 0-1, E. Goulding 0-1.
Wexford: A. English, R. Rackard, N. O'Donnell, M. Morrissey, J. English (capt), W. Rackard, J. Morrissey, S. Hearne, E. Wheeler, Padge Kehoe, M. Codd, T. Flood, T. Ryan, N. Rackard, T. Dixon.
Cork: M. Cashman, J. Brohan, J. Lyons, A. O'Shaughnessy (capt), M. Fouhy, W. J. Daly, P. Philpott, E. Goulding, P. Dowling, M. Regan, J. Hartnett, P. Barry, C. O'Shea, T. Kelly, C. Ring. *Subs*: V. Twomey for O'Shaughnessy, G. Murphy for Hartnett.

1957
SCORERS:
Kilkenny: W. Dwyer 2-0, M. Kenny 0-5, M. Kelly 1-1, D. Rockett 1-0, S. Clohosey 0-2, D. Heaslip 0-1, M. Walsh 0-1.
Waterford: P. Grimes 1-6, D. Whelan 2-2, J. Kiely 0-2, F. Walsh 0-1, T. Cheasty 0-1.
Kilkenny: O. Walsh, T. Walsh, J. Walsh, J. Maher, P. Buggy, M. Walsh, J. McGovern, J. Sutton, M. Brophy, D. Heaslip, M. Kenny, M. Kelly (capt), D. Rockett, W. O'Dwyer, S. Clohosey. *Sub*: B. Walsh for Sutton.
Waterford: R. Roche, T. Cunningham, A. Flynn, J. Barron, M. O'Connor, M. Óg Morrissey, S. Power, J. O'Connor, P. Grimes (capt), M. Flannelly, T. Cheasty, L. Guinan, F. Walsh, J. Kiely, D. Whelan.

1958
SCORERS:
Tipperary: D. Nealon 1-2, L. Keane 1-1, L. Devaney 1-0, A. Wall 1-0, Jimmy Doyle 0-3, T. Larkin 0-2, L. Connolly 0-1.
Galway: T. Kelly 1-2, P. J. Lawless 1-0, J. Fives 0-2, T. Sweeney 0-1.
Tipperary: J. O'Grady, M. Byrne, M. Maher, K. Carey, J. Finn, A. Wall (capt), John Doyle, J. Hough, T. English, D. Nealon, T. Larkin, Jimmy Doyle, L. Keane, L. Devaney, L. Connolly.
Galway: M. Sweeney, F. Spillane, P. Burke, S. Cullinane (capt), J. Duggan,

J. Fives, F. Benson, J. Salmon, P. J. Lally, T. Sweeney, J. Young, T. Kelly, P. J. Lawless, W. O'Neill, T. Conway. *Subs*: E. Dervan for Spillane, M. Fox for Young.

1959
SCORERS:
Waterford: F. Walsh 0-5, T. Cheasty 0-5, S. Power 1-0, P. Grimes 0-3, L. Guinan 0-2, J. Kiely 0-2.
Kilkenny: T. O'Connell 3-0, R. Carroll 1-2, W. Dwyer 1-1, P. Kelly 0-1, S. Clohosey 0-1.
Waterford: E. Power, J. Harney, A. Flynn, J. Barron, M. Lacey, M. Óg Morrissey, J. Condon, S. Power, P. Grimes, L. Guinan, T. Cheasty, F. Walsh (capt), C. Ware, D. Whelan, J. Kiely. *Subs*: M. Flannelly for Condon, T. Cunningham for Ware.
Kilkenny: O. Walsh, T. Walsh, J. Walsh, J. Maher, P. Buggy, M. Walsh, J. McGovern, M. Brophy, P. Kelly, D. Heaslip, R. Carroll, M. Fleming, S. Clohosey (capt), W. Dwyer, T. O'Connell. *Subs*: T. Kelly for McGovern, J. Sutton for Fleming, Fleming for Sutton, M. Kelly for Brophy.

1959 Replay
SCORERS:
Waterford: T. Cheasty 2-2, F. Walsh 0-8, M. Flannelly 1-1, L. Guinan 0-1.
Kilkenny: W. Dwyer 0-5, D. Heaslip 1-1, E. Keher 0-2, S. Clohosey 0-1, M. Walsh 0-1.
Waterford: E. Power, J. Harney, A. Flynn, J. Barron, M. Lacey, M. Óg Morrissey, J. Condon, S. Power, P. Grimes, M. Flannelly, T. Cheasty, F. Walsh (capt), L. Guinan, T. Cunningham, J. Kiely. *Subs*: M. O'Connor for Lacey, D. Whelan for Cunningham.
Kilkenny: O. Walsh, T. Walsh, J. Walsh, J. Maher, P. Buggy, T. Kelly. J. McGovern, P. Kelly, M. Walsh, D. Heaslip, M. Fleming, S. Clohosey (capt), R. Carroll, W. Dwyer, T. O'Connell. *Subs*: E. Keher for McGovern, M. Kelly for Fleming.

1960
SCORERS:
Wexford: Padge Kehoe 1-7, O. McGrath 1-2, T. Flood 0-3, J. Morrissey 0-1, J. Harding 0-1, J. O'Brien 0-1.
Tipperary: T. Ryan 0-3, L. Devaney 0-2, T. Moloughney 0-2, A. Wall 0-2, T. English 0-1, Jimmy Doyle 0-1.

Wexford: P. Nolan, J. Mitchell, N. O'Donnell (capt), T. Neville, J. English, W. Rackard, J. Nolan, E. Wheeler, J. Morrissey, J. O'Brien, Padge Kehoe, S. Quaid, O. McGrath, J. Harding, T. Flood. *Subs*: S. Power for Quaid, M. Morrissey for Power.

Tipperary: T. Moloney, M. Hassett, M. Maher, K. Carey, M. Burns, A. Wall (capt), John Doyle, T. English, T. Ryan, Jimmy Doyle, L. Devaney, D. Nealon, L. Connolly, T. Moloughney, S. McLoughlin. *Subs*: W. Moloughney for McLoughlin, N. Murphy for English.

1961

SCORERS:

Tipperary: Jimmy Doyle 0-9, D. Nealon 0-3, M. O'Gara 0-2, T. Moloughney 0-1, J. McKenna 0-1.

Dublin: W. Jackson 1-2, Achill Boothman 0-5, L. Shannon 0-3, Des Foley 0-1, Bernard Boothman 0-1.

Tipperary: D. O'Brien, M. Hassett (capt), M. Maher, K. Carey, M. Burns, A. Wall, John Doyle, M. O'Gara, T. English, Jimmy Doyle, L. Devaney, D. Nealon, J. McKenna, W. Moloughney, T. Moloughney. *Subs*: T. Ryan for McKenna, J. Hough for O'Gara, S. McLoughlin for Wall.

Dublin: J. Gray, D. Ferguson, N. Drumgoole (capt), L. Foley, L. Ferguson, C. Hayes, S. Lynch, D. Foley, F. Whelan, Achill Boothman, M. Bohan, L. Shannon, Bernard Boothman, P. Croke, W. Jackson. *Sub*: E. Malone for Bohan.

1962

SCORERS:

Tipperary: S. McLoughlin 1-2, Jimmy Doyle 0-4, D. Nealon 0-3, T. Moloughney 1-0, T. Ryan (Killenaule) 1-0, L. Connolly 0-1.

Wexford: Padge Kehoe 0-4, E. Wheeler 1-1, J. O'Brien 1-0, P. Lynch 0-2, T. Flood 0-2, O. McGrath 0-1, W. Rackard 0-1.

Tipperary: D. O'Brien, John Doyle, M. Maher, K. Carey, M. O'Gara, A. Wall, M. Burns, T. English, L. Devaney, Jimmy Doyle (capt), J. McKenna, T. Ryan (Killenaule), D. Nealon, T. Moloughney, S. McLoughlin. *Subs*: L. Connolly for O'Gara, T. Ryan (Toomevara) for Jimmy Doyle.

Wexford: P. Nolan, T. Neville, N. O'Donnell, E. Colfer, J. English, W. Rackard (capt), J. Nolan, P. Wilson, M. Lyng, J. O'Brien, Padge Kehoe, P. Lynch, O. McGrath, E. Wheeler, T. Flood.

1963

SCORERS:

Kilkenny: E. Keher 0-14, T. Murphy 2-1, T. Walsh 2-0, S. Cleere 0-2.

Waterford: S. Power 3-0, M. Flannelly 2-0, P. Grimes 1-4, F. Walsh 0-2, M. Dempsey 0-1, J. Condon 0-1.

Kilkenny: O. Walsh, P. Larkin, C. Whelan, M. Treacy, S. Cleere (capt), T. Carroll, M. Coogan, P. Moran, S. Clohosey, D. Heaslip, J. McGovern, E. Keher, T. Walsh, W. Dwyer, T. Murphy. *Sub*: O. Gough for McGovern.

Waterford: E. Power, T. Cunningham, A. Flynn, J. Byrne, L. Guinan, M. Óg Morrissey, J. Irish, M. Dempsey, J. Condon (capt), M. Flannelly, T. Cheasty, F. Walsh, S. Power, J. Barron, P. Grimes. *Subs*: P. Flynn for E. Power, J. Meaney for Condon, M. Walsh for Byrne.

1964

SCORERS:

Tipperary: Jimmy Doyle 0-10, D. Nealon 3-0, J. McKenna 1-0, S. McLoughlin 1-0, M. Keating 0-2, M. Roche 0-1.

Kilkenny: T. Walsh 1-2, J. Teehan 1-0, E. Keher 0-2, P. Moran 0-2, S. Cleere 0-1, T. Forrestal 0-1.

Tipperary: J. O'Donoghue, John Doyle, M. Maher, K. Carey, M. Burns, A. Wall, M. Murphy (capt), T. English, M. Roche, Jimmy Doyle, L. Kiely, M. Keating, D. Nealon, J. McKenna, S. McLoughlin. *Subs*: L. Devaney for Kiely, M. Lonergan for Maher.

Kilkenny: O. Walsh, C. Whelan, P. Dillon, P. Larkin, P. Henderson, T. Carroll, M. Coogan, P. Moran, S. Buckley (capt), S. Cleere, J. Teehan, E. Keher, T. Walsh, T. Forrestal, T. Murphy. *Subs*: W. Murphy for Coogan, D. Heaslip for Murphy.

1965

SCORERS:

Tipperary: S. McLoughlin 2-1, Jimmy Doyle 0-6, J. McKenna 0-5, L. Kiely 0-2, T. English 0-1, L. Devaney 0-1.

Wexford: J. O'Brien 0-4, M. Codd 0-3, D. Shannon 0-3.

Tipperary: J. O'Donoghue, John Doyle, M. Maher, K. Carey, M. Burns, A. Wall, L. Gaynor, T. English, M. Roche, Jimmy Doyle (capt), L. Kiely, L. Devaney, D. Nealon, J. McKenna, S. McLoughlin.

Wexford: P. Nolan, W. O'Neill, D. Quigley, E. Colfer, V. Staples, T. Neville (capt), W. Murphy, P. Wilson, M. Byrne, J. O'Brien, J. Nolan, R. Shannon,

P. Quigley, M. Codd, J. Foley. *Subs*: E. Wheeler for J. Nolan, O. McGrath for
P. Quigley.

1966

SCORERS:

Cork: C. Sheehan 3-0, S. Barry 0-4, Justin McCarthy 0-3, Gerald McCarthy
0-1, Charlie McCarthy 0-1.

Kilkenny: E. Keher 0-7, T. Walsh 1-0, J. Dunphy 0-1, S. Buckley 0-1, J. Teehan
0-1.

Cork: P. Barry, P. Doolan, T. O'Donoghue, D. Murphy, A. Connolly,
J. O'Sullivan, P. Fitzgerald, Justin McCarthy, M. Waters, S. Barry,
J. O'Halloran, Gerald McCarthy (capt), Charlie McCarthy, C. Sheehan,
J. Bennett.

Kilkenny: O. Walsh, P. Henderson, J. Lynch (capt), J. Treacy, S. Cleere,
T. Carroll, M. Coogan, P. Moran, J. Teehan, E. Keher, C. Dunne, S. Buckley,
J. Dunphy, P. Dillon, T. Walsh. *Subs*: T. Murphy for Dillon, P. Carroll for
Murphy.

1967

SCORERS:

Kilkenny: T. Walsh 1-2, P. Moran 1-0, M. Brennan 1-0, E. Keher 0-3,
C. Dunne 0-2, R. Blanchfield 0-1.

Tipperary: D. Nealon 2-0, Jimmy Doyle 0-5, M. Roche 0-2.

Kilkenny: O. Walsh, T. Carroll, P. Dillon, J. Treacy (capt), S. Cleere,
P. Henderson, M. Coogan, P. Moran, J. Teehan, E. Keher, T. Walsh,
C. Dunne, J. Bennett, J. Lynch, M. Brennan. *Subs*: R. Blanchfield for Keher,
P. Carroll for T. Walsh, J. Kinsella for Bennett.

Tipperary: J. O'Donoghue, John Doyle, K. Carey, N. O'Gorman, M. Burns,
A. Wall, L. Gaynor, T. English, M. Roche (capt), D. Nealon, J. Flanagan,
L. Devaney, Jimmy Doyle, M. Keating, S. McLoughlin. *Subs*: L. Kiely for
McLoughlin, M. Lonergan for Burns, P. J. Ryan for English.

1968

SCORERS:

Wexford: Jack Berry 2-2, A. Doran 2-1, P. Lynch 1-3, J. O'Brien 0-2.

Tipperary: J. Doyle 1-5, M. Keating 1-3, S. McLoughlin 1-1, L. Devaney 0-2,
M. Burns 0-1.

Wexford: P. Nolan, T. Neville, E. Kelly, E. Colfer, V. Staples, D. Quigley (capt), W. Murphy, P. Wilson, D. Bernie, P. Lynch, A. Doran, C. Jacob, J. O'Brien, S. Whelan, J. Berry. *Sub*: J. Quigley for Whelan.

Tipperary: J. O'Donoghue, J. Costigan, N. O'Gorman, J. Gleeson, M. Burns, M. Roche (capt), L. Gaynor, P. J. Ryan, D. Nealon, M. Keating, J. Ryan, J. Doyle, J. McKenna, S. McLoughlin, L. Devaney. *Sub*: F. Loughnane for Doyle.

1969

SCORERS:

Kilkenny: E. Keher 0-8, M. Brennan 1-1, J. Millea 1-0, M. Coogan 0-3, P. Kavanagh 0-1, P. Moran 0-1, M. Lawlor 0-1.

Cork: Charlie McCarthy 1-6, E. O'Brien 1-1, Gerald McCarthy 0-1, P. Hegarty 0-1.

Kilkenny: O. Walsh, T. Carroll, P. Dillon, J. Treacy, W. Murphy, P. Henderson, M. Coogan, M. Lawlor, F. Cummins, C. Dunne, P. Delaney, E. Keher (capt), J. Millea, M. Brennan, T. Murphy. *Subs*: P. Kavanagh for Dunne, P. Moran for Delaney, S. Buckley for T. Murphy.

Cork: P. Barry, A. Maher, T. O'Donoghue, D. Murphy (capt), D. Clifford, W. Walsh, Gerald McCarthy, D. Coughlan, R. Tuohy, T. Ryan, C. Cullinane, P. Hegarty, Charlie McCarthy, R. Cummins, E. O'Brien. *Subs*: J. O'Halloran for O'Brien, J. Murphy for Tuohy, S. Looney for Ryan.

1970

SCORERS:

Cork: Charlie McCarthy 1-9, E. O'Brien 3-1, T. Ryan 0-6, W. Walsh 1-2, C. Cullinane 1-0, Gerald McCarthy 0-2, R. Cummins 0-1.

Wexford: A. Doran 2-0, Pat Quigley 2-0, Dan Quigley 1-0, M. Butler 0-3, D. Bernie 0-3, T. Byrne 0-2, M. Jacob 0-1, M. Browne 0-1.

Cork: P. Barry (capt), A. Maher, P. McDonnell, J. Horgan, D. Clifford, P. Hegarty, C. Roche, Gerald McCarthy, S. Looney, T. Ryan, W. Walsh, C. Cullinane, Charlie McCarthy, R. Cummins, E. O'Brien. *Sub*: S. Murphy for Clifford.

Wexford: P. Nolan, E. Colfer, M. Collins (capt), T. Neville, M. Browne, Dan Quigley, T. O'Connor, D. Beirne, M. Jacob, Martin Quigley, Pat Quigley, John Quigley, M. Butler, A. Doran, J. Berry. *Subs*: T. Byrne for Butler, J. Russell for Neville.

1971

SCORERS:

Tipperary: M. Keating 0-7, R. Ryan 2-0, J. Flanagan 1-2, D. Ryan 1-1, N. O'Dwyer 1-0, F. Loughnane 0-4, P. J. Ryan 0-2, P. Byrne 0-1.

Kilkenny: E. Keher 2-11, M. Murphy 1-1, E. Byrne 1-0, K. Purcell 1-0, F. Cummins 0-2.

Tipperary: P. O'Sullivan, L. King, J. Kelly, J. Gleeson, T. O'Connor (capt), M. Roche, L. Gaynor, P. J. Ryan, S. Hogan, F. Loughnane, N. O'Dwyer, D. Ryan, J. Flanagan, R. Ryan, M. Keating. *Subs*: Jimmy Doyle for Hogan, P. Byrne for Flanagan.

Kilkenny: O. Walsh, P. Larkin, P. Dillon, J. Treacy, W. Murphy, P. Henderson (capt), M. Coogan, F. Cummins, P. Lalor, M. Murphy, P. Delaney, E. Keher, M. Brennan, K. Purcell, E. Byrne. *Subs*: P. Moran for W. Murphy, P. Cullen for Brennan, E. Carroll for Larkin.

1972

SCORERS:

Kilkenny: E. Keher 2-9, L. O'Brien 0-5, F. Cummins 1-0, P. Delaney 0-3, M. Crotty 0-2, K. Purcell 0-2, P. Henderson 0-1, J. Kinsella 0-1, M. Murphy 0-1.

Cork: R. Cummins 2-3, M. Malone 2-1, S. O'Leary 1-1, C. McCarthy 0-4, C. Roche 0-2.

Kilkenny: N. Skehan (capt), P. Larkin, P. Dillon, J. Treacy, P. Lalor, P. Henderson, E. Morrissey, L. O'Brien, F. Cummins, M. Crotty, P. Delaney, J. Kinsella, E. Byrne, K. Purcell, E. Keher. *Subs*: M. Murphy for Byrne, M. Coogan for Larkin, P. Moran for Kinsella.

Cork: P. Barry, A. Maher, P. McDonnell, B. Murphy, F. Norberg (capt), S. Looney, C. Roche, Justin McCarthy, D. Coughlan, Gerald McCarthy, M. Malone, P. Hegarty, Charlie McCarthy, R. Cummins, S. O'Leary. *Subs*: T. O'Brien for Norberg, D. Collins for Hegarty.

1973

SCORERS:

Limerick: R. Bennis 0-10, M. Dowling 1-1, E. Grimes 0-4, F. Nolan 0-2, E. Rea 0-2, J. McKenna 0-1, B. Hartigan 0-1.

Kilkenny: C. Dunne 0-7, P. Delaney 1-1, M. Crotty 0-3, L. O'Brien 0-2, M. Brennan 0-1.

Limerick: S. Horgan, W. Moore, Pat Hartigan, J. O'Brien, Phil Bennis, E. Cregan, S. Foley, Richie Bennis, E. Grimes (capt), Bernie Hartigan,

M. Dowling, L. O'Donoghue, F. Nolan, E. Rea, J. McKenna. *Sub*: T. Ryan for Bernie Hartigan.

Kilkenny: N. Skehan, P. Larkin, N. Orr, P. Cullen, P. Lalor, P. Henderson, B. Cody, F. Cummins, L. O'Brien, C. Dunne, P. Delaney (capt), P. Broderick, M. Crotty, J. Lynch, M. Brennan. *Subs*: K. Purcell for Broderick, W. Harte for Cummins, J. Kinsella for Lynch.

1974

SCORERS:

Kilkenny: E. Keher 1-11, M. Brennan 1-2, P. Delaney 1-0, K. Purcell 0-2, P. Henderson 0-1, W. Fitzpatrick 0-1, M. Crotty 0-1, L. O'Brien 0-1.

Limerick: R. Bennis 0-5, L. O'Donoghue 1-0, E. Rea 0-3, J. McKenna 0-2, M. Ruth 0-1, E. Grimes 0-1, F. Nolan 0-1.

Kilkenny: N. Skehan, P. Larkin, N. Orr (capt), J. Treacy, P. Lalor, P. Henderson, T. McCormack, F. Cummins, L. O'Brien, M. Crotty, P. Delaney, W. Fitzpatrick, M. Brennan, K. Purcell, E. Keher.

Limerick: S. Horgan, W. Moore, Pat Hartigan, J. O'Brien, T. Ryan, E. Cregan, S. Foley (capt), Bernie Hartigan, E. Grimes, J. McKenna, R. Bennis, M. Ruth, L. O'Donoghue, E. Rea, F. Nolan. *Subs*: P. Kelly for Bernie Hartigan, Phil Bennis for Ryan, P. Fitzmaurice for McKenna.

1975

SCORERS:

Kilkenny: E. Keher 2-7, L. O'Brien 0-5, M Crotty 0-5, M. Brennan 0-2, F. Cummins 0-1, P. Delaney 0-1, P. Henderson 0-1.

Galway: G. Coone 0-6, F. Burke 1-0, P. J. Qualter 1-0, P. J. Molloy 0-3, J. Connolly 0-1.

Kilkenny: N. Skehan, P. Larkin, N. Orr, B. Cody, P. Lalor, P. Henderson, T. McCormack, F. Cummins, L. O'Brien, M. Crotty, P. Delaney, W. Fitzpatrick (capt), M. Brennan, K. Purcell, E. Keher.

Galway: M. Conneely, N. McInerney, J. Clarke, P. Lally, J. McDonough, S. Silke, I. Clarke, J. Connolly (capt), S. Murphy, G. Coone, F. Burke, P. J. Molloy, M. Barrett, P. J. Qualter, P. Fahy. *Subs*: M. Connolly for Barrett, Ted Murphy for Lally, S. Grealish for S. Murphy.

1976

SCORERS:

Cork: P. Moylan 0-10, Charlie McCarthy 1-3, Ray Cummins 1-2, J. Barry-Murphy 0-4, S. O'Leary 0-1, M. Malone 0-1.

Wexford: Martin Quigley 2-1, M. Butler 1-4, E. Buggy 0-5, A. Doran 1-0, John Quigley 0-1.

Cork: M. Coleman, B. Murphy, P. McDonnell, M. O'Doherty, P. Barry, J. Crowley, D. Coughlan, Gerald McCarthy, P. Moylan, M. Malone, Brendan Cummins, J. Barry-Murphy, Charlie McCarthy, Ray Cummins (capt), S. O'Leary. *Subs*: E. O'Donoghue for O'Leary, J. Horgan for Barry.

Wexford: J. Nolan, T. O'Connor, W. Murphy, J. Prendergast, L. Bennett, M. Jacob, Colm Doran, E. Buggy, Billy Rowsome, J. Murphy, Martin Quigley, John Quigley, N. Butler, Tony Doran (capt), C. Keogh. *Subs*: Declan Rowsome for Kehoe, M. Casey for Billy Rowsome.

1977

SCORERS:

Cork: Gerald McCarthy 0-6, Charlie McCarthy 0-5, S. O'Leary 1-2, J. Barry-Murphy 0-2, T. Cashman 0-1, R. Cummins 0-1.

Wexford: E. Buggy 1-4, M. Butler 1-2, T. Doran 1-0, J. Quigley 0-1, C. Keogh 0-1.

Cork: M. Coleman, B. Murphy, M. O'Doherty (capt), J. Horgan, D. McCurtain, J. Crowley, D. Coughlan, T. Cashman, T. Crowley, M. Malone, Gerald McCarthy, J. Barry-Murphy, Charlie McCarthy, R. Cummins, S. O'Leary. *Subs*: P. Moylan for Malone, T. Murphy for Gerald McCarthy.

Wexford: J. Nolan, T. O'Connor, W. Murphy, J. Prendergast, L. Bennett, M. Jacob, Colm Doran, D. Bernie, E. Buggy, C. Kehoe, Martin Quigley, M. Butler, John Quigley, Tony Doran (capt), J. Murphy. *Subs*: J. Russell for Prendergast, M. Casey for Murphy, E. Walsh for Bernie.

1978

SCORERS:

Cork: Charlie McCarthy 0-7, J. Barry-Murphy 1-1, Gerald McCarthy 0-2, T. Crowley 0-2, T. Cashman 0-1, S. O'Leary 0-1, R. Cummins 0-1.

Kilkenny: L. O'Brien 0-4, W. Fitzpatrick 1-1, K. Fennelly 1-0, M. Brennan 0-2, J. Hennessy 0-1.

Cork: M. Coleman, B. Murphy, M. O'Doherty, J. Horgan, D. McCurtain, J. Crowley, D. Coughlan, T. Cashman, P. Moylan, J. Barry-Murphy, Gerald

McCarthy, T. Crowley, Charlie McCarthy (capt), R. Cummins, S. O'Leary. *Subs*: J. Allen for Cashman, E. O'Donoghue for O'Leary.

Kilkenny: N. Skehan, P. Prendergast, P. Larkin, R. O'Hara, J. Hennessy, G. Henderson (capt), R. Reid, F. Cummins, L. O'Brien, K. Fennelly, M. Crotty, W. Fitzpatrick, M. Brennan, B. Cody, M. Ruth. *Subs*: T. Malone for Fennelly, P. Henderson for O'Brien.

1979

SCORERS:

Kilkenny: L. O'Brien 1-7, M. Brennan 1-1, J. Hennessy 0-1, W. Fitzpatrick 0-1, M. Crotty 0-1, Kevin Fennelly 0-1.

Galway: N. Lane 1-0, P. J. Molloy 0-3, Joe Connolly 0-2, F. Gantley 0-2, S. Mahon 0-1.

Kilkenny: N. Skehan, P. Larkin, P. Prendergast, John Henderson, R. Reid, Ger Henderson, Nickey Brennan, J. Hennessy, F. Cummins, Ger Fennelly (capt), W. Fitzpatrick, L. O'Brien, Mick Brennan, M. Crotty, M. Ruth. *Subs*: Kevin Fennelly for Crotty, R. O'Hara for Prendergast.

Galway: S. Shinnors, N. McInerney, C. Hayes, A. Fenton, J. McDonagh (capt), S. Silke, I. Clarke, John Connolly, S. Mahon, B. Forde, F. Burke, Joe Connolly, P. J. Molloy, N. Lane, F. Gantley. *Subs*: S. Linnane for Forde, M. Whelan for Burke.

1980

SCORERS:

Galway: B. Forde 1-5, Joe Connolly 0-4, P. J. Molloy 1-0, N. Lane 0-3, John Connolly 0-2, J. Ryan 0-1.

Limerick: E. Cregan 2-7, J. McKenna 1-1, B. Carroll 0-1.

Galway: M. Conneely, C. Hayes, N. McInerney, J. Cooney, S. Linnane, S. Silke, S. Coen, Michael Connolly, S. Mahon, F. Burke, Joe Connolly (capt), P. J. Molloy, B. Forde, John Connolly, N. Lane. *Subs*: F. Gantley for Michael Connolly, J. Ryan for Molloy.

Limerick: T. Quaid, D. Murray, L. Enright, Dom Punch, L. O'Donoghue, M. Carroll, S. Foley (capt), J. Carroll, David Punch, Paudie Fitzsimmons, J. Flanagan, W. Fitzmaurice, O. O'Connor, J. McKenna, E. Cregan. *Subs*: P. Herbert for M. Carroll, B. Carroll for Flanagan, E. Grimes for Fitzmaurice.

1981

SCORERS:

Offaly: P. Delaney 0-5, P. Carroll 1-1, J. Flaherty 1-1, P. Horan 0-2, L. Currams 0-2, D. Owens 0-1.

Galway: Joe Connolly 0-8, N. Lane 0-3, S. Mahon 0-2, Michael Connolly 0-1, P. J. Molloy 0-1.

Offaly: D. Martin, T. Donoghue, E. Coughlan, P. Fleury, A. Fogarty, P. Delaney, G. Coughlan, J. Kelly, L. Currams, P. Kirwan, B. Bermingham, M. Corrigan, P. Carroll, P. Horan (capt), J. Flaherty. *Subs*: D. Owens for Kirwan, B. Keeshan for Donoghue.

Galway: M. Conneely, S. Coen, N. McInerney, J. Cooney, S. Linnane, S. Silke (capt), I. Clarke, Michael Connolly, S. Mahon, F. Gantley, Joe Connolly, P. J. Molloy, B. Forde, John Connolly, N. Lane. *Subs*: F. Burke for Gantley, P. Ryan for Forde.

1982

SCORERS:

Kilkenny: C. Heffernan 2-3, W. Fitzpatrick 0-6, R. Power 0-4, Ger Fennelly 1-1, Liam Fennelly 0-2, J. Hennessy 0-1, K. Brennan 0-1.

Cork: P. Horgan 0-5, R. Cummins 0-3, E. O'Donoghue 1-0, T. O'Sullivan 0-2, T. Crowley 0-2, T. Cashman 0-1.

Kilkenny: N. Skehan, John Henderson, B. Cody (capt), R. O'Hara, Nickey Brennan, Ger Henderson, P. Prendergast, J. Hennessy, F. Cummins, R. Power, Ger Fennelly, Kieran Brennan, W. Fitzpatrick, C. Heffernan, Liam Fennelly.

Cork: G. Cunningham, Brian Murphy, M. O'Doherty, J. Blake, J. Buckley, John Crowley, D. McCurtain, T. Cashman, Tim Crowley, T. O'Sullivan, P. Horgan, J. Barry-Murphy (capt), S. O'Leary, R. Cummins, E. O'Donoghue. *Subs*: B. Óg Murphy for Buckley, K. Hennessy for O'Sullivan, F. Collins for McCurtain.

1983

SCORERS:

Kilkenny: W. Fitzpatrick 0-10, L. Fennelly 1-0, R. Power 1-0, G. Henderson 0-2, C. Heffernan 0-1, H. Ryan 0-1.

Cork: B. Óg Murphy 0-5, T. Mulcahy 1-0, S. O'Leary 1-0, J. Buckley 0-3, K. Hennessy 0-2, E. O'Donoghue 0-1, F. Collins 0-1.

Kilkenny: N. Skehan, John Henderson, B. Cody, R. O'Hara, J. Hennessy,

Ger Henderson, P. Prendergast, F. Cummins, Ger Fennelly, R. Power, K. Brennan, Liam Fennelly (capt), W. Fitzpatrick, C. Heffernan, H. Ryan. *Sub*: P. Lannon for Power.

Cork: G. Cunningham, B. Murphy, D. O'Grady, D. McCurtain, P. Horgan, John Crowley, T. Cashman, J. Buckley, J. Fenton, B. Óg Murphy, K. Hennessy, Tim Crowley, T. Mulcahy, J. Barry-Murphy (capt), E. O'Donoghue. *Subs*: F. Collins for Fenton, T. O'Sullivan for Mulcahy, S. O'Leary for Murphy.

1984

SCORERS:

Cork: J. Fenton 0-7, S. O'Leary 2-1, T. O'Sullivan 0-6, K. Hennessy 1-0, T. Mulcahy 0-1, P. Hartnett 0-1.
Offaly: Mark Corrigan 1-2, P. Delaney 0-4, P. Carroll 0-4, P. Horan 0-2.
Cork: G. Cunningham, D. Mulcahy, D. O'Grady, J. Hodgins, T. Cashman, John Crowley, D. McCurtain, J. Fenton (capt), P. Hartnett, K. Hennessy, Tim Crowley, T. O'Sullivan, T. Mulcahy, J. Barry-Murphy, S. O'Leary.
Offaly: D. Martin, L. Carroll, E. Coughlan, P. Fleury (capt), Aidan Fogarty, P. Delaney, Ger Coughlan, T. Conneely, J. Kelly, Mark Corrigan, B. Bermingham, P. Carroll, Declan Fogarty, P. Horan, J. Dooley. *Subs*: Paddy Corrigan for Bermingham, P. Kirwan for Dooley.

1985

SCORERS:

Offaly: P. Cleary 2-0, Paddy Corrigan 0-5, P. Horan 0-3, Mark Corrigan 0-2, B. Bermingham 0-1.
Galway: P. J. Molloy 1-6, B. Lynskey 0-2, M. McGrath 0-1, J. Cooney 0-1, N. Lane 0-1, T. Keady 0-1.
Offaly: J. Troy, A. Fogarty, E. Coughlan, P. Fleury (capt), T. Conneely, P. Delaney, G. Coughlan, D. Owens, J. Kelly, Paddy Corrigan, B. Bermingham, Mark Corrigan, P. Cleary, P. Horan, J. Dooley. *Subs*: D. Fogarty for Owens, B. Keeshan for Conneely.
Galway: P. Murphy, Ollie Kilkenny, C. Hayes, S. Linnane, P. Finnerty, A. Keady, Tony Kilkenny, M. Connolly (capt), S. Mahon, M. McGrath, B. Lynskey, J. Cooney, B. Forde, N. Lane, P. J. Molloy. *Subs*: J. Murphy for McGrath, A. Cunningham for Forde, M. Haverty for Connolly.

1986

SCORERS:

Cork: K. Hennessy 2-1, J. Fenton 1-4, T. Mulcahy 1-1, K. Kingston 0-2, J. Barry-Murphy 0-2, T. Cashman 0-1, T. O'Sullivan 0-1, G. Fitzgerald 0-1.
Galway: T. Keady 0-5, J. Cooney 0-4, P. J. Molloy 1-1, J. Commins 1-0, M. Naughton 0-2, P. Finnerty 0-1, S. Mahon 0-1, P. Murphy 0-1.
Cork: G. Cunningham, D. Mulcahy, R. Browne, J. Crowley, P. Hartnett, Tom Cashman (capt), D. Walsh, J. Fenton, Jim Cashman, T. McCarthy, T. Mulcahy, A. O'Sullivan, G. Fitzgerald, J. Barry-Murphy, K. Hennessy. *Sub*: K. Kingston for Fenton.
Galway: J. Commins, S. Linnane, C. Hayes, Ollie Kilkenny, P. Finnerty, A. Keady, G. McInerney, S. Mahon, P. Piggott, Tony Kilkenny, B. Lynskey, M. Naughton, A. Cunningham, J. Cooney, N. Lane (capt). *Subs*: P. J. Molloy for Piggott, M. Connolly for Mahon, P. Murphy for Cunningham.

1987

SCORERS:

Galway: J. Cooney 0-5, N. Lane 1-0, S. Mahon 0-2, T. Keady 0-2, M. McGrath 0-1, M. Naughton 0-1, A. Cunningham 0-1.
Kilkenny: G. Fennelly 0-7, H. Ryan 0-1, T. Lennon 0-1.
Galway: J. Commins, S. Linnane, C. Hayes (capt), Ollie Kilkenny, P. Finnerty, A. Keady, G. McInerney, S. Mahon, P. Malone, M. McGrath, J. Cooney, M. Naughton, E. Ryan, B. Lynskey, A. Cunningham. *Subs*: N. Lane for Naughton, P. J. Molloy for Cunningham, Tony Kilkenny for McGrath.
Kilkenny: Kevin Fennelly, J. Hennessy, P. Prendergast (capt), John Henderson, L. Walsh, Ger Henderson, Seán Fennelly, Ger Fennelly, L. Ryan, K. Brennan, C. Heffernan, R. Power, P. Walsh, Liam Fennelly, H. Ryan. *Subs*: T. Lennon for Walsh, L. McCarthy for Power.

1988

SCORERS:

Galway: N. Lane 1-0, P. Malone 0-3, G. McInerney 0-2, M. Naughton 0-2, M. McGrath 0-2, T. Keady 0-2, J. Cooney 0-1, B. Lynskey 0-1, E. Ryan 0-1, C. Hayes 0-1.
Tipperary: N. English 0-6, Declan Ryan 0-4, D. O'Connell 0-2, Aidan Ryan 0-1, P. Delaney 0-1.
Galway: J. Commins, S. Linnane, C. Hayes (capt), Ollie Kilkenny, P. Finnerty, A. Keady, G. McInerney, M. Coleman, P. Malone,

A. Cunningham, J. Cooney, M. Naughton, M. McGrath, B. Lynskey, E. Ryan. *Subs*: N. Lane for Cunningham, Tony Kilkenny for Naughton, G. Burke for Lynskey.

Tipperary: K. Hogan, P. Delaney, C. O'Donovan, J. Heffernan, Bobby Ryan, N. Sheehy, J. Kennedy, Colm Bonnar, J. Hayes, Declan Ryan, D. O'Connell, J. Leahy, P. Fox, N. English (capt), Aidan Ryan. *Sub*: Cormac Bonnar for Hayes.

1989

SCORERS:

Tipperary: N. English 2-12, Declan Ryan 1-3, P. Fox 1-2, J. Leahy 0-3, D. Carr 0-2, M. Cleary 0-2.

Antrim: Brian Donnelly 1-1, O. McFetridge 0-3, A. McCarry 1-0, D. Armstrong 1-0, Terence McNaughton 0-2, P. McKillen 0-1, L. McKeegan 0-1, D. McKillop 0-1.

Tipperary: K. Hogan, J. Heffernan, C. O'Donovan, N. Sheehy, Conal Bonnar, Bobby Ryan (capt), J. Kennedy, Colm Bonnar, D. Carr, J. Leahy, Declan Ryan, M. Cleary, P. Fox, Cormac Bonnar, N. English. *Subs*: J. Hayes for Cormac Bonnar, D. O'Connell for Leahy, Aidan Ryan for Cleary.

Antrim: N. Patterson, G. O'Kane, Terence Donnelly, Des Donnelly, James McNaughton, D. McKinley, L. McKeegan, P. McKillen, D. McMullan, C. Barr, A. McCarry, O. McFetridge, D. Armstrong, Brian Donnelly, Terence McNaughton. *Subs*: Danny McNaughton for McMullan, D. McKillop for O'Kane, M. Sullivan for McKinley.

1990

SCORERS:

Cork: J. Fitzgibbon 2-1, K. Hennessy 1-4, T. Mulcahy 1-2, M. Foley 1-1, T. McCarthy 0-3, T. O'Sullivan 0-2, G. Fitzgerald 0-1, K. McGuckin 0-1.

Galway: J. Cooney 1-7, N. Lane 0-4, M. Naughton 0-4, B. Lynskey 1-0, E. Ryan 0-2, T. Keady 0-1, M. McGrath 0-1, A. Cunningham 0-1, M. Coleman 0-1.

Cork: G. Cunningham, J. Considine, D. Walsh, S. O'Gorman, S. McCarthy, J. Cashman, K. McGuckin, B. O'Sullivan, T. McCarthy, G. Fitzgerald, M. Foley, T. O'Sullivan, T. Mulcahy (capt), K. Hennessy, J. Fitzgibbon. *Subs*: C. Casey for B. O'Sullivan, D. Quirke for McGuckin.

Galway: J. Commins, D. Fahy, S. Treacy, O. Kilkenny, P. Finnerty, T. Keady, G. McInerney, M. Coleman, P. Malone, A. Cunningham, J. Cooney (capt),

M. Naughton, M. McGrath, N. Lane, E. Ryan. *Subs*: T. Monaghan for Malone, B. Lynskey for Cunningham.

1991
SCORERS:

Tipperary: M. Cleary 1-6, P. Fox 0-5, Aidan Ryan 0-2, Bobby Ryan 0-1, Declan Ryan 0-1, J. Leahy 0-1.

Kilkenny: D. J. Carey 0-9, E. Morrissey 0-3, R. Power 0-1, L. Fennelly 0-1, L. McCarthy 0-1.

Tipperary: K. Hogan, P. Delaney, N. Sheehy, Michael Ryan, Colm Bonnar, Bobby Ryan, Conal Bonnar, D. Carr (capt), Aidan Ryan, M. Cleary, Declan Ryan, J. Leahy, P. Fox, Cormac Bonnar, N. English. *Subs*: C. Stakelum for Cormac Bonnar, D. O'Connell for English.

Kilkenny: M. Walsh, B. Hennessy, J. Henderson, L. Simpson, L. Walsh, P. Dwyer, E. O'Connor, R. Power, M. Phelan, J. Power, C. Heffernan (capt), D. J. Carey, E. Morrissey, L. Fennelly, L. McCarthy. *Subs*: A. Ronan for McCarthy, L. Ryan for J. Power.

1992
SCORERS:

Kilkenny: D. J. Carey 1-4, L. McCarthy 1-1, J. Power 1-0, M. Phelan 0-2, L. Fennelly 0-1, C. Heffernan 0-1, A. Ronan 0-1.

Cork: T. O'Sullivan 0-3, S. McCarthy 0-3, G. Manley 1-0, T. McCarthy 0-2, C. Casey 0-1, T. Mulcahy 0-1, K. Hennessy 0-1, B. Corcoran 0-1.

Kilkenny: M. Walsh, Eddie O'Connor, P. Dwyer, L. Simpson, L. Walsh, P. O'Neill, Willie O'Connor, M. Phelan, B. Hennessy, L. McCarthy, J. Power, D. J. Carey, E. Morrissey, L. Fennelly (capt), J. Brennan. *Subs*: C. Heffernan for Brennan, A. Ronan for Morrissey.

Cork: G. Cunningam, S. O'Gorman, D. Mulcahy, B. Corcoran, C. Casey, J. Cashman, D. Walsh, P. Buckley, S. McCarthy, T. McCarthy, T. Mulcahy, T. O'Sullivan, G. Fitzgerald (capt), J. Fitzgibbon, K. Hennessy. *Subs*: P. Hartnett for Walsh, G. Manley for Fitzgerald, M. Foley for Buckley.

1993
SCORERS:

Kilkenny: P. J. Delaney 1-4, A. Ronan 1-2, D. J. Carey 0-4, L. McCarthy 0-3, E. Morrissey 0-2, B. Hennessy 0-1, J. Power 0-1.

Galway: J. Rabbitte 0-4, J. Cooney 0-4, P. Malone 0-3, L. Burke 1-0, M. McGrath 0-2, P. Kelly 0-2.

Kilkenny: M. Walsh, Eddie O'Connor (capt), P. Dwyer, L. Simpson, L. Keoghan, P. O'Neill, Willie O'Connor, B. Hennessy, M. Phelan, L. McCarthy, J. Power, D. J. Carey, E. Morrissey, P. J. Delaney, A. Ronan. *Subs*: J. Brennan for Morrissey, T. Murphy for Phelan, C. Heffernan for Delaney.

Galway: R. Burke, P. Cooney, S. Treacy, M. Killilea, T. Helebert, G. McInerney, P. Kelly, M. Coleman, P. Malone, B. Keogh, J. McGrath, J. Cooney, M. McGrath (capt), J. Rabbitte, L. Burke. *Subs*: J. Campbell for J. McGrath, P. Finnerty for Keogh.

1994

SCORERS:

Offaly: Johnny Dooley 1-4, Joe Dooley 1-2, Billy Dooley 0-5, P. O'Connor 1-0, Johnny Pilkington 0-2, John Troy 0-1, Declan Pilkington 0-1, M. Duignan 0-1.

Limerick: D. Quigley 2-3, G. Kirby 0-6, C. Carey 0-2, M. Houlihan 0-1, L. O'Connor 0-1.

Offaly: Jim Troy, S. McGuckin, K. Kinahan, M. Hanamy (capt), Brian Whelehan, H. Rigney, K. Martin, Johnny Pilkington, D. Regan, Johnny Dooley, John Troy, Joe Dooley, Billy Dooley, B. Kelly, Declan Pilkington. *Subs*: J. Errity for McGuckin, M. Duignan for Regan, P. O'Connor for Joe Dooley.

Limerick: J. Quaid, S. McDonagh, Mike Nash, J. O'Connor, D. Clarke, G. Hegarty, Declan Nash, C. Carey, M. Houlihan, F. Carroll, G. Kirby (capt), M. Galligan, T. J. Ryan, B. Heffernan, D. Quigley. *Sub*: L. O'Connor for Galligan.

1995

SCORERS:

Clare: F. Tuohy 0-4, E. Taffe 1-0, S. McMahon 0-3, J. O'Connor 0-2, A. Daly 0-1, O. Baker 0-1, F. Hegarty 0-1, G. O'Loughlin 0-1.

Offaly: Johnny Dooley 0-5, M. Duignan 1-0, Johnny Pilkington 1-0, D. Regan 0-1, John Troy 0-1, Billy Dooley 0-1.

Clare: D. Fitzgerald, M. O'Halloran, Brian Lohan, Frank Lohan, L. Doyle, S. McMahon, A. Daly (capt), J. O'Connor, O. Baker, F. Tuohy, P. J. O'Connell, F. Hegarty, S. McNamara, C. Clancy, G. O'Loughlin. *Subs*: E. Taffe for McNamara, C. Lyons for Clancy, A. Neville for Taffe.

Offaly: D. Hughes, S. McGuckin, K. Kinahan, M. Hanamy, Brian Whelehan, H. Rigney, K. Martin, Johnny Pilkington (capt), D. Regan, Johnny Dooley, J. Troy, M. Duignan, Joe Dooley, Billy Dooley, P. O'Connor. *Subs*: Declan Pilkington for P. O'Connor, B. Kelly for Joe Dooley.

1996
SCORERS:

Wexford: T. Dempsey 1-3, G. Laffan 0-3, L. O'Gorman 0-2, M. Storey 0-2, E. Scallan 0-1, L. Murphy 0-1, J. O'Connor 0-1.

Limerick: B. Foley 0-4, C. Carey 0-3, G. Kirby 0-2, D. Quigley 0-1, F. Carroll 0-1, T. J. Ryan 0-1, D. Clarke 0-1, O. O'Neill 0-1.

Wexford: D. Fitzhenry, C. Kehoe, G. Cush, John O'Connor, R. Guiney, L. Dunne, L. O'Gorman, A. Fenlon, George O'Connor, R. McCarthy, M. Storey (capt), L. Murphy, T. Dempsey, G. Laffan, E. Scallan. *Subs*: B. Byrne for L. Murphy, P. Finn for Guiney, P. Codd for Laffan.

Limerick: J. Quaid, S. McDonagh, Mike Nash, Declan Nash, D. Clarke, C. Carey (capt), M. Foley, M. Houlihan, S. O'Neill, F. Carroll, G. Kirby, B. Foley, Owen O'Neill, D. Quigley, J. Ryan. *Subs*: P. Tobin for Owen O'Neill, B. Tobin for Ryan, T. Herbert for Foley.

1997
SCORERS:

Clare: J. O'Connor 0-7, N. Gilligan 0-3, O. Baker 0-2, C. Lynch 0-2, D. Forde 0-2, L. Doyle 0-1, S. McMahon 0-1, C. Clancy 0-1, G. O'Loughlin 0-1.

Tipperary: T. Dunne 0-6, E. O'Neill 1-1, J. Leahy 0-3, L. Cahill 1-0, B. O'Meara 0-1, M. Cleary 0-1, C. Gleeson 0-1.

Clare: D. Fitzgerald, M. O'Halloran, Brian Lohan, Frank Lohan, L. Doyle, S. McMahon, A. Daly (capt), O. Baker, C. Lynch, J. O'Connor, C. Clancy, P. J. O'Connell, N. Gilligan, G. O'Loughlin, F. Tuohy. *Subs*: T. Hegarty for Tuohy, D. Forde for O'Connell, B. Murphy for Hegarty.

Tipperary: B. Cummins, Paul Sheehy, Noel Sheehy, Michael Ryan, L. Sheedy, Colm Bonnar, Conal Bonnar, T. Dunne, C. Gleeson (capt), L. McGrath, Declan Ryan, J. Leahy, M. Cleary, E. O'Neill, B. O'Meara. *Subs*: Aidan Ryan for McGrath, L. Cahill for Cleary.

1998

SCORERS:

Offaly: Brian Whelehan 1-6, J. Errity 1-2, J. Troy 0-3, M. Duignan 0-2, Joe Dooley 0-2, J. Pilkington 0-1.

Kilkenny: D. J. Carey 0-5, C. Carter 1-1, B. McEvoy 0-3, K. O'Shea 0-2, P. Larkin 0-1, A. Comerford 0-1.

Offaly: S. Byrne, Simon Whelehan, K. Kinahan, M. Hanamy, Brian Whelehan, H. Rigney (capt), K. Martin, J. Pilkington, Johnny Dooley, M. Duignan, J. Troy, Gary Hanniffy, Billy Dooley, J. Errity, Joe Dooley. *Subs*: P. Mulhare for Hanniffy, Darren Hanniffy for Billy Dooley, J. Ryan for Johnny Dooley.

Kilkenny: J. Dermody, T. Hickey (capt), P. O'Neill, W. O'Connor, M. Kavanagh, C. Brennan, L. Keoghan, P. Larkin, P. Barry, D. J. Carey, A. Comerford, B. McEvoy, K. O'Shea, P. J. Delaney, C. Carter. *Subs*: N. Maloney for O'Shea, S. Ryan for Comerford, J. Costelloe for Kavanagh.

1999

SCORERS:

Cork: J. Deane 0-3, T. McCarthy 0-3, S. McGrath 0-3, M. Landers 0-1, A. Browne 0-1, K. Murray 0-1, B. O'Connor 0-1.

Kilkenny: H. Shefflin 0-5, A. Comerford 0-2, C. Carter 0-2, J. Power 0-1, D. Byrne 0-1, B. McEvoy 0-1.

Cork: D. Óg Cusack, F. Ryan, D. O'Sullivan, J. Browne, W. Sherlock, B. Corcoran, S. Óg Ó hAilpín, M. Landers (capt), M. O'Connell, T. McCarthy, F. McCormack, N. Ronan, S. McGrath, J. Deane, B. O'Connor. *Subs*: A. Browne for Ronan, K. Murray for Landers.

Kilkenny: J. McGarry, P. Larkin, C. Brennan, W. O'Connor, M. Kavanagh, P. O'Neill, P. Barry, A. Comerford, D. Byrne (capt), D. J. Carey, J. Power, B. McEvoy, K. O'Shea, H. Shefflin, C. Carter. *Subs*: P. J. Delaney for Power, N. Moloney for Carter.

2000

SCORERS:

Kilkenny: D. J. Carey 2-4, H. Shefflin 1-3, C. Carter 1-3, D. Byrne 0-4, E. Brennan 1-0, A. Comerford 0-1.

Offaly: Johnny Dooley 0-8, J. Pilkington 1-1, Joe Dooley 0-1, B. Murphy 0-1, G. Hanniffy 0-1, Brian Whelehan 0-1, P. Mulhare 0-1.

Kilkenny: J. McGarry, M. Kavanagh, N. Hickey, W. O'Connor (capt), P. Larkin, E. Kennedy, P. Barry, A. Comerford, B. McEvoy, D. Byrne, J. Power, J. Hoyne, C. Carter, D. J. Carey, H. Shefflin. *Subs*: Canice Brennan for McEvoy, Eddie Brennan for C. Brennan.

Offaly: S. Byrne, Simon Whelehan, K. Kinahan, N. Claffey, Brian Whelehan, J. Errity, K. Martin, Johnny Dooley (capt), G. Oakley, J. Pilkington, G. Hanniffy, B. Murphy, M. Duignan, J. Ryan, Joe Dooley. *Subs*: D. Franks for Claffey, J. Troy for Ryan, P. Mulhare for Murphy.

2001

SCORERS:

Tipperary: E. Kelly 0-7, M. O'Leary 2-1, T. Dunne 0-5, L. Corbett 0-2, D. Ryan 0-1, P. O'Brien 0-1, J. Carroll 0-1.

Galway: E. Cloonan 1-5, F. Healy 1-2, K. Broderick 0-5, Mark Kerins 0-2, J. Rabbitte 0-1.

Tipperary: B. Cummins, T. Costello, P. Maher, P. Ormonde, E. Corcoran, D. Kennedy, Paul Kelly, T. Dunne (capt), E. Enright, M. O'Leary, J. Carroll, L. Corbett, Eoin Kelly, D. Ryan, E. O'Neill. *Subs*: D. Fahy for Costello, P. O'Brien for O'Neill, M. Ryan for Paul Kelly, C. Gleeson for Kennedy.

Galway: M. Commins, G. Kennedy, Michael Healy, O. Canning, D. Hardiman, L. Hodgins (capt), C. Moore, D. Tierney, R. Murray, J. Rabbitte, Mark Kerins, K. Broderick, Alan Kerins, E. Cloonan, Fergal Healy. *Subs*: B. Higgins for Hardiman, O. Fahy for Rabbitte.

2002

SCORERS:

Kilkenny: H. Shefflin 1-7, D. J. Carey 1-6, Martin Comerford 0-1, E. Brennan 0-1, Andy Comerford 0-1, J. Coogan 0-1, D. Lyng 0-1, B. McEvoy 0-1, C. Carter 0-1.

Clare: S. McMahon 0-6, J. O'Connor 0-4, C. Lynch 0-2, N. Gilligan 0-2, G. Considine 0-2, T. Griffin 0-1, A. Quinn 0-1, O. Baker 0-1.

Kilkenny: J. McGarry, M. Kavanagh, N. Hickey, P. Larkin, R. Mullaly, P. Barry, J. J. Delaney, Andy Comerford (capt), D. Lyng, J. Hoyne, H. Shefflin, J. Coogan, E. Brennan, Martin Comerford, D. J. Carey. *Subs*: C. Carter for Coogan, B. McEvoy for Hoyne, J. Power for Brennan.

Clare: D. Fitzgerald, Brian Quinn, Brian Lohan (capt), Frank Lohan, D. Hoey, S. McMahon, Gerry Quinn, J. Reddan, C. Lynch, J. O'Connor, T. Griffin, A. Markham, T. Carmody, N. Gilligan, D. Forde. *Subs*: O. Baker for

Reddan, G. Considine for Forde, Andrew Quinn for Markham, C. Plunkett for Baker.

2003

SCORERS:

Kilkenny: M. Comerford 1-4, H. Shefflin 0-6, T. Walsh 0-3, D. Lyng 0-1.
Cork: J. Deane 0-5, Setanta Óg Ó hAilpín 1-0, Niall McCarthy 0-2, Timmy McCarthy 0-1, Ben O'Connor 0-1, Jer O'Connor 0-1, S. McGrath 0-1.
Kilkenny: J. McGarry, M. Kavanagh, N. Hickey, J. Ryall, S. Dowling, P. Barry, J. J. Delaney, D. Lyng, Paddy Mullaly, H. Shefflin, J. Hoyne, T. Walsh, D. J. Carey (capt), Martin Comerford, E. Brennan. *Subs*: C. Phelan for Walsh, Andy Comerford for Ryall, Richard Mullally for Paddy Mullally, J. Coogan for Brennan.
Cork: D. Óg Cusack, W. Sherlock, D. O'Sullivan, P. Mulcahy, T. Kenny, R. Curran, Seán Óg Ó hAilpín, J. Gardiner, M. O'Connell, Ben O'Connor, Niall McCarthy, Timmy McCarthy, Setanta Óg Ó hAilpín, J. Deane, A. Browne (capt). *Subs*: Jer O'Connor for O'Connell, S. McGrath for Ben O'Connor.

2004

SCORERS:

Cork: J. Deane 0-5, Ben O'Connor 0-3, Niall McCarthy 0-3, Brian Corcoran 0-2, K. Murphy (Sarsfields) 0-2, Jer O'Connor 0-1, T. Kenny 0-1.
Kilkenny: H. Shefflin 0-5, M. Comerford 0-2, J. Fitzpatrick 0-1, D. Lyng 0-1.
Cork: D. Óg Cusack, W. Sherlock, D. O'Sullivan, B. Murphy, J. Gardiner, R. Curran, S. Óg Ó hAilpín, T. Kenny, Jer O'Connor, Ben O'Connor (capt), Niall McCarthy, Timmy McCarthy, K. Murphy (Sarsfields), B. Corcoran, J. Deane. *Sub*: J. Browne for Murphy.
Kilkenny: J. McGarry, M. Kavanagh, N. Hickey, J. Ryall, T. Walsh, P. Barry, J. J. Delaney, D. Lyng, K. Coogan, H. Shefflin, J. Hoyne, D. J. Carey, J. Fitzpatrick, M. Comerford (capt), E. Brennan. *Subs*: C. Phelan for Fitzpatrick, S. Dowling for Coogan.

2005

SCORERS:

Cork: Ben O'Connor 1-7, T. Kenny 0-3, J. Deane 0-3, B. Corcoran 0-2, Jer O'Connor 0-2, Timmy McCarthy 0-2, Niall McCarthy 0-1, J. Gardiner 0-1.
Galway: G. Farragher 0-8, A. Kerins 0-3, D. Hayes 1-0, Fergal Healy 0-2, Niall Healy 0-1, D. Tierney 0-1, D. Hardiman 0-1.

Cork: D. Óg Cusack, B. Murphy, D. O'Sullivan, P. Mulcahy, J. Gardiner, R. Curran, S. Óg Ó hAilpín (capt), T. Kenny, Jer O'Connor, Kieran Murphy (Sarsfields), Niall McCarthy, Timmy McCarthy, Ben O'Connor, B. Corcoran, J. Deane. *Subs*: N. Ronan for Kieran Murphy (Sarsfields), Kieran Murphy (Erin's Own) for N. McCarthy.

Galway: L. Donoghue (capt), D. Joyce, T. Óg Regan, O. Canning, D. Hardiman, S. Kavanagh, D. Collins, Fergal Healy, D. Tierney, R. Murray, D. Forde, A. Kerins, G. Farragher, Niall Healy, Damien Hayes. *Subs*: K. Broderick for Niall Healy, Kevin Hayes for Forde.

2006

SCORERS:

Kilkenny: H. Shefflin 0-8, A. Fogarty 1-3, M. Comerford 0-1, D. Lyng 0-1, J. Fitzpatrick 0-1, R. Power 0-1, E. Brennan 0-1.

Cork: Ben O'Connor 1-4, J. Deane 0-6, Niall McCarthy 0-1, Jer O'Connor 0-1, J. Gardiner 0-1.

Kilkenny: J. McGarry, M. Kavanagh, N. Hickey, J. Tyrrell (capt), T. Walsh, J. Tennyson, J. Ryall, D. Lyng, J. Fitzpatrick, E. Brennan, M. Comerford, E. Larkin, R. Power, H. Shefflin, A. Fogarty. *Subs*: W. O'Dwyer for Larkin, R. Mullally for Lyng.

Cork: D. Óg Cusack, P. Mulcahy (capt), D. O'Sullivan, B. Murphy, J. Gardiner, R. Curran, S. Óg Ó hAilpín, T. Kenny, Jer O'Connor, Timmy McCarthy, Niall McCarthy, N. Ronan, Ben O'Connor, B. Corcoran, J. Deane. *Subs*: K. Murphy (Sarsfields) for Ronan, W. Sherlock for Mulcahy, C. Naughton for Timmy McCarthy, C. O'Connor for K. Murphy, C. Cusack for Kenny.

2007

SCORERS:

Kilkenny: E. Brennan 1-5, H. Shefflin 1-2, R. Power 0-4, E. Larkin 0-4, T. Walsh 0-2, J. Fitzpatrick 0-1, A. Fogarty 0-1.

Limerick: A. O'Shaughnessy 0-7, Ollie Moran 1-3, D. O'Grady 0-2, Niall Moran 0-1, S. O'Connor 0-1, M. Fitzgerald 0-1.

Kilkenny: P. J. Ryan, M. Kavanagh, N. Hickey, J. Tyrrell, T. Walsh, B. Hogan, J. J. Delaney, D. Lyng, J. Fitzpatrick, W. O'Dwyer, M. Comerford, E. Larkin, E. Brennan, H. Shefflin (capt), A. Fogarty. *Subs*: J. Tennyson for Hickey, R. Power for O'Dwyer, M. Fennelly for Shefflin.

Limerick: B. Murray, D. Reale (capt), S. Lucey, S. Hickey, P. Lawlor, B. Geary, M. Foley, D. O'Grady, Mike O'Brien, M. Fitzgerald, Ollie Moran, S. O'Connor, A. O'Shaughnessy, B. Begley, D. Ryan. *Subs*: Niall Moran for Mike O'Brien, James O'Brien for O'Connor, Pat Tobin for Fitzgerald, Kevin Tobin for Ryan, M. O'Riordan for Lawlor.

2008
SCORERS:
Kilkenny: E. Brennan 2-4, H. Shefflin 0-8, E. Larkin 1-4, T. J. Reid 0-4, D. Lyng 0-3, A. Fogarty 0-3, R. Power 0-2, J. Fitzpatrick 0-2.
Waterford: E. Kelly 1-9, J. Mullane 0-3, D. Bennett 0-1.

Kilkenny: P. J. Ryan, M. Kavanagh, N. Hickey, J. Tyrrell, T. Walsh, B. Hogan, J. J. Delaney, J. Fitzpatrick (capt), D. Lyng, H. Shefflin, M. Comerford, E. Larkin, E. Brennan, R. Power, A. Fogarty. *Subs*: T. J. Reid for Comerford, D. J. McGarry for Ryan.
Waterford: C. Hennessy, A. Kearney, Declan Prendergast, E. Murphy, T. Browne, Ken McGrath, K. Moran, M. Walsh (capt), J. Nagle, D. Shanahan, S. Molumphy, Seamus Prendergast, Eoin McGrath, J. Mullane, E. Kelly. *Subs*: J. Kennedy for Seamus Prendergast, D. Bennett for Shanahan, P. Flynn for Eoin McGrath, T. Feeney for Declan Prendergast, S. O'Sullivan for Nagle.

CAPTAINS

Only one man was more than twice presented with the old Liam MacCarthy Cup—Christy Ring, the legendary Cork hurler. He took his place in history after he led the Rebel County to a successful defence of the trophy in 1954 against Wexford. That was a historic day in more ways than one for Ring as he was also the first man to win eight All-Ireland senior medals in hurling or football. Ring's first year as a MacCarthy Cup-winning captain was in 1946, when Kilkenny were well beaten in the final. He had to wait until 1953 for his next success as a victorious captain. Galway lost that year to Cork and the following September came that big day for Ring. In addition to captaining his county for the third time and winning his eighth medal, he became the first to lead two MacCarthy Cup-winning teams in successive years.

The first hurler to receive the MacCarthy Cup twice was a Cork man, Seán Óg Murphy. He was the county skipper in the wins of 1926 and 28.

Four years later Jimmy Walsh took the first step on the road to the double as Kilkenny's team leader in a triumph over Clare for the 1932 final. Walsh was captain again in the 1939 final, the game now invariably referred to as the 'Thunder and Lightning final', and in which Kilkenny had one of their famous one point wins over Cork.

Mick Mackey, undoubtedly Limerick's greatest-ever hurler, became the third man to lead a county team to a brace of MacCarthy Cup triumphs when he captained the Shannonsiders to their triumphs of 1936 and 40.

The fifties saw the emergence of Wexford, and when the Model County made the long-awaited breakthrough by beating Galway for the 1955 crown, the man who stepped up to receive the trophy was Nick O'Donnell, a native of Kilkenny, and a substitute on the Noreside team that won the 1947 crown. O'Donnell took his place in the small group of captains on the double after Wexford caused one of the biggest upsets of MacCarthy Cup games by beating strongly fancied Tipperary for the 1960 championship.

Next into the exclusive ranks was Jimmy Doyle. He led Tipperary to their title wins of 1962 and 65.

Then came a long gap until the late eighties when a new member joined this exclusive company. Conor Hayes led Galway to their MacCarthy Cup wins of 1987 and 88 and is the only westerner to skipper two trophy-winning sides. He also ranks as the last hurler to be twice presented with the cup. He played at full back in each title-winning side.

Anthony Daly, who led Clare to their first MacCarthy Cup win in 1995, now ranks as the last hurler to lead a county to their initial cup triumph. That success, of course, was in the era of the new trophy. That was Clare's first All-Ireland senior hurling title win since 1914.

Captain of the first 80 minute winning team was Cork goalkeeper Paddy Barry in the 1970 win over Wexford. Billy Fitzpatrick skippered Kilkenny to success over Galway in the first 70 minute tie in 1975.

There was no further entrant to the ranks of two-time winning captains up until the old Liam MacCarthy Cup was replaced by a new trophy, for the 1992 All-Ireland championship. When Kilkenny beat Cork that year, captained by Liam Fennelly, he earned a unique ranking in the annals of the MacCarthy Cup. He was the Leinster county's team leader in 1983 so is the only hurler to have led old and new MacCarthy Cup-winning teams.

Anthony Daly led Clare to a memorable victory in 1995 when he captained the side that beat Offaly for the county's first All-Ireland senior title since 1914. Then in 1997 he carved out his own slice of history when he captained Clare to victory over Tipperary to become the first to be twice presented with the new trophy.

Back to Liam Fennelly. He maintained a family tradition when in 1983 he joined the captains' table. Four years earlier his brother Ger led Kilkenny to their 'coming of age' All-Ireland senior title and their fourteenth cup victory. The Fennellys became the first brothers to captain MacCarthy Cup-winning teams. Incidentally, both were 25 on each occasion.

Bob McConkey was the first man presented with the old Liam MacCarthy Cup on 4 March 1923 as Limerick's skipper for the 1921 final win over Dublin.

Only two finals since then were played outside Croke Park. The first was when Jim Lanigan skippered Tipperary in their 1937 win over Kilkenny at Killarney. The second was when John Fenton captained Cork to their 1984 win over Offaly at Semple Stadium, Thurles, where the game was played as part of the GAA Centenary Year celebrations.

The list of captains contains two with the same Christian name and surname. Paddy Barry (Sarsfields) led Cork from left full forward to their 1952 win over Dublin and went on to win further national awards in 1953 and 54 when Ring was captain. Paddy Barry (St Vincent's) was Cork's leader and goalkeeper in 1970 in the first 80 minute final.

All-Ireland winning captains

1921	B. McConkey (Limerick)
1922	W. Dunphy (Kilkenny)
1923	M. Kenny (Galway)
1924	F. Wall (Dublin)
	non playing captain
1925	J. Leahy (Tipperary)
1926	S. Óg Murphy (Cork)
1927	M. Gill (Dublin)
1928	S. Óg Murphy (Cork)
1929	D. Barry-Murphy (Cork)
1930	J. J. Callanan (Tipperary)
1931	E. Coughlan (Cork)
1932	J. Walsh (Kilkenny)
1933	E. Doyle (Kilkenny)
1934	T. Ryan (Limerick)
1935	L. Meagher (Kilkenny)
1936	M. Mackey (Limerick)
1937	J. Lanigan (Tipperary)
1938	M. Daniels (Dublin)
1939	J. Walsh (Kilkenny)
1940	M. Mackey (Limerick)
1941	C. Buckley (Cork)
1942	J. Lynch (Cork)
1943	M. Kennefick (Cork)
1944	S. Condon (Cork)
1945	J. Maher (Tipperary)
1946	C. Ring (Cork)
1947	D. Kennedy (Kilkenny)
1948	J. Ware (Waterford)
1949	P. Stakelum (Tipperary)
1950	S. Kenny (Tipperary)

1951	J. Finn (Tipperary)
1952	P. Barry (Cork)
1953	C. Ring (Cork)
1954	C. Ring (Cork)
1955	N. O'Donnell (Wexford)
1956	J. English (Wexford)
1957	M. Kenny (Kilkenny)
1958	A. Wall (Tipperary)
1959	F. Walsh (Waterford)
1960	N. O'Donnell (Wexford)
1961	M. Hassett (Tipperary)
1962	Jimmy Doyle (Tipperary)
1963	S. Cleere (Kilkenny)
1964	M. Murphy (Tipperary)
1965	Jimmy Doyle (Tipperary)
1966	Gerald McCarthy (Cork)
1967	J. Treacy (Kilkenny)
1968	D. Quigley (Wexford)
1969	E. Keher (Kilkenny)
1970	P. Barry (Cork)
1971	T. O'Connor (Tipperary)
1972	N. Skehan (Kilkenny)
1973	E. Grimes (Limerick)
1974	N. Orr (Kilkenny)
1975	B. Fitzpatrick (Kilkenny)
1976	R. Cummins (Cork)
1977	M. O'Doherty (Cork)
1978	Charlie McCarthy (Cork)
1979	Ger Fennelly (Kilkenny)
1980	Joe Connolly (Galway)
1981	P. Horan (Offaly)
1982	B. Cody (Kilkenny)
1983	Liam Fennelly (Kilkenny)
1984	J. Fenton (Cork)
1985	P. Fleury (Offaly)
1986	T. Cashman (Cork)
1987	C. Hayes (Galway)
1988	C. Hayes (Galway)

1989   B. Ryan (Tipperary)
1990   T. Mulcahy (Cork)
1991   D. Carr (Tipperary)
1992   Liam Fennelly (Kilkenny)
1993   E. O'Connor (Kilkenny)
1994   M. Hanamy (Offaly)
1995   A. Daly (Clare)
1996   M. Storey (Wexford)
1997   A. Daly (Clare)
1998   H. Rigney (Offaly)
1999   M. Landers (Cork)
2000   W. O'Connor (Kilkenny)
2001   T. Dunne (Tipperary)
2002   A. Comerford (Kilkenny)
2003   D. J. Carey (Kilkenny)
2004   B. O'Connor (Cork)
2005   S. Óg Ó hAilpín (Cork)
2006   J. Tyrrell (Kilkenny)
2007   H. Shefflin (Kilkenny)
2008   J. 'Cha' Fitzpatrick (Kilkenny)

Appendix 4 ∾

WINNING RANKINGS

Kilkenny's win in the 2008 All-Ireland senior hurling championship final earned them the top spot in the rankings in the Liam MacCarthy Cup Roll of Honour with 24 triumphs. They are one ahead of Cork.

24 Kilkenny: 1922, 32, 33, 35, 39, 47, 57, 63, 67, 69, 72, 74, 75, 79, 82, 83, 92, 93, 00, 02, 03, 06, 07, 08

23 Cork: 1926, 28, 29, 31, 41, 42, 43, 44, 46, 52, 53, 54, 66, 70, 76, 77, 78, 84, 86, 90, 99, 04, 05

16 Tipperary: 1925, 30, 37, 45, 49, 50, 51, 58, 61, 62, 64, 65, 71, 89, 91, 01

5   Limerick: 1921, 34, 36, 40, 73
    Wexford: 1955, 56, 60, 68, 96

4   Galway: 1923, 80, 87, 88
    Offaly: 1981, 85, 94, 98

3   Dublin: 1924, 27, 38

2   Clare: 1995, 97
    Waterford: 1948, 59

BIBLIOGRAPHY/SOURCES

Irish Independent
Irish Press
Evening Press
The Irish Times
Cork Examiner
Tipperary Star

National Library
Pearse Street Library staff
Raheny Library staff

Calmac Publishing, *Seán Óg, His Own Story*
Comhairle Laighean, *Cead Bliain de Chluichi Gaelacha*
Fullam, Brendan, *Off the Field and On*
Fullam, Brendan, *The Final Whistle*
Horgan, Tim, *Cork's Hurling Story*, 1997
Irish Independent, *Famous All-Irelands*
McCann, Owen, *The Shell Book of the McCarthy Cup*, Oisín Publications, 1993
Murphy, Seán, *Jackie Power*
O'Ceallaigh, Seamus and Seán Murphy, *One Hundred Years of Glory: A History of Limerick GAA*, 1987
Ryall, Tom, *Kilkenny: The GAA Story 1884–1984*
Smith, Raymond, *The Complete Handbook of Gaelic Games*

INDEX